Simon Perkins of the Western Reserve

Oil painting by Allen Smith, Jr., used by permission of Case Western Reserve University.

Simon Perkins (1771–1844)

Simon Perkins

OF THE WESTERN RESERVE

Mary Lou Conlin

The Western Reserve Historical Society

1968

Copyright © 1968 by The Western Reserve Historical Society,
Cleveland, Ohio. All rights reserved.

Printed in the United States of America.

Library of Congress Catalogue Card Number 67–25320.

Distributed by The Press of Case Western University,
Cleveland, Ohio 44106.

The Western Reserve Historical Society Publication Number 120.

Preface

*U*NTIL NOW, historians have known Simon Perkins principally as the first president of the first bank in the Western Reserve and as one of the founders of Akron. He played, however, a great and important part in molding the future of the Western Reserve, and his part is now revealed in this book.

The book was envisioned as a contribution to our knowledge of the history of this region by Ralph Perkins of Cleveland, great-grandson of Simon Perkins and a trustee of The Western Reserve Historical Society, 1937–1963. He died, however, before plans for the book could be realized. Subsequently, members of his family graciously provided funds for the preparation of a book on Simon Perkins, leaving the Society complete freedom in the choice of an author, and the author complete freedom in presenting the subject.

We are happy, indeed, to have as writer of this book a person so competent and so familiar with the history of the region as Mary Lou Conlin. We are very much indebted to her. She drew in part upon the extensive manuscripts in The Western Reserve Historical Society, especially the Simon Perkins papers.

We acknowledge the financial support of the Clara Belle Ritchie Fund in publication of the book and the co-operation of The Press of Case Western Reserve University in handling the details of publication.

Frederick C. Crawford, *President*
Meredith B. Colket, Jr., *Director*

The Western Reserve Historical Society
Cleveland, Ohio

Acknowledgments

The author wishes to express her appreciation to the Henry Huntington Library, the Connecticut Historical Society, the Connecticut State Library, the New London County Historical Society, and the libraries of Harvard, Yale, Princeton, and Johns Hopkins universities for permission to use, and quote from, manuscripts in their possession. She is most indebted, however, to The Western Reserve Historical Society for unlimited use of the Society's excellent manuscript collection and to The Press of Case Western Reserve University for valuable editorial assistance.

Mary Lou Conlin

Contents

Foreword   xi

1. "To a day spent with Perkins—2.00"   1

2. "July 4, 1798—arrived at the mouth of Conneott."   13

3. "People are very much pleasd."   20

4. "What kind of Christianity is this, or where is it to be found?"   38

5. "We have a singular kind of Republicanism in this County."   48

6. "God in his mercy keep me & mine from such a Revolution."   65

7. "It is of the first importance . . . that you fall, not by the hands of each other. You are to each other friends and not enemies."   74

8. "Good as a Western Reserve Bank bill." . .   95

9. "Permit me to congratulate you on your great popularity . . . you were appointed Commissioner of the C. Fund without a dissenting voice." . .   107

10. "Pitch of anarchy." 121

11. "The poor against the rich." 133

12. "A melancholy tale." 145

    Afterword 150

    Notes 154

    Bibliography 193

    Index 206

Foreword

*A*FTER HE HAD EXPLORED the lands along Lake Erie's southern shore, Simon Perkins said there was "nothing wanting to make this a profitable purchase, but to have the proprietors resolute and determine it should be so."

And when the venture began in 1795, the proprietors of Connecticut's Western Reserve were indeed resolute and determined to settle the land and watch it grow not only in value but into a state they planned to call New Connecticut. Before many years had passed, however, some of the proprietors began to fall away from the original goals: Moses Cleaveland differed with his fellow proprietors and became so careless and slow in the management of the property that he actually delayed settlement; and all too often proprietors like Joseph Williams, Joseph Howland, Oliver Phelps, and Ephraim Root found their financial obligations more than they could meet and were forced to give up their lands.

The venture might well have been a financial fiasco for all the proprietors and the dream of statehood long in being realized had it not been for the resolution and determination of Simon himself. For forty-six years he served the Western Reserve and the state of Ohio in various capacities: land agent, arbiter, jurist, postmaster, Indian negotiator, soldier, banker, and developer of roads, canals, cities, and various social institutions. Often, too, he was the catalyst and advisor to those who led in the West.

A large man—six feet, he once told a friend, was "the length I always boasted"—he gained a reputation for being firm, even stern. But he treasured his wife as only the western pioneer learned to, and he loved their children and concerned himself with their welfare almost to the point of obsession. There was, too, an understanding twinkle in his brown eyes that explains why his friends' children came to him and readily accepted his advice, counsel, and admonition.

But he lived, 1771–1844, in a turbulently changing country: As a child, he experienced the American Revolution; as a youth, he knew the formation of the United States; as a man, he participated in the westward movement, the War of 1812, the decline of Federalism, and the rise of Jacksonian democracy. Since he gained wealth and considerable influence over both the affairs of his state and the finances of its citizens, he found himself subjected to the "poor against the rich" doctrine that marked the Jackson era. Because his own actions had been guided by his belief that "one ounce of character is worth" more to a man "than a waggonload of money," he found intolerable the criticisms leveled against him and the financial system he represented. And for a brief time, he openly opposed those who, in his view, resorted to anarchy in an effort to level the so-called aristocracy of the country. But finally—old, disillusioned, and even somewhat bitter—he gave up the struggle against the forces of democracy and brought to a close the businesses and activities he had once thought vital to the Western Reserve.

But this is the way it began. . . .

Simon Perkins of the Western Reserve

Men of wonderful charm they were, but they were singularly lacking in an understanding of the spirit of their times and country. They fell, as we shall find, because they neither had nor sought contact with the average man, and sternly set themselves against the over-whelming current of democracy.

Claude G. Bowers, *Jefferson and Hamilton, The Struggle for Democracy in America* (Boston and New York: Houghton Mifflin Company, 1925), p. vi.

1.

To a day spent with Perkins—2.00

Moses Cleaveland, Erie Company Expense Account of 1798

*M*ay 22, 1795," said Simon Perkins, "was the first time I left home for to travel new Countries."[1] Then a hardy twenty-three-year-old who liked an outdoor life and the exercise of riding on horseback, he left his family's farm home in Lisbon, Connecticut, and journeyed to New York state to survey and sell wild lands owned by his Connecticut friends and relatives.

His knowledge of surveying, carefully recorded in a small leatherbound book he could carry in his pocket, was apparently self-taught; and he learned by experience during the three summers of 1795–1797 that he spent in New York how to make out land contracts, record deeds, and collect debts and taxes. He soon learned there were difficulties involved in landowning; but he was convinced, as were so many men of that period, that land was a good investment. He was even willing to gamble on this conviction, and he accepted land as part payment for his services. By March 17, 1798, when he was wintering at his Lisbon home, he had established a small business in Tioga, New York, to handle the sale of his own and his clients' lands in that state.

It was very stormy that March day, but "a short thick set man with a broad face, rather dark, or brown complexion" journeyed from his home in Canterbury to Norwich, Connecticut, on business with the newly formed Erie Company. Some of his acquaintances said this man looked like an Indian, and they called him Ol'

Molock; others, of course, addressed Moses Cleaveland by his Connecticut Militia title of General. But it was said by his friends that "he was capable of going through thick or thin in the business in which he was engaged." [2]

Cleaveland's pressing business that stormy day was the employment of an agent to handle the exploration, survey, and sale of the western lands of the Erie Company. Cleaveland, Daniel Lathrop Coit, and Joseph Perkins held as Trustees of this Company more than 125,000 acres [3] of Connecticut's Western Reserve lands that had been drawn by the nineteen members of the Erie Company through their investment in the Connecticut Land Company, a coalition of companies formed in 1795 to purchase the property from the state of Connecticut. The members of the Erie Company wanted an agent on their land early that summer to meet the many buyers who were expected. A Company meeting had, in fact, already been "warned" for April 2 to settle his instructions; [4] and so it was urgent that an agent now be employed by the three Trustees.

Daniel Lathrop Coit, Treasurer-Trustee of the Company, lived with his wife and five children in a large white gambrel-roofed house in Norwich.[5] He was, at forty-three, a financially successful importer of drugs; and he had combined with his brother-in-law Joseph Howland and two friends, Elias and John Morgan, to invest $81,863 in the Western Reserve lands.[6] Like Cleaveland, Coit was optimistic about the future of the western country. He had pooled in the Erie Company, in fact, over 29,000 acres [7] of his land. A beak-nosed man with a receding hairline, Coit had a gentle sense of humor and a great amount of patience with the shortcomings of others. And he would need both humor and patience when Cleaveland and other proprietors caviled over Company affairs or divisions of, as he called it, "the promised land."

The third Trustee, Joseph Perkins, was a cousin to Simon and a Brigade-Major in the Twentieth Regiment of Connecticut's Militia. The Major, uniformed in his blue coat and buff trousers, inspected his Regiment when it held its festive drills in front of his house on Norwich's Town Plain.[8] The Major's occupation, however, was general store-owner and merchant-shareholder with his uncle Andrew Perkins in vessels engaged in the West Indies trade. Lumber, provisions, and livestock were exported by the Andrew and Joseph Perkins Company from the wharf in that part of Norwich called Chelsea Landing; rum, molasses, sugar, wine, coffee, cotton, tobacco, indigo, and salt were imported from the West Indies to be sold by the Perkins Company at its store near the Landing.[9]

Daniel Coit and The Major knew about Simon's experience as a land agent; and they of course knew that he came from an old and highly respected family. Simon was descended from the John Perkins who, according to family records, arrived in America with Roger Williams in 1631. Descendants of John Perkins had first settled in Norwich and then purchased, in 1695, a nearby thousand-acre point of land between the Quinebaug and Shetucket rivers. Here, partly because of the difficulty of crossing the Shetucket to attend meetings in Norwich but also because of their opposition to the revivalism at one time encouraged by the Congregational Church, the Perkins family founded a separate congregation called the Newent Society. Some members of the family, like The Major, eventually returned to Norwich to live; but Simon's branch of the family had stayed on the point that the townspeople called "Perkins Crotch" and that became part of the village of Lisbon.[10]

Whether Cleaveland knew Simon before 1798 is not known, but the three Trustees agreed upon Simon's ability, judgment, and integrity. Coit would steadily write Simon, in the coming years, ". . . my confidence in your judgment being great, and in your integrity perfect . . . do as you think best." [11] And it was decided that Simon should spend March 29 with Cleaveland, to discuss the Erie Company affairs.

Cleaveland, a Yale graduate and attorney, was to draw up the Company's agreement with and instructions to their agent. As a result of his own 1796 surveying trip as General Agent for the Connecticut Land Company, Cleaveland could give Simon firsthand information about conditions on the Reserve. Since he was also a Director of the Connecticut Land Company as well as a Trustee of the Erie Company, he could, in addition, acquaint Simon with the history of the property and the problems involved in its sale and settlement.

The property had, in fact, an interesting and unique history. By the terms of a charter granted to the colony of Connecticut by Charles II in 1662, that colony was given land bounded on the east by Narragansett Bay, on the north by the Massachusetts colony line, on the south by the waters of the Atlantic, and on the west by the unlocated South Seas.[12] This charter was intended to settle boundary disagreements which then existed between Connecticut and the colonies of Rhode Island and New Haven. Although these disagreements were settled shortly thereafter,[13] Connecticut soon acquired new land-claim conflicts when Charles granted to his brother James, Duke of York, in 1664, and to William Penn, in 1681, lands which lay within the vaguely stipulated western bounds of Connecticut's charter.[14] And the Pennsylvania conflict reached near-war proportions.

By 1773, the Connecticut-based Susquehanna Land Company had planted a colony in the fertile Wyoming Valley. Connecticut expressed her intention to protect her claim to this land by making the Valley part of her Westmoreland County. Since the Valley was also claimed by Pennsylvania under her 1681 charter, the Land Company's colony was opposed by the Pennamites, even to the point of actual combat. There was some respite in this conflict during the Revolution, but in 1778 the colonists suffered defeat by British troops and a nearly total massacre by Indian fighters led by the maniacal Queen Esther. Injustice seemed added to injury when, in 1782, the Trenton Federal Court ruled in favor of Pennsylvania's claim to the Valley.[15]

When the various colonies, during and following the Revolution, ceded their land claims to the newly formed confederacy, Connecticut again asserted her charter rights by reserving an area between the 41° and 42°2′ parallels of North Latitude and extending 120 miles westward from the western boundary of

Pennsylvania.[16] This area, which would be part of the future state of Ohio, was first called Connecticut's Western Reserve, then New Connecticut, and finally the Western Reserve.

Congress accepted this reservation, after some effort on the part of Arthur St. Clair and other delegates to the Continental Congress to add a proviso that the acceptance would not affect the Trenton decision.[17] But this acceptance did not settle the state's title to the land. Legislators from other states questioned whether Congress, never having owned the land in the first place, could release it to Connecticut; they questioned whether New York and Virginia had ceded their claims to the land; and they questioned whether Connecticut's territorial and juridical rights, even if agreed to, were in turn assignable.[18]

Related to this complex title problem was the additional matter of establishing a civil government over the Reserve. Connecticut, because of the disastrous Wyoming Valley experience, extended no laws over the territory and would even refuse, at a later date, to name the territory a county of Connecticut. The Reserve therefore had no provision for recording deeds nor any means of enforcing any contracts that might be entered into. And while Connecticut was willing to cede juridical rights and permit the extension of the Northwest Territory government over the Reserve, the problem was to separate the right to govern from the right to the soil.

Consequently, the stubbornly fought for western lands proved, for many years, less an asset than a liability to Connecticut. In fact, a later proprietor said the property was "a pretty large white elephant, too large for Connecticut to manage at such a distance." [19] In addition to the title-juridical tangle, the British did not immediately evacuate the area as agreed to in the treaty ending the Revolutionary War, the Indian claims to the land remained to be quieted, and the Connecticut General Assembly could not or did not decide upon the disposition of the money that would be received from the sale of the Reserve. In 1787 Samuel Holden Parsons was appointed to survey the lands; in 1788 he agreed to purchase 24,000 acres called the Salt Springs tract, but he drowned the following year and his purchase offer only complicated the sale of the land.[20] In 1792 Connecticut granted the western half-million acres, called the Sufferers' Lands or the Firelands, to those of her citizens who had suffered property losses by fire during the Revolution.[21] But it was not until 1795 that the remaining estimated 3,000,000-acre tract was at last purchased by a coalition of investors formed by Oliver Phelps.

Phelps had previously organized companies in 1792 and 1793 to purchase the Reserve, but his applications to the Connecticut General Assembly were turned down, as he said, because "the business at that time was not in a situation that a purchase could be effected." It was not until Jay's Treaty assured the removal of the British from the area, Wayne's control of the Indians fore-shadowed the Treaty of Greenville, and the Connecticut General Assembly determined to establish a permanent school fund with the proceeds from the land that Connecticut, according to Phelps, "put the business in a train for an actual sale." [22]

The Assembly appointed a committee of eight and ordered the sale advertised in all the Connecticut newspapers and also in those of Boston, Providence, New York, Albany, and Philadelphia even though, as Phelps discovered, the Assembly intended to confine the sale to Connecticut citizens. "This being the case," wrote Phelps, who then spent more time at his Canandaigua, New York, residence than he did at his Suffield, Connecticut, home, "I found it necessary to connect with the citizens of this State and designed to have purchased the whole." [23]

But when the day of the sale—August 5, 1795—arrived, Phelps discovered "the whole State convened at Hartford. Not less than twelve different Companies formed for the purpose within the State of Connecticut" were gathered for the bidding, and there were "nearly as many companies from New York, Pennsylvania, Massachusetts, etc." In Phelps's opinion, "the purchase could not be effected on any reasonable terms without uniting all the companies in this State," and they were "obliged . . . to coalese, 'til we had cut it up into small share, hardly worth holding."

As far as the out-of-state companies were concerned, Phelps

"did not apprehend any danger . . . as we knew they could not purchase without paying the whole purchase money down . . . but as they might serve to raise the price, we thought better to make some small sacrifice to get rid of them, than to risk their raising the price." [24]

Such a small sacrifice was made on August 12 when John Livingston and associates from New York offered $1,255,000 for the lands, which exceeded the August 11 bid of $1,150,000 made by Phelps's coalition, and agreed that Connecticut citizens might participate to the amount of one-half the purchase. This was not the first time Phelps had met Livingston over land affairs in the United States. Livingston had previously opposed Phelps over the 2,500,000-acre Phelps-Gorham Purchase in New York, and Phelps had then come to an agreement with Livingston by his technique of sharing the purchase.[25] So when the Connecticut committee seized upon the supposed advantage of renewed competition and announced "they had concluded to wait till 5 o'clock in the afternoon and that they were determined to close with the best offer that might then be made exceeding in value the sum of 1,260,000 interest after two years," [26] Phelps—along with William Hart, Samuel Mather Junior, Ebenezer Huntington, Moses Cleaveland, Elisha Hyde, Matthias Nicholl, and Gideon Granger Junior—seized upon the recess to meet with Livingston. And by five o'clock, Phelps's coalition had secured Livingston's agreement to withdraw his bid in return for the future sale to him of all land in excess of 3,000,000 acres which should be discovered in the still unexplored and unsurveyed Western Reserve tract.[27]

When the out-maneuvered state committee reconvened at five o'clock and found Livingston's bid withdrawn, they proposed to close a contract with Phelps's coalition if $50,000 were added to the original bid. With the competition eliminated, the coalition was naturally reluctant to increase its offer.

A train of reasoning on the subject took place [reported the committee], pending which a gentleman from Berkshire County . . . was introduced to the Committee, who informed them that he was just

{7}

arrived in town, that he represented a number of Gentlemen . . . who wished to become purchasers of the Connecticut Reserve, and wished to know if an offer could be received. . . . The Committee then resolved that they were at liberty to receive further offers unless the Agents of the State companies should close with the proposal made them by the State Committee.[28]

With the competition renewed and faced with the necessity of dividing the purchase into even smaller shares to eliminate this eleventh-hour opposition, Phelps's coalition, which would be called the Connecticut Land Company, agreed to the $1,200,000 asked by the committee and finally secured the purchase of the Western Reserve.[29]

In September, forty-eight of the proprietors posted fifteen per cent security for the purchase and received, as tenants in common, thirty-five quitclaim deeds granting them "all right, title and interest, juridical and territorial, in and to the lands" of the Western Reserve. These forty-eight proprietors, who deeded the land in trust to John Morgan, Jonathan Brace, and John Caldwell, actually represented 204 persons at the time of the first partition of the land in 1798.[30] And even these 204 investors represented, in turn, still other investors. The Major, for example, was not listed among the 204 investors drawing land in 1798 but was represented in the Connecticut Land Company by his cousin John Kinsman.

With their non-warranted deeds to the land the trustees and proprietors acquired, of course, the old title-juridical problem. The problem was, in fact, even more complicated in 1795 than it had been, for Arthur St. Clair, now Governor of the Northwest Territory, had proclaimed the Western Reserve part of Washington County and had extended over it, although only in theory, the government of the Northwest Territory. This was not satisfactory to the Connecticut Land Company because it contradicted the juridical and by implication the title rights granted in their deeds from Connecticut. And Zephaniah Swift—Connecticut Land Company proprietor, Yale graduate, Federalist in the House of Representatives, attorney, and author of *The System of Laws of*

Connecticut—[31] went to Philadelphia to consult with his friends in Congress about the title.

In December, 1795, Swift wrote confidently to Phelps:

On the fullest examination, I am convinced we may consider our title to the purchase to be unquestionable, that the Reserve has by everybody been considered as belonging to Connecticut, and that Congress will neither interfere with, or obstruct the Settlement, or disapprove of our taking possession of it.[32]

Swift was less successful, however, regarding an "application to the Executive of the United States for appointment of Commissioners to hold a Treaty for the purpose of extinguishing the Indian right to that part of the Connecticut Reserve not included in the late Treaty made by General Wayne." He wrote to Phelps regarding the unquieted Indian claim to the land west of the Cuyahoga River:

I have conversed with Col. Pickering, the late Secretary of War & now Secretary of State & Mr. Wolcott the Secretary of the Treasury who are decidedly of the opinion, that in so short a time after making a Treaty with the Indians, it would be highly improper to propose another Treaty for the purpose of purchasing more of their lands. It seems now to be a principle assumed by the Executive to make use of method to conciliate the affections of the Indians and to convince them that there is a disposition in the Government not only to treat them with justice and humanity, but also to avoid any encroachments of their Territory. It is supposed that a perpetual performance of the late Treaty, & the avoidance of every measure calculated to excite their Jealousy, may establish that harmony & confidence which are now beginning to take place, but it is strongly apprehended that a proposition to buy more of their lands so soon after we have guaranteed it, to them by a solemn Treaty, would wholly destroy their confidence in the Government, & possibly involve us in another war . . . that it is best to suffer things to remain in their present arrangements, 'til such confidence is gained by the Indians & such an intercourse opened with them that the proposition can be made without exciting any suspicion respecting the good faith & Integrity of the Government.[33]

Swift had then been told that

there are no Indians residing on that part of the Reserve to which the Indian title has been extinguished, [and he concluded that] we may proceed to survey the country & establish Settlements on Lake Erie with as much safety as it can be done any where in the United States. I am confident that we need neither fear any interruption from the Indians nor any claim from any quarter to the Land. As the Settlements can be made without any embarrasment or dispute with respect to the title, I apprehend they can be carried on with much greater advantage than in almost any other new country, for in general the mode of granting new lands has been such, as to involve the titles in Intricacy & confusion.[34]

The Connecticut Land Company then proceeded to arrange for the survey and sale of the land east of the Cuyahoga River. Six townships of 16,000 acres each were to be sold as soon as possible to meet the expenses of the Directors and of Moses Cleaveland's surveying party of 1796. But sales were slow and the proprietors had to be taxed or assessed repeatedly for Company expenses. Dissension among the proprietors is indicated by the January, 1797, appointment of committees to investigate the Directors' accounts, the expenses of Cleaveland's party, and the causes that prevented the 1796 party from completing the survey of the land east of the Cuyahoga River into five-mile square townships.[35] The proprietors were anxious to partition the land; and in 1797 a second surveying party, headed by Seth Pease and Seth Hart, was sent to the Reserve. Finally—by January, 1798—the land was readied for partition among the proprietors.

The mode of partition was quite complex. Each of the four townships that were considered "best" by the equalizing committee had been surveyed into 100 lots of approximately 160 acres each. Three thousand dollars in purchase money entitled a Connecticut Land Company investor to one of these 400 lots. Fourteen other townships and fractional townships located on Lake Erie, the Cuyahoga River, the Tuscarawas River, and on the Portage Path (so called because the Indians had made the Path in porting their canoes between the Cuyahoga and Tuscarawas Rivers) were set aside as "equalizing" townships. This left ninety-three townships to be partitioned among the members of the Company. Only eight of these townships were considered the "average" of the tract and had no "equalizing" land attached. To all the other townships varying amounts of land in the equalizing townships were attached. The sum of $12,903.23 entitled an investor or group of investors to one of the approximately 16,000-acre townships with, if any, its attached equalizing land. A tract of land in Towns 2 and 3 of Ranges 3 and 4—the Salt Springs tract—was excluded from the partition because it was claimed by the heirs of General Parsons, based on his 1788 agreement to purchase the property.[36]

There were many disadvantages, however, to a partition of the property. For one thing, further expenses involved in the survey, sale, and settlement of the land would become the responsibility of the individual proprietors or groups of proprietors who would continue to hold their land in combination. Since the partition would be effected by a drawing, many of the proprietors would, as an additional disadvantage, own widely separated pieces of land. Moreover, some proprietor must inevitably draw land he considered of less value than the average of the tract, in spite of efforts of the equalizing committee to establish equal drafts. And finally, the partition of the land would result in possibly disastrous competition for sales.

Consequently, some of the proprietors, "being desirous of taking such steps in regard to such partition as shall conduce to the benefit of the concerned," agreed to recombine their interests and form the Erie Company. These proprietors felt that "uniting our interest in one common Stock, and in the partition drawing together as one common Stock will have a tendency to equalize our respective shares . . . and sales can be better managed by suitable Agents, than by the concern[ed] Individually." [37]

Perhaps by chance, but possibly by design, the brothers Asahel [Asael] and Jabez Adams were among the members of the Erie Company. And when the Connecticut Land Company proprietors gathered at Hartford in January, 1798, for the alphabetically conducted partition of their lands, Company Clerk Ephraim Root drew from the box of numbered draft slips on behalf of the brothers Adams, for the Erie Company, the first twenty-eight 160-acre lots in the four allotted townships.[38]

Hopefully the drafts for other Erie Company members would be for land adjacent to or near that drawn in common. But when the partition was completed, the members of the Erie Company held land scattered from the Pennsylvania boundary on the east to the Cuyahoga River on the west, and from the southern almost to the northern boundary of the Reserve.

Exploring this widespread property would be both difficult and slow. But after he had spent March 29 with Cleaveland, Simon Perkins was willing and even eager to undertake the task.

After that day it remained only for the Erie Company members to settle, in their April 2 meeting, the instructions to their agent, Simon Perkins.

2.

July 4, 1798—

arrived at the mouth of Conneott.

Simon Perkins, Surveying Book, 1795

*I*T WAS A SUCCESSFUL and illustrious group that gathered in the
Norwich Courthouse on April 2 at one o'clock for the first
officially "warned" meeting of the Erie Company.

Some of the group—The Major, Colonel Christopher Leffingwell, Joseph Howland, Joseph Williams, and Lynde McCurdy
—had been associated during the Revolution in a short-lived
organization that seized and sold for charitable purposes all the
smuggled British goods they could discover.[1] Colonel Leffingwell,
dignified-looking in his high narrow-brimmed hat and long
tight-waisted coat,[2] had also distinguished himself during the
Revolution for his service as a member of the Committee of
Correspondence and for his bravery as Captain of a light infantry
troop which went to the defense of neighboring New London. An
energetic business man, Leffingwell had established in Norwich a
paper mill, a chocolate mill, and a highly successful stocking-
weaving factory with a yearly production of twelve to fifteen
hundred pairs of worsted, cotton, linen, and silk stockings.[3]

Joseph Howland and Joseph Williams were equally successful
in the shipping business. Howland owned, with some of his relatives, the ship "Charlotte" and a fleet of brigs, schooners, and
sloops which carried livestock and other cargo to the West Indies.

Howland's shipping business was so well known that in 1801 and 1802 the warring British and French would both seek contracts with him to supply their forces in the West Indies.[4] Joseph Williams was the principal owner of six trading vessels, one of which—the "Snow"—was made entirely of American materials. Williams' vessels were primarily engaged in the West Indies trade, but his sloop "Prosperity" carried on a profitable trade with the northern ports of South America.[5]

Several others of the group were, like The Major, successful merchants: from Lynde McCurdy one could buy fine broadcloths, laces, and even Indian, Damascus and Persian silks;[6] from John Kinsman, brother-in-law to Simon and a Representative in the Connecticut General Assembly, one could buy a hat made in Kinsman's own shop.[7]

Among the illustrious of the group there was, in addition to Zephaniah Swift, Senator Uriah Tracy. Tracy owned a store in Norwich with Joseph Coit,[8] also a member of the Erie Company, and was an attorney, a former member of Connecticut's General Assembly, and a congressional associate of Hamilton, Ames, and Adams.[9]

And there was also Samuel Huntington Junior, the adopted son, nephew, and namesake of the late Samuel Huntington who had signed the Declaration of Independence and for more than ten years had been Governor of Connecticut. The junior Huntington had been educated at Dartmouth and Yale, had traveled in Europe, and was in 1798 an attorney in Norwich with offices in the Courthouse.[10] With his background and education he could presumably look forward to a successful political career in Connecticut. But of late his headstrong espousal of Jeffersonian principles had made him unpopular with his Federalist friends and neighbors.

Asahel [Asael] and Jabez Adams, Penuel Cheney, Erastus and Thomas Huntington, Daniel Lathrop, and William Wheeler Williams completed the membership of the Erie Company.[11]

As might be expected, the nineteen hard-working and ambitious proprietors were very demanding in their instructions to young Simon Perkins. According to the documents drawn up by Cleaveland, Simon was to be on the land in July and "continue there three months and longer if . . . the business of the Company shall require . . . to imploy his time . . . in Selling, Surveying laying out and exploring." [12]

The Company agreed to pay Simon "two dollars pr day and his necessary expenses" for supplies, provisions, a horse, and "men hired or imployed in the services of the Company." But Simon, on his part, agreed to purchase "one thousand acres of the lands in said Reserve" at a price of $1.50 for the first 240 acres and $1 per acre thereafter. The land was to be selected in two tracts within specified townships and he was "to settle on one of said tracts of said land, or in his room to have settled thereon a family, and also another family on the other tract within one year . . . and build on each tract a good log or frame house and clear and sow with English grain six acres the first year, on the first mentioned tract." If there should be good mill seats on either of the tracts he selected, Simon was also to "build in 1 year a sawmill and in two years a gristmill." The only option Simon had relevant to this land was that he need not contract for more acreage the first summer than the amount of his wages. [13]

Moreover, as if the selling, surveying, laying out, exploring, settling, and building duties were not enough, Simon was also instructed to find William Wheeler Williams, one of the Erie Company proprietors who had decided to settle on the Reserve and would precede Simon there. Because the Company was eager to promote settlement, they had agreed that Williams might take in one parcel the nearly 1,300 acres to which his investment entitled him and to thus sever his connection with the Company. On his part, Williams had agreed to take three men on the land "to build a log house . . . clear as much land and get into the ground from twenty to forty acres" of wheat. In the summer following, "which will be in the year 1799," he agreed to build a gristmill and a sawmill, "in the township on which he shall settle."[14] When Simon found Williams, he was to measure off the land he had chosen and see that he was fulfilling his Erie Company agreement.

The terms of sale Simon was to follow were as demanding as his duties, considering the shortage of money in the country and the physical difficulties involved in settling new land. He was restricted from selling any land at less than $1 per acre, and he was to secure "five to ten pr Cent" of the purchase money or a note on interest at the time of sale. The balance of payment was due in three years, but interest compounded at six per cent was due annually. In addition, Simon was to restrict purchases to "actual Settlers, who must condition to do settling duties, not less than those for which you have conditioned."[15]

But the most nearly insurmountable of the proprietors' conditions was their stipulation that Simon could give purchasers, on fulfillment of the terms of purchase, a deed that would be only "so far a warranty as to warrant all the title that the State of Connecticut had to the land."[16] Since the title of Connecticut was by no means warranted, potential settlers would soon prove wary of purchasing land in the Reserve, contrary to Zephaniah Swift's opinion, and would turn elsewhere for settlement.

Simon had to be optimistic about the future of the western country and the potential value of the Western Reserve lands when he signed, on April 14, the terms imposed by the Erie Company. But his decision to leave his comfortable familiar surroundings and the business already established in Tioga to go into wild, unexplored, and lawless country where, as the Trustees pointed out, "many circumstances will occur, many unknown exigencies be found to be provided for,"[17] may also have been influenced by his personal responsibility for his mother and younger brother.

Simon had, for a man of twenty-six, considerable family responsibility. His father had died in 1778, following service as a Lieutenant in the Revolution, and had left to his wife, Olive Douglass Perkins, and their five children "122 acres of Land with a Dwelling house, Corn house, barn & gristmill," located on the

Quinebaug-Shetucket point of land, a third interest in a "pot ash house," the livestock of the farm, two swarms of bees, all his other goods, and "533 Continental Dollars." [18] The estate was appraised in 1778 at slightly over £1,398,[19] but the actual money was "not worth a Continental" only a few years later.

Simon had taken over the management of this property at an early age, although he was undoubtedly helped and possibly educated by his Yale graduate grandfather, Dr. Joseph Perkins, who lived on the adjoining farm.[20] Under Simon's management the property apparently provided the family with the necessities of life, but it is improbable that the family of six had many extra comforts. And by 1798, although his three sisters were married—Olive, the eldest in the family, to Christopher Starr; Rebecca, two years younger than Simon, to John Kinsman; and Joanna, twenty-two, to Samuel Lovett—[21] Simon was still responsible not only for his mother but for the care of his twenty-year-old brother, Daniel Bishop.

Bishop had begun studying at Yale in 1794.[22] At that time, the three buildings of the college were surrounded by "a grotesque group" of establishments, which included a "poor house and house of correction, and the public jail . . . used alike for criminals, for maniacs and debtors . . . where the moans of innocent prisoners, the curses of felons, and the shrill screams and wild laughter of the insane were sometimes mingled with the sacred songs of praise and with the voice or prayer, rising from the academic edifices." [23] Here Bishop, like other students of the time, pored over his Greek, Latin, and Hebrew books and soon became, as his brother-in-law Christopher Starr phrased it, alternately "very talkative then again silent—sometimes troublesome and sometimes peaceable." [24]

Simon blamed Bishop's illness on his excessive study at Yale, and for the rest of his life he would be opposed, as a consequence, to the kind of education that required close attention to books and study of the dead languages. Simon had arranged for a kind of care that few mentally disturbed persons then received: He insisted that Bishop be fed, clothed, kept warm and clean, and treated kindly at all times. Simon did not believe, as did most of the persons willing to care for his brother, that it mattered not to Bishop whether his bodily needs were attended to; nor did Simon believe that confining him in a cage or beating him was the only way to control Bishop during his troublesome periods. And when Simon made ready to leave Connecticut he was able, fortunately, to depend upon his brothers-in-law, especially the kindly Christopher Starr, to see that Bishop's care was continued and that his mother was looked after.

Finally, on April 19, with the "best wishes" of Cleaveland, The Major, and Daniel Coit for his "prosperity, Health, and safe return," [25] Simon left home for "New Connecticut."

His way took him first to the Connecticut Land Company's office in the Hartford Courthouse where, on April 24, he copied from Ephraim Root's notes the division the Company had established for Township 8 Range 7,[26] which was then called Canton and would later be called Claridon. This township was owned jointly by Daniel Coit, Uriel Holmes, Nathaniel Patch, and Martain Smith.[27] The division of the township would be disputed by Holmes, who would claim that his share was mostly worthless swamp and his equalizing land without value. And Simon's attempt to settle this dispute so the land could be brought into market would be the first of many long and bitter land disputes he would handle during his years on the Reserve.

From Hartford Simon proceeded to Owego, New York. Here he employed James Pumpelly, Reuben Forgason, and Daniel McQuigg to assist him in surveying the Erie Company lands. Here too he bought a supply of kettles, pans, and tin cups for himself and his men and arranged to have their provisions of flour, pork, and wheat shipped from Owego to the Reserve via Oswego to Niagara—where every item had to be unloaded and carried by land around the falls—and thence to Presque Isle.[28]

On June 21, Simon left his Tioga land business in the hands of friends and proceeded with his surveyors, according to Elisha Whittlesey's later account of the journey, "through the wilderness of Western New York" to Buffalo. Here, Whittlesey says, they obtained a batteau with which they "coasted up Lake Erie." [29] Finally, on July 4, 1798, Simon at last "arrived at the mouth of Conneott." [30]

It was exactly two years before that Moses Cleaveland's party of fifty men, women, and children "took possession" of the Connecticut Reserve by encamping at this same creek. In commemoration of the beginning of the settlement of the "good & promised land" which "in time may raise her head amongst the most enlightened & improved States," Cleaveland's party christened the spot Port Independence and "fired a Federal salute of 15 rounds & then the 16th in honor of New Connecticut." [31]

No such celebration marked Simon's arrival in 1798, but it was nevertheless an important day: From that day until his death in 1844, Simon would influence the settlement and development of the Western Reserve.

3.

People are very much pleasd.

Simon Perkins, Letter to the Trustees, June 18, 1800

*I*N TIME MOST of the townships of the Reserve were named after Connecticut towns or for the owner of the land. But in 1798 many locations on the Reserve were still designated by township and range numbers. The townships were numbered every five miles from south to north; the ranges were numbered every five miles from east to west. Thus Conneaut Creek, located near the northeast boundary of the Reserve, was in Town 14 Range 1.

The prevailing Lake Erie winds had formed a sand bar that stretched from the west bank partly across the mouth of Conneaut Creek. And although Lake Erie's waves often rose over this protective barrier to smash destructively against the Creek's eastern beach and the bluff overlooking it, all the parties sent out by the Connecticut Land Company had landed at this place.

Cleaveland's party had built a cabin—named Stow's Castle in honor of Joshua Stow, who was in charge of the supplies stored at that place—on the bluff overlooking a bend in the Creek a short distance from its mouth, and had helped build another cabin nearby that the James Kingsbury family occupied in the winter of 1796. When Pease's party arrived in 1797, they found Mrs. Kingsbury in very poor health, and the Kingsburys' child, to whom Cleaveland had wanted to give a lot for being the first white child born on the Reserve, had died during the winter. Pease moved the desperate family on to Cleveland with his party.

Consequently, when Turhand Kirtland, one of a 1798 Connecticut Land Company party of thirty-seven that included three women and eight children plus various livestock and a dog, arrived at the Creek on May 28, just ahead of Simon's party, he found the cabins and a nearby Indian village deserted.[1]

Kirtland, who would soon become the Connecticut Land Company's agent on the Reserve, had come to survey and settle the towns in which he had a proprietary interest and to assist in cutting a road from the Pennsylvania line of Town 13 Range 1 [Litchfield] to the "capital city" that Cleaveland's party had laid out on Lake Erie and along the east side of the Cuyahoga River in Town 7 Range 12 [Cleveland]. Major Amos Spafford, a member of both the 1796 and 1797 surveying parties, had a contract with the Connecticut Land Company to run the line for the road. Kirtland, William Law, and Lucius Tuttle were to cut the road into Range 6; Spafford and Lemuel Clark were to cut the road from Range 6 into "Cleaveland," [2] as the "capital city" had been named, in honor of Moses Cleaveland. And on the day of Simon's arrival at the deserted Creek, Kirtland, "a tall but rather spare built" man who possessed "a fund of dry humor," [3] was celebrating—in the log house in Town 7 Range 7 [Burton] that he had christened "Umberville's Coffee House" in honor of its inhabitants—not only Independence Day but the completion of this "Girdled Road." [4]

According to his instructions, Simon proceeded to make his "pitch" along this road at its intersection in the Erie Company's Town 10 Range 8 [Concord] with a second Connecticut Land Company road, being cut by John Young, that ran south from the Girdled Road to the Salt Springs tract in Town 3 Range 3 [Weathersfield].[5] This seemed an ideal location for a land agent, for presumably most of the prospective settlers would make use of the roads in exploring the Reserve.

During the summer John Partridge Bissell, who had been surveying with Seth Pease in New York, and Amos Loveland, who had journeyed to the Reserve from Vermont, joined Simon's party.[6] Together the men built a house that was referred to as

Perkins' Camp, cleared land to plant grain, and carried their surveying chains through heavy brush and rank weeds to measure off the Erie Company's land.

And it was, for the most part, promising land. Although the hills of the northern part of the Reserve made that land unsuitable for raising stock, the soil seemed good for a variety of crops. Further south, the land was higher, flatter, and better suited to grazing. Here too, the plentiful timber was sometimes sparser, and thus the land could be more easily cleared for planting. Most of the land was well watered by the rivers and streams that flowed north and south, falling away from the dividing ridge that stretched from northeast to southwest across the Reserve. In places such as Town 2 Range 11 [Portage], there were several lakes that promised an abundant supply of water; but in other places, Town 8 Range 7 [Canton-Claridon] being one of them, the trickling streams left swampy land of dubious value.

It was hard and often disagreeable work for Simon and his men to make their way through the unbroken country. And even when he rested, Simon had maps to draw and field notes to write that recorded essential data about the soil, water, and wood he found:

Made explore of Lot No 4 in No 9 8th R began at a post set for the NE corner which post stands about 25 links S. of the road . . . soil very good but Stonney . . . passed two creeks . . . Timber has been Basswood Hickery Maple Beach Chesnut Butternut and Blk Walnut and W. Oak and some Whitewood . . . thick herbage all the way . . . a handsome Cr. sufficient for a mill runs N. . . .[7]

There was a problem, too, with William Wheeler Williams. For Williams decided to settle on a Connecticut Land Company lot near Cleveland [8] instead of on Erie Company land. And in 1799, instead of building the mill the Erie Company had planned on to improve their townships, Williams would begin a mill at what would be called Newburgh. This was a setback to the Company's settlement program; but with no government on the Reserve, Simon had no legal means of enforcing Williams' Erie Company agreement.

But as he explored and surveyed the Erie Company's lands, Simon found settlers who were clearing land, building houses, and planting crops. Thomas Sheldon, Amos Spafford, Lemuel Clark, Lorenzo Carter, Nathaniel Doan, and the Kingsbury, Stiles and Gun families were living at Cleveland. In Town 11 Range 5 Alexander Harper had begun a settlement called Harpersfield. And after establishing the Thomas Umberville family in Town 7 Range 7 [Burton], Kirtland had gone on to Town 1 Range 1 [Poland] and built himself a log house.

Late that summer Ephraim Quinby and Richard Storer rode over from Washington County, Pennsylvania, to buy land in Town 4 Range 4 [Warren] from two of its proprietors, John Leavitt and Ebenezer King. And Richard Storer hired a squatter named Joseph McMahon to begin clearing his land for planting the following spring.

But Simon found that the largest settlement was in Town 2 Range 2 [Youngstown], which had been bought from the Connecticut Land Company in 1796 by John Young of Whitestown, New York. The proximity of this land to the town of Pittsburgh made it attractive to settlers; and here the Indians' friend and former Pennsylvanian James Hillman, the fiery Irishman Daniel Sheehy, and some ten families from Washington County, Pennsylvania, had settled, cleared land, and begun laying out a village according to Young's plan.

Once during the summer, probably by following the Indian path which lay along Big Beaver Creek, Simon left the Reserve and went to Fort McIntosh on the Ohio River. Here there was a fort "made of strong stockades—with bastions, and mounted with one six pounder . . . well selected as a point for a small military force always in readiness to pursue, or intercept the war parties of the Indians, who frequently made incursions into the settlements." [9] But since the Reserve was not under the protection of the Fort, Simon and the settlers could expect no help against an Indian attack. The Fort was useful only as a source of supplies; and on occasion that use was further limited to flour, as Simon found. For fresh meat the surveyors and settlers were sometimes reduced to killing and roasting the rattlesnakes which infested the Reserve.

Finally, in October, Simon settled his debts with Mrs. Henry Brown for doing his washing and mending and for making him a pair of trousers.[10] Then he started home "by the way of Presque Isle, Gennesee, Owego, & Minisink." [11]

Simon could report to the Erie Company proprietors, following his arrival in Norwich on November 27, that he found the prospect of sale and settlement good, but he had made land contracts during the summer with only three persons: Amos Loveland for $762.50; Henry Brown for $347.15; and James Hillman for $62.74. He had received in cash payment on these contracts just $13. And in payment of his own contract for a little over 829 acres at $946.83, Simon turned over his summer's wages and put himself in debt to the Company for the remaining $524.24 at six per cent annual interest.[12] The Company might be satisfied with the surveying, exploring, and settling duties performed by Simon, but they obviously could not have considered the summer's expedition an immediate financial success.

In addition, a new problem had developed and an old problem had been renewed, during Simon's months on the Reserve, that would further complicate efforts to sell and settle the land. The new problem was with Cleaveland who, already at odds with his associates in the Connecticut Land Company, also differed with the Erie Company Trustees and delayed Simon's next journey to the Reserve; the old problem was renewed opposition to the proprietors' claim to the land.

The proprietors of the Connecticut Land Company had already expressed their dissatisfaction with Cleaveland's management of the 1796 surveying party by appointing committees—in January, 1797—to investigate his expenses and the failure of the party to complete the surveying of the land east of the Cuyahoga River.[13] Moreover, since Directors like Phelps wanted to set a high price on the land, there was no doubt displeasure over Cleaveland's long-credit, $1 per acre sale of a township to some of the members of the 1796 surveying party, in order to settle what one of the party later said was a "mutiny or what would now be called a strike for higher wages."[14]

But worst of all, on his way to the Reserve Cleaveland had negotiated a treaty with Joseph Brant, the educated chief of the Mohawks, and some chiefs of the Seneca tribes; and in doing so not only violated the advice given to Zephaniah Swift in 1795 [15] but also an act passed by Congress in May, 1796, that forbade making unauthorized treaties with the Indians.[16] Cleaveland not only gave the Indians "ten or twelve hundred dollars worth of goods" [17] when he met with them at Buffalo Creek, but he evidently offered to help Brant seek an annuity from Congress [18] and agreed to pay Brant $1,500 on behalf of the Connecticut Land Company. It was generally believed that the payment was to be contingent upon the failure of Congress to grant Brant the annuity.[19]

And Brant did, in fact, try to get the annuity from Congress. In February, 1797—at the very time the Connecticut Land Company committees were questioning Cleaveland's expenses and his conduct of the surveying party—Brant went to Philadelphia for this purpose.[20] But Cleaveland did not go to help him, as he had evidently promised the Indian; [21] and Brant did not see, as he later wrote, any of the "great men" there.[22] He felt, in fact, that no one paid much attention to him. And he received no annuity from Congress.

Following Brant's unsuccessful bid for an annuity, Cleaveland's treaty or contract, as the Company chose to call it, became a source of dispute among the Mohawk and Seneca tribes.

Finally, on January 30, 1798, the Company voted to deposit money with Israel Chapin, Superintendent of Indian Affairs at Canandaigua, in order to pay the treaty. But at the same meeting they terminated Cleaveland's appointment as Agent by voting to have him turn over to Ephraim Root all the contracts he had made in 1796.[23]

Cleaveland then became short-tempered and petulant with Erie Company Trustee Daniel Coit. He delayed signing Simon's 1798 expense account and giving formal agreement to an advance of money to Simon for his 1799 trip to the Reserve. Then after Cleaveland's delay had forestalled Simon's April departure for three weeks and possibly cost him sales to settlers who would want to plant spring crops, Coit gave Simon the money he needed and evidently protested to Cleaveland about his lack of civility in the matter. Cleaveland, in turn, disputed Coit's right to advance Simon money and wrote testily to Coit:

Sir, you certainly need not call me to acknowledge what I have so repeatedly done at all time—that you and your Family have treated me not only with cevility, but the greatest and most unfeignd politeness. You could not have hit a nerve suseptable of a quicker touch . . . am now informed by you the first time that you were Treasurer of the Company and add to it a precious peice of knowledge that as Treasurer . . . you had a right to receive & pay out money without myne or Major Perkins consent . . . you tell me you informd me what Money would be wanted to pay our Agent and I did not make any objection & Major Perkins gave his Verbal consent.

And then, considering his delay in the affair, a final petulance:

I might say not any of Mr Perkins Letters . . . were communicated or directed to me that I have seen nothing but scraps & memorandums of Monies & Taxes Recepts & expenditures and you wrote Letters to our Agent without consulting me.[24]

Thereafter Simon carefully addressed his letters to all three Trustees at Norwich, and Coit or The Major sent them on to Cleaveland, often by personal messenger. But Cleaveland would continue to delay Company documents and decisions in the years ahead: At one time Simon would be kept waiting over a year for a properly executed power of attorney that Cleaveland had agreed to send him; and another time The Major would be left cooling his heels in Canterbury after Cleaveland had said he would meet him there to discuss Uriel Holmes's proposal for dividing the land in Town 8 Range 7, and that affair would consequently continue to cause trouble for Simon and the Erie Company.

Perhaps it was the problems that resulted from Cleaveland's season on the Reserve that deterred the proprietors from setting up their own government over the land; perhaps it was a realistic appraisal of the enormity of the task. In any event, except for the unexecuted motion made by Pierpont Edwards, son of Jonathan Edwards, that the Connecticut Land Company establish a college out of the proceeds from the Company's six townships,[25] the proprietors made no effort to found or organize any institutions on the Reserve. And as early as January, 1797, the proprietors were willing to cede their juridical rights to the Reserve.

Following the precedent of the Susquehanna Land Company's Wyoming Valley colony, the proprietors first requested the Connecticut General Assembly to erect the Reserve into a county to be administered at the sole expense of the Connecticut Land Company. The Assembly refused the proprietors' request, but the legislators agreed that Senators Uriah Tracy and James Hillhouse might present a bill in Congress ceding Connecticut's juridical rights to the United States. Once this was accomplished, the proprietors could accept the government of the Northwest Territory without jeopardizing their land claim and could work for statehood under the provisions of the Northwest Ordinance.

But as Simon learned on his return to Connecticut in the fall of 1798, Tracy's first attempt to secure Senate consideration of the bill had been unsuccessful. In the winter of 1799, Tracy finally managed to get the bill engrossed, but consideration in the House was postponed from the Fifth to the Sixth Congress.[26] And when Simon returned to the Reserve in May, 1799, he found the Company's efforts had renewed the old title question.

There is a report in Circulation I am told and has gaind much credit in Washington County Pennsylvania that the Connecticut title for this land is not good which has prevented many people from coming to this Countery. [And he warned the Trustees]: If this should continue to influence the minds of the People I fear that the articles of agreement which I have generally given . . . will not be satisfactory with out such further addition as to make it a compleat warranted title. I think it would be a great misfortune, [he added], to have any preventative to the pleasing prospect of immediate Settlement. All the Proprietors now in the Countery have resolved to give Contracts for warrantee deeds.[27]

Only two weeks later, Simon again wrote the Trustees:

It is current that Mr [Albert] Gallatin has said the title is not good. An observation of that Kind, coming from the Pole Star of the Western part of Pennsylvania together with the intrigues of Pennsylvania Landholders has been sufficient to prevent many people from coming to this countery . . . my Contracts will not be satisfactory if this report should continue . . . please to write me particularly on the subject.[28]

While he waited for an answer, Simon made eleven sales agreements and was able, in August, to report that his total contracts amounted to $5,497.[29] This was a considerable accomplishment, for in addition to arriving later in the spring than he had planned and the deterring effect of the title problem, suiting a prospective settler with a lot took, as one proprietor said, "the Patience of Job—the wisdom of Solomon & the strength of Sampson—to pass over in good humour the whims etc. of these . . . the quibbles of those & to remove the difficulties of others by tramping till they are satisfyed." [30]

But on most of Simon's contracts there was to be no cash paid until late autumn. In fact, only one settler made a down payment on his land, and that was in a yoke of oxen and a cow.[31] And as time passed Simon would often have to accept butter, a horse, or even a few yards of cloth for a settler's payment of his contract. When that happened, because of the highly complicated chain of debts involved in the Reserve, the financial welfare of the settlers, proprietors, and ultimately, of the schools of Connecticut would come to depend upon Simon's ability to accept such farm produce or property and convert it to specie or paper acceptable to eastern creditors and their banks.

And during the summer of 1799 it was already evident that the people of the Reserve were depending upon Simon for more than just land: Simon went with John Young and some of Youngstown's settlers to "fix on a place for a Burying ground"; [32] and he met with Young, Hillman, and Daniel Sheehy to "arbitrate" Sheehy's disagreement with John Young over obtaining a deed for the land Sheehy had bought from Young.[33]

Simon had ridden his horse to the Reserve that summer over the southern road through Pennsylvania to Pittsburgh and then through the woods to Youngstown. This route was more economical and less difficult than the frequently stormy Lake Erie trip. And it was evident even in 1798 that the early settlers, many of whom were from Pennsylvania, preferred the southeastern farm land at $1 or $2 per acre over Cleveland lots at $50 or even $25. It was also significant to the settlement pattern of the Reserve that the southeastern townships were more conveniently located for obtaining supplies from Fort McIntosh and Pittsburgh and for future shipping of produce to New Orleans, where the United States had now secured the right of deposit from Spain, via the Ohio and Mississippi rivers. And so Simon moved his headquarters to Youngstown, where he boarded with John Young and his wife, and cut roads and made his contracts for the most part in the Erie Company's adjacent Town 2 Range 1 [Coitsville] and Town 3 Range 2 [Liberty]. He did not neglect fulfilling his agreement in Town 10 Range 8, for he arranged with Richard Gifford to build an "improvement" on the property.[34] But Simon's decision to develop the townships in the southeastern corner of the Reserve added to the factors that favored that part of the purchase for early settlement.

And it seemed the Reserve was alive with settling activity that summer, in spite of the title "slander," as Simon termed it. Town 4 Range 4 [Warren] added several families to its population when some of Quinby's and Storer's neighbors in Washington County, Pennsylvania, followed them onto the Reserve. But there were still very few people on the great expanse of land, and Simon often felt lonely and isolated. In September he noted quietly: "Tuesday 17th was 28 years of age." [35] Another time he pleaded with The Major: "Believe me Sir I have not heard from any Son of Adam in Connecticut . . . if you have not time to write more please to write your name and send me that, that I may know there is yet one man Alive." [36]

Then, as the title rumor raged unchecked through the Reserve and buyers grew wary of his contracts, the only unwarranted ones still being given in the Reserve, Simon begged the Trustees, "Gentlemen If you have any Respect for your property, your Agent, or anything else in this Countery do be so kind as to answer this letter." [37]

At last, on September 22, John Kinsman arrived in Youngstown with an appendix to Simon's instructions. But it was a disappointment. Simon, confident that the proprietors' claim to the land was valid, had hoped to give warranted deeds. His new instructions, however, only gave him the additional option of taking land in Connecticut in exchange for Reserve land. "I observe from the caution which governd you in wording it that you are no gamblers," he said to the Trustees. "Am sorry that it was quite so limited . . . was it not for the Clamor about the title Lands would sell as fast as to equal the wishes of the proprietors." [38]

But the proprietors were definitely concerned about Simon's reports, for interest was coming due on their debts to Connecticut and payment depended heavily on the sale of the land. And that winter—spearheaded by Uriah Tracy of the Erie Company in the Senate and by Jonathan Brace, Trustee of the Connecticut Land Company, in the House—the proprietors prepared to fight through Congress a bill that would cede Connecticut's jurisdiction to the United States but yet validate their title to the land.

The title fight soon became involved in the politics of the day. The people of the country were already split into Federalist and Republican camps that reflected the economic, sectional, and ideological differences between Alexander Hamilton, Washington's young Secretary of the Treasury, and Thomas Jefferson, Washington's Secretary of State and former minister to France. In the economic area the two men differed over Hamilton's plans to assume state Revolutionary War debts, establish a Bank of the United States, and protect fledgling manufacturing interests by tariffs; sectionally, they differed over Hamilton's favoring of New England-mercantile interests and Jefferson's favoring of Southern-agrarian interests; ideologically, they differed over federal versus state rights as well as over industrial versus agrarian concepts of the United States. Their ideological differences were even reflected in the sides they took in the British-French conflict that would soon embroil most of Europe in war: Hamilton sympathized with the British, and Jefferson sympathized with the French.[39] Hamilton, according to Bowers, believed "democracy could only lead to anarchy," and relied on "strong government supported by wealth." [40] Jefferson, on the other hand, had "absolute faith in democracy." [41]

Like others throughout the country, the Connecticut Land Company proprietors were split into Federalist and Republican camps. The merchants who had been injured by French paralyzation of shipping were firmly in the Federalist camp of Hamilton. But others were just as strongly allied with the Republican followers of Jefferson: Gideon Granger, who had invested heavily in the Connecticut Land Company and held much of his land in combination with Oliver Phelps, was then stumping Connecticut for the Jeffersonians; [42] Samuel Huntington Junior was openly supporting that party and had incurred the wrath of Director Roger Newberry—whom Huntington thereafter referred to as "Granny" Newberry, an "old superannuated bigot." [43]

The correspondence of the proprietors and records of the debates in Congress show that both parties were interested in predominating in the settlement of the Reserve, but the Connecticut Land Company proprietors were willing temporarily to set aside party differences for the vital task of securing their title to the Western Reserve. "I am sure that this time," said Gideon Granger, "when both parties want all their friends—is the best calculated for success." [44] And so Tracy sought the support of John Marshall and other Federalists in the Senate; Brace sought the support of William Henry Harrison and Federalists in the House; and Granger took up lodgings at the Frances Hotel in Philadelphia, where "The Vice President [Jefferson] & Republican Senators & Representatives reside," and was "sedulously tho not ostensibly attentive" to securing the support of the Jeffersonians.[45]

In the House, where the act then lay, Brace had been busy

enlisting the "interest in our service of Mr. Harrison Member from the Northwest Teritory," and Brace was able to report before consideration of the act began that Harrison "enters heartily into the business of our concern and promises me to do all in his power to aid the matter through." [46]

Brace had also been busy "collecting and arranging papers" relating to Connecticut's claim to the Reserve, and he had some anxious days when The Major, who had gone to Zephaniah Swift's house in Windham "for the Reserve papers," reported that the elderly Mrs. Swift

appeared to have no knowledge respecting them, [but that] after examining a long time . . . she recollected that Mr. Swift not long before he left home put up a large bundle of papers some printed & some written & requested Genrl. Cleaveland to call for them to carry to you, but thinks that Gen Cleaveland did not take them . . . she remembers that Mr Swift gave Major Ripley some papers to carry to you which she took to be the same. I wrote Genrl Cleaveland from Windham if they were in his possession or he had any knowledge respecting them to send to me this day without fail, but have heard nothing from him . . . I should be glad to hear that you have made an important discovery in Ripley's desk.[47]

But Brace did not find the papers. Whether Cleaveland ever had them cannot be known; Brace finally used some pertinent papers he found in the library in Philadelphia, and wrote Ephraim Root for copies of relevant Connecticut legislation and affidavits of the "Number of towns surveyd—in how many settlements have been commenced—the principal roads cut—the Genl amount of money advanced by the Company & by individuals in payment of Interest & other expenditures." [48]

Simon had by that time returned to Lisbon for the winter and could provide Root with the firsthand information he needed. And in John Marshall's March, 1800, report on the cession bill, it was stated—based, no doubt, on information provided by Simon—that settlements had been begun in thirty-five of the ninety-three townships east of the Cuyahoga, that there were about 1,000 settlers, that mills had been built, and that 700 miles of roads had been cut. It was also stated in this report that the proprietors, individually and collectively, had spent, in addition to interest on their payments for the land, $80,000 in the development and settlement of the Reserve.[49] Yet the title to the land continued to be questioned, and Simon waited in Lisbon to learn whether he would return to the Reserve.

In Philadelphia the party lines drew taut and tempers flared. "The real state of the parties," wrote Granger, "is inexpressible and shall never be entrusted to paper by me."[50] And Uriel Holmes wrote threateningly:

I learn from Phila. that a Report is circulated & believed among the Members of Congress that the Company has sent them a Democrat who has told the Demos in Congress that the Settlement on the Reserve is to be a Democratic one—And that he shall set up for a Representative from that Country. Who the rascal & fool is I can not lern, it is sayd not to be Granger. But the Report has alarmed the Federal Members and has rendered the issue of our Question quite uncertain again, whereas it before had become beyond doubt in our favor. If you can lern or suspect who the person is that made the observation, do write to him that he is crazy & that he must retract the whole or have his Throat cut. Do make a cast immediately of the Property which is holden by Democrats and send on to Brace. . . .[51]

Brace had found, in the meantime, that all the Federalist members could not be relied on, and he enlisted the support of Albert Gallatin, Republican minority leader, who was anxious to bring Connecticut's Wyoming Valley land claims to an end. On March 15, 1800, Brace sent Root a "copy of a Bill agreed between us & Pennsylvania yesterday."[52]

This bill provided that Connecticut would renounce forever any claims under her charter to territory west of the eastern line of New York, except for the Western Reserve. This meant, in effect, that Connecticut would no longer pursue the right of soil claims of some 13,000 colonists then living in the Wyoming Valley and that neither would Connecticut continue to claim, on behalf of the proprietors of the Connecticut Gore Land Company, a disputed two-mile-wide gore of land, lying within the 42°2' limits of Connecticut's charter, that stretched across the southern boundary of New York. This land had been given to Jeremiah Halsey and Andrew Ward in 1795 as payment for finishing the new Hartford courthouse, and New York had naturally disputed the claim to the land.[53] But the setting of Connecticut's territorial renunciation line at the eastern boundary of New York would concede this gore to New York and assure Pennsylvania of an end to the Wyoming Valley claims. In return, Connecticut quite naturally expected both Pennsylvania and New York to vote for the cession act.

On March 21 Marshall reported for the committee appointed on the subject that the cession of the lands ought to be accepted,[54] and the act was "referred to a Committee of the Whole House." Then in April, opposition to the "part which goes to conciliate and adjust the right of Pennsylvania to some of the land in question" developed. Some members of Congress also objected to "the principle of the bill." Finally Gallatin "moved a proviso which specially went to prevent the bill being construed to draw into question the conclusive settlement of the dispute between the States of Pennsylvania and Connecticut, by the decree of the Federal Court at Trenton, or to impair the right of Pennsylvania."[55]

After that, in a last ditch effort, the opposition in the House tried to show "the invalidity of the claim of Connecticut to the land in question,"[56] and in the Senate tried to amend the act to send the question of title to the Supreme Court for decision.[57]

But on April 28, 1800—with the shrill-voiced John Randolph of Roanoke having objected to the end to an act which would eventually lead to the establishment of more states in the Union—the "Act to Authorize the President of the United States to Accept, for the United States, a Cession of Jurisdiction of the Territory West of Pennsylvania, commonly called the Western Reserve of Connecticut" was approved. President John Adams was to deliver "letters patent" to the state of Connecticut for the "use and benefit of the persons holding and claiming under the State of Connecticut . . . the soil of that tract of land . . . called the Western Reserve of Connecticut," and Connecticut was to renounce all claims under her charter to any other land west of the eastern boundary of New York, in addition to ceding her jurisdiction over the Reserve to the United States. A final proviso specified that the act should not be interpreted as a pledge on the part of the United States to extinguish any Indian claims to the land.[58]

Following approval of the Act, the Directors of the Connecticut Land Company nominated the civil officers of the Reserve, and Governor Trumbull of Connecticut was asked to attach his recommendations to the list. It was at first thought that Huntington, who was now planning to move to the Reserve, would carry the list to St. Clair,[59] Governor of the Northwest Territory. But the Directors, perhaps influenced by Huntington's politics or by "Granny" Newberry's personal opposition, decided to have the list delivered by Federalist John Stark Edwards, "a heavy, fleshy man" [60] who was the son of Pierpont Edwards.[61]

In the meantime Erie Company proprietors Christopher Leffingwell, Uriah Tracy, Joseph Coit, Samuel Huntington Junior, Joseph Howland, Daniel Lathrop, Lynde McCurdy, Joseph Williams, and Erastus Huntington had signed a petition, which they delivered to The Major at his store near the Landing, that instructed the Trustees to send immediately to the Reserve "Mr Simon Perkins who . . . is as proper and Eligible a person as we can possibly procure for the purpose of negotiating for our Company." [62] And Simon, accompanied by John Kinsman and Moses Cleaveland's brother Camden, left at once for the Reserve.

They arrived at Youngstown on June 16 and that same day a meeting was held "to agree on the place where the County should be established." Then on June 19, according to Turhand Kirtland, he met with "Esqs. [Judson] Canfield, [John] Young, & [Ebenezer] King . . . at [Jonathan] Fowlers" in Town 1 Range 1 [Poland] "to advise where the County should be with Mr. Edwards." [63]

After this meeting Edwards proceeded to a conference with St. Clair in Cincinnati. On July 10 St. Clair proclaimed the Reserve

Trumbull County and "fix'd on Warren," as Simon said, "for the place where the courts are to be held." [64]

By July 27 Edwards was back at Ephraim Quinby's in Warren with the Governor's commissions for the civil officers.

The Governor told Mr. Edwards [Huntington wrote from Youngstown to Daniel Coit], he could not constitutionally appoint any person to an office who was not a Resident in the Territory, & desired him to strike out of the Company's nomination all who had not been on the land . . . Mr. Edwards in striking out the Justices struck out some that had been Residents for some time but which through some mistake, he was unacquainted with. [65]

Otherwise, the officers of new Trumbull County, which encompassed that part of the Reserve lying east of the Cuyahoga River and was named for the Governor of Connecticut, stood as nominated by the Connecticut Land Company Directors.

Five long and expensive years after the purchase of the Reserve, the proprietors and the people who had purchased from them at last had title to their land and the protection of an established government. Since the appointed officers were all nominees of the Connecticut Land Company, the proprietors had to some extent succeeded in establishing their own government. But since the officers were all residents of the Reserve, the settlers had at least a measure of self-government, although it was not a government they had had any hand in choosing.

The settlement of the title-juridical problem was looked upon by someone like Uriel Holmes as a great victory for the proprietors. No other Company had ever had their land title assured to them by congressional and presidential action. And Holmes, primarily concerned with profiting on his land, wrote to Root that the proprietors now stood on "high ground" and could congratulate themselves on being the undisputed owners of a "quantum sufficit of this Earth." [66] Huntington, who had planned to carve a Jeffersonian New Connecticut out of the wilderness of the Reserve, spoke of the title settlement as the "loss of paradise." [67] But Simon, who was concerned with the people and their feelings, said that the "People are very much pleasd to know that their title is established and permanent." [68]

With the title at last settled and government established, Simon should have found the sale of land easier. But although he was able to write the Trustees that he believed he had "sold more than any other man in the County," Simon felt he had not sold as much land that summer "as I had reason to think I might."

The people, as Simon later explained, had become "afraid to visit and settle in this land of promise" [69] because "we have been so unfortunate as to have two Indians killd by some foolish Whiskey fellows." [70]

4.

What kind of Christianity is this, or where is it to be found?

Governor Arthur St. Clair, Address to the Legislature of the Northwest Territory, November 5, 1800

*T*HAT SAME JULY, 1800, only a few days after the Reserve was established as Trumbull County, Joseph McMahon went to the Salt Springs with some other settlers to make salt.

The salt works was a two- or three-acre piece of ground containing a plank vat, "7 or 8 feet square & about 3 feet deep," which was full of water and kettles for making salt. Around the works were the remains of cabins and stone furnaces, said to have been built by Parsons in 1788. Pieces of broken kettles, decayed timber, and rotten tree stumps also lay scattered about the works.[1]

By this time, only a few Indians were still on the Reserve. The Eries had long since disappeared from the shores of the lake which bore the tribe's name. And the Wyandots, Delawares, Ottawas, Mohicans, and Shawnees had almost all journeyed further west. Across from Cleveland, on the west bank of the Cuyahoga River, there was still a small village of Ottawas, and a few straggling Tuscarawas and Seneca Indians still moved peacefully about among the Reserve settlers.[2]

Not once in his many months on the Reserve had Simon complained of any difficulty between the Indians and the white settlers. In fact, it was not unusual for Indians to come to the Salt Springs, where they would boil water alongside the white settlers to eke out a precious bit of salt that was needed to preserve their meat. And that July a party of Indians had camped "about 60 rods up the Salt Spring run Ravine, at an old camping ground." [3] But this time, according to Leonard Case's account of the affair:

The Indians got whiskey and had a general drunken revel in which McMahan and some other whites joined. The whiskey of the Indians having been exhausted, the whites were not satisfied, but sent to Quinby's at Warren and obtained a small further supply. The Indians suspected this, but the whites denied it and would not let the Indians have any.

A few days later, McMahon went to take care of Richard Storer's corn. The Indians came to McMahon's house and "began to tease" McMahon's wife "to serve as squaw, and finally threatened to kill her and the children." McMahon returned, talked to the Indians, and got their promise to leave his wife alone. But when he went again to Storer's farm, the Indians once more threatened Mrs. McMahon and one Indian, so the story is told, "struck one of the children with the handle of his tomahawk."

On Saturday afternoon, July 19, Mrs. McMahon started with the children to Storer's farm. On her way, she met her husband in front of Case's house; and after talking things over they decided to go to Storer's to discuss the problem.

On Sunday morning, after spending the night at Storer's, McMahon went "among the settlers along the Mahoning" and asked them "to go with him and make a permanent settlement of the difficulty." McMahon got about thirteen men and two boys to go with him. Among them were Ephraim Quinby, Richard Storer, and two brothers named Filles who later recounted their view of the affair to Leonard Case. Except for the two boys, all the members of the party had guns; and it was about ten o'clock that Sunday morning that the party passed by Case's house on its way to the Indian encampment at the Salt Springs.

When the party reached the run below the Indian camp, "Mr.

{ 39 }

Quinby, who in those times was generally looked up to as a kind of leader, called a halt. It was agreed that he should go up to the camp and see what the difficulty was and return and let [the party] know. . . . He passed on to the camp. There the Indians lay lolling about. Among them were Captain George, a Tuscarawa who spoke English, and John Winslow, a Seneca called 'Spotted John' because he was part white."

Quinby asked Captain George "what was the difficulty between him and McMahan and his family." The Indian answered, " 'Oh, Jo dam fool. The Indians dont want to hurt him or his family. [The whites] drank up all the Indians whiskey and then wouldn't let the Indians have any of theirs. [The Indians] were a little mad but don't care any more about it. [Mrs. McMahon and family] may come back and live as long as they like; the Indians wont hurt them!' "

When Quinby went back, his party had "sauntered up the path in the ravine along the run," and he met them coming up the bank. All except McMahon and the two boys stopped. Quinby said, " 'Stop, Jo,' " but McMahon and the boys went on to the camp.

The party could see the Indian camp, "some 12 or 15 rods distant," from the bank where they stood. "Capt George was sitting on the root of rather a large tree, when McMahon approached him. The other Indians, some five or six, and several squaws and papooses were lolling round about the camp."

After this point, McMahon's justification for the murder is debated in the accounts of the period. But Case, basing his account on the Filles brothers' observations and their comment that Captain George said he had already killed nineteen white men and wanted to make it twenty, felt McMahon acted in self-defense.

McMahon stood in front of Captain George, according to Case's story, and said, " 'Are you for peace or war? Yesterday you had your men, now I have got mine.' "

[There was] a tomahawk . . . sticking in the body of the tree, immediately above the head of George. He sprang to his feet, seized the tomahawk and was in the act of swinging it as if to sink it into

Jo's head, when Jo, being too near to shoot, jumped backward, brought his rifle to bear and instantly shot George in the breast. . . .

The blood spurted nearly to McMahan. McMahan cried out, "Shoot! Shoot!" to the men standing in open view without any thing to screen them.

At the same instant, the Indians jumped up, caught their rifles, treed and aimed at the whites. Of course the whites brought their rifles to bear, Storer among the rest. Several of their guns were snapped, but . . . the morning had been drizzling with rain and the guns were damp [and missed fire]. Storer saw John Winslow aiming, as he supposed, at him, and without further reflection threw his rifle into position . . . and fired.

At the same moment Winslow's squaw was endeavoring to screen herself and papooses behind the same tree with Winslow and was directly behind him. Winslow's hips were all of him that was exposed. Storer's ball passed through them and, passing on, broke a boy's arm, passed under the cords of the neck of [Winslow's] girl, and grazed the throat of his squaw.

At the camp, after the shooting . . . all was confusion among the whites as well as the Indians.

Between one and two o'clock the whites went back to Warren, and passed Case's farm "at rather a fast pace." The Indians, they said, had "dug slight holes, covered the dead with dirt and leaves" and, except for the wounded squaw and her children, had "fled for the woods expecting the whites would be after and murder them."

The wounded squaw took her children to James Hillman's place near Youngstown. This was a distance of nine miles, but it was said she arrived there with her children in her arms an hour and a half after the killing.

After that, "the report of the affray . . . spread like wildfire." Kirtland heard that "Joseph McMahon & the people of Warren had killed two Indians . . . in hasty & inconsiderate manner." [4] Huntington heard about the affair only a few days later when he was thirty miles below Youngstown, on his way to the Reserve.

We were informed it might be dangerous to come on to the Reserve [he wrote], as the settlers had been killing Indians & the whole settlement was in a state of confusion. Upon enquiry it appeared that the mischief had been done by a Vagabond Irishman from Pennsylvania, with little or no provocation from the Indians.[5]

"By 3 or 4 o'clock of the same day," said Case, the killing "had brought Hillman, John Young, and some others to Warren." Simon, who boarded again that summer with Young, was no doubt in the group.

That night, "the whites, supposing that the Indians would be upon them for vengeance, gathered in squads for safety. They mostly met at Quinby's. All kept guard and look-out."

The following day McMahon was arrested and put in jail at Pittsburgh.

Some of the inhabitants [said Case] thought that Storer ought to be arrested also. The gathering was at his place. . . . He quietly observed what was going on around him. He concluded from what he saw and heard, that he too might perhaps be arrested and put on trial and on reflection believing that would be inconvenient, he, about four o'clock in the afternoon, walked into his cabin, put on his hat, took down his rifle from its place on the hooks, [and] quietly walked off before them all, saying he must go to look for his cows and went west to the woods. No one molested him or tried in any way to hinder him.

James Hillman had traded with the Indians for some time, and the people now "prevailed upon Hillman to follow the Indians and endeavor to make some arrangement with them." A day or two later he took the wounded Indian boy and

followed the trail of the Indians through the woods to their camp. They had been so much frightened that . . . when Hillman came in sight they fled to the woods, and even with the aid of the boy, [Hillman] found it difficult to induce the Indians to return to their camp . . . Hillman made with them a temporary arrangement upon which the whites returned to their houses and the Indians to their hunting.

Simon, for the Erie Company, bore the expense of the conference Hillman had arranged with the Indians for July 30 at John Young's house. On July 29 the Indians began to gather. An interpreter had been sent for and he arrived "in company with one Indian chief & his lady on horseback." By the following day, "about 300 people" but only ten Indians had assembled at Youngstown.[6]

Huntington got to Youngstown in time to witness the affair with Simon and the crowd of settlers. And he wrote to Daniel Coit:

Mr. Young, on behalf of the Settlers, addressed [the Indians] in pacific terms, assuring them that the conduct of the Murderers was highly disapproved of by all the White people, that McMahon would be tried by our courts, & that the Treaty provided that mode, as the only one that could be adopted. He concluded by assuring them that it was the sincere wish of the White people to live in perfect friendship & harmony with their Brethern the red people.[7]

The Indian chief then spoke and the interpreter conveyed the message to the settlers that "the Indians were perfectly satisfyed to wait for the ordinary mode of Justice," and that "they consider it a quarrel in which Individuals only were consernd and not the mass of either nation." [8] The result of the conference, as Huntington reported, "was an Agreement to keep bright the chain of friendship & to leave McMahon to the Laws." [9]

Following this conference the settlers gave up their nightly watches at Quinby's and returned to their own homes. Then the newly appointed officers of Trumbull County proceeded with the business of establishing a government.

Town 4 Range 4 [Warren] having been "fix'd upon" for the county seat, it had next to be decided where the public buildings should be located. The original proprietors of Warren were Ashbell King, Simon Kendall, John Leavitt, Erastus Granger, Oliver Sheldon, Sylvanus Griswold, Matthew Thomson, and Reuben Bardwell. Like the Erie Company proprietors, these men had pooled their land to form the Cuyahoga and Big Beaver Land Company.[10] A considerable amount of the southeastern portion of the township—along the banks of the Mahoning, "where the lands, especially the bottoms, are generally good" [11] and where the settlers were convenient to the transportation and communication afforded by the Mahoning River and the Salt Springs road—had been sold to Quinby, Storer, and their friends who had followed them from Pennsylvania. But the proprietors of Warren township ignored this concentration of population and "laid out a town plot in the Center of the township," according to Simon, "and are very desirous that the public buildings should be there." [12]

Simon was well aware that the money for public buildings must either be contributed by the proprietors or raised by public subscription. He was quick to see and point out to Joseph Howland, who owned the township adjacent on the east to Warren township, that locating the buildings for the convenience and benefit of two townships could be expected to increase contributions to the cause. "With a little exertion," he wrote, "I am very much of opinion that . . . the place where the Courthouse shall be . . . may be fix'd on the East side of Mahoning and about 30 [chains?] from Howland west line and about two miles from the South line, which if that should be the case would benefit your township almost as much as it would the other." [13]

The county officers evidently agreed with Simon, and they overruled the Warren proprietors' original plan. When the first Court of Quarter Sessions met on August 25, 1800, it was between Ephraim Quinby's corncribs, east of the Mahoning and near the Howland west line. The court spent August 27, 28, and 29 "in hearing proposals viewing the ground & of fixing on a place for the Seat of Justice in Warren . . . many places were mentioned, but the east side the Mahoning near Esqr. Quinbies house was determined upon by the Court." [14]

Choosing the site of the public buildings was not, however, the only business that concerned Simon during the Court's five-day session. Simon was also one of a committee that established areas of legal jurisdiction by dividing Trumbull County, or that part of the Western Reserve lying east of the Cuyahoga River, into eight townships that each encompassed several of the five-mile square townships surveyed by the Connecticut Land Company. The Court then appointed a Constable over each of the eight townships.

And Simon was, in addition, named Foreman of the Grand Jury that was summoned to hear "Information . . . lodged by the State attorney against Joseph Mahan [McMahon] & Richard Storer." The Grand Jury met at once and "found bills against each of them for the Murder of two Indians at the Salt Springs & processes were ordered to be issued against them to be apprehended and holden in close custody until the [Government] should order a . . . Court of [Oyer] & Terminer to be held to try them." [15]

On September 11 Simon went to Pittsburgh, evidently to attend to McMahon's return to the Reserve for trial. By the night of Monday, September 15, Simon was back at Youngstown with the prisoner and "the sheriff & an escort of 25 troops from the Garrison at Pittsburgh" [16] that had guarded McMahon.

Then on Wednesday the court opened and the Grand Jury, with Simon still Foreman, was summoned and "had bills of indictment laid before them" by the State's Attorney. On Thursday the Jury "found bills," the prisoner was "brought in traverse," and a "Jury summoned & impannelled" for the trial." [17] On Friday and Saturday the witnesses against the prisoner were examined and the case was argued. Then on Saturday evening, September 20, the people gathered at Youngstown to hear the verdict.

It was, as Simon said, "a considerable collection of people." [18] Governor Arthur St. Clair was there, for the first murder trial in new Trumbull County was an important occasion. George Tod, Yale graduate and recently admitted counsellor at law on the Reserve, was there, for he was attorney for the people in McMahon's trial. Benjamin Tappan and John S. Edwards, also admitted as counsellors by the first Court of Quarter Sessions, were there, for they had aided Steel Sample as attorneys for McMahon. And Simon, Samuel Huntington, Calvin Pease, Turhand Kirtland, and a nephew of Mrs. Moses Cleaveland mingled with the other settlers—the men dressed in homespun shirts and buckskin trousers, and the women in linsey-woolsey or buckskin dresses—who came from miles away to hear the verdict.

And the verdict of not guilty "was very surprising to the people," according to Simon. McMahon, he insisted, ought to have been punished. But, "There is so great a proportion of people here who have such a prejudice against the Indians that it is almost impossible to do them Justice." [19]

The verdict was surprising to St. Clair too, for according to the angered Governor

the homicide was clearly proved, and . . . committed with deliberate malice . . . yet the perpetrator was acquitted. . . . It has long been a disgrace to the people of all the States, bordering upon the Indians, both as men and as Christians, that while they loudly complained of every injury or wrong received from [the Indians] . . . they were daily offering to [the Indians] injuries and wrongs of the most provoking and atrocious nature, for which I have not heard that any person was ever brought to due punishment, and all proceeding from the false principle that, because [the Indians] had not received the light of the gospel, they might be abused, cheated, robbed, plundered and murdered at pleasure, and the perpetrators, because professed Christians, ought not to suffer for it.

And then he demanded: "What kind of Christianity is this, or where is it to be found?" [20]

But St. Clair's concern over conditions on the Reserve was not limited to prejudice against the Indians. He also cried out against the individuals who held lands in "large quantities" and "sold . . . in parcels on credit." It was a "not improbable evil," according to St. Clair, that because "the greatest part of the people are their debtors," that the great landholders had it "in their power to influence the whole elections in the country, and instead of a representation of the people we should have a representation of the great land holders only, who no doubt would serve their interests in preference to those of the whole people." [21]

St. Clair proposed to guard against the "not improbable evil" of landholder influence by substituting the ballot for the *viva voce* method of voting then used in the Territory. And as a result of the prejudiced McMahon verdict, the Legislature soon passed the act sought by St. Clair that provided for a jury of forty-eight freeholders of not more than 100 acres each in trials involving the murder of an Indian by a white person.[22]

And it was true, of course, that the large landholders were exerting a considerable influence over affairs on the Reserve. The Connecticut Land Company Directors had, after all, named the officers of Trumbull County; and those officers had admitted lawyers to practice, decided legal divisions of the county, and determined where the county buildings should be located—a matter of considerable importance in determining land values. And it was also true that although expediency and practicality were involved, Simon, with the interest of Joseph Howland in mind, helped influence the latter decision. But as far as selling land on credit was concerned, the evil of that system would be felt by the proprietors before it was felt by the settlers.

The policy established by the proprietors was, as Simon wrote the men who sought his help in selling their land, not to commence suits against the settlers for the collection of money due for land. As a consequence of this leniency, which was predicated on attracting settlers to the area, many proprietors were now pressed for money to pay their own debts, and some were already ruined: On September 6, 1800, Hannah Huntington wrote to her husband that Jonathan Devotion, a Connecticut Land Company proprietor, had had "every thing even to his wife's clothing . . . attach'd"; on September 28 she said that General Joseph Williams, Erie Company proprietor, had "Fail'd for an immense sum" and "There is hardly a man in the Landing but will feel it more or less." [23]

As Hannah told her husband that year of 1800, "There [have] been many changes . . . Friends & riches have taken to themselves wings & flown away. God in his mercy keep me & mine from such a Revolution." [24]

5.

We have a singular kind of Republicanism in this County.

Simon Perkins, Letter to Benjamin Gorham, September 3, 1805

*T*HE CHANGES IN the East and the settlers' fear of and prejudice against the Indians would soon create problems for Simon, but in the meantime there were changes on the Reserve and in Simon's life.

With title and government established, the proprietors began to send their sons west or to journey west themselves. Often the proprietors sent their sons to "the promised land" because it was thought heroic and character-building for a young man to go to the new country and live among the noble savages. Pierpont Edwards, writing to his son John Stark when the young man visited the Reserve in 1799, said:

Your enterprise has done you infinite credit, not only among your acquaintances but among all who have heard of it. I do not believe you could have done any act which would at a stroke have made you so important in the Eyes of the world as your going to the Reserve. All ascribe to you that firmness, enterprize, ambition, and perseverance, which must in a few years make you to be considered the father of that Country.[1]

And William Law sent his sons, William Junior and Jonathan, to the Reserve to sell his lands there even though William Junior preferred reading Butler's *Hudibras* or the Bible and building a

Windsor chair or a desk from a bread trough,[2] and Jonathan preferred delivering Jonathan Edwards' sermon "And he left his garment in her hand and fled and got him out,"[3] to tramping through the woods with a quibbling lot seeker.

The proprietors themselves journeyed west for various reasons: Sometimes they planned, like Samuel Huntington, to establish themselves politically through residence in the western country; sometimes they planned, like Daniel Coit, to provide potential settlers in the East with firsthand knowledge of Reserve conditions.

On January 10, 1801, Samuel Huntington, who was even more eager than Edwards to be the "father" of the new country, said the "atmosphere of Connecticut is infectious—particularly Norwich," and he made ready to "get out of it as soon as I can."[4] Huntington found it difficult, however, to obtain land where he wanted to settle. On the eve of the location of the county seat at Warren he had written to Joseph Howland suggesting a trade of the Huntingtons' big wide-porched colonial house in Norwich for some of Howland's land adjacent to the Warren township line.[5] But as Huntington's luck would have it, Simon had already written his letter to Howland about the probable location of the county seat; and Howland, knowing the land was worth more than Huntington offered, turned down the proposal. The land Huntington was apportioned in the partial division made by the Erie Company in February, 1801, did not suit him for his home. Then he decided he liked the preponderance of Yankees in Cleveland and made a proposal to the Directors of the Connecticut Land Company to buy land there. Included in his proposal was an offer to clear the mouth of the Cuyahoga for shipping and to build a distillery in the stagnating capital city. But Huntington's proposal was turned down, amid Moses Cleaveland's strenuous objections in Huntington's behalf.[6] Finally Huntington bought land in Youngstown from John Young, and Simon was asked to see that a house was made ready for the Huntington family.

Hannah was ecstatic over having her frequently absent husband "safe in my longing arms" after his trip to the Reserve. She told him that "blest with you and my children New Connecticut will be paradise." [7] She bustled about the Norwich house readying their entourage of "4 horses in hack, 4 horses in waggon & 2 horses rode—10 horse in all & 15 souls, Men Women & children." According to Christopher Leffingwell, who dropped in on the Huntingtons to witness the preparations, Hannah kept "her flesh" through the busy days, but "Sammy," said Leffingwell, grew thin in the process of selling their house and auctioning off their furniture. [8]

Hannah was still enthusiastic about the venture even when, after a journey of over forty days, the Huntingtons arrived at the Youngstown house prepared by Simon; and even when, shortly after, some secret arrangements enabled Huntington to purchase 200 acres in and around Cleveland and the entourage packed up and spent another nine days journeying through the wilderness from Youngstown to their new home on Lake Erie. Such families, commented Leffingwell, "would soon people the whole Reserve," for "Hannah will probably add six more in 7 or 8 years." [9]

That same summer Daniel Coit made the first of several visits to Simon on the Reserve. And he started toward home more enthusiastic than ever about "the promised land." When he stopped at Pittsburgh, Coit was pleased to hear that Gideon Granger, whose party loyalty Jefferson had rewarded with the appointment of Postmaster General, had named Simon the first postmaster on the Reserve. Besides being pleased about Simon's honor, Coit felt the establishment of regular mail service would be good news to relay to potential settlers.

But Coit was shocked to find, during his homeward journey, that not everyone shared his high opinion of the Reserve. A friend named "Gardiner" had spread some "tough stories" about the Reserve following his visit there:

Huntington's cattle have been driven 40 miles during the summer to find water, there being scarcely a brook in the Country . . . is said to have paid five hundred dollars at Pittsburg for furniture and that he is spending what little he has got left, is cheated by Mr Young and every one who deals with him, and that the fever and ague will kill him at the lake and his family be returned to their friends in Norwich for maintenance in two years.[10]

And although Huntington laughed off the stories as "Gardner-isms" and told Coit that if he could see the visitor's whisky bill at Lorenzo Carter's Cleveland hotel "you would believe there was no water in Cuyahoga or the Lake," [11] Coit still feared the tales would affect the westward migration.

He disliked even more, however, the "pompous description" of the Reserve that he later found in the *Alexandria Gazette*.

We are told [Coit said], that the County had not a white Inhabitant in it at the close of the last Century . . . and that now there are Thirteen Thousand Inhabitants, twenty or thirty Grist mills & many more Saw mills and free schools in great numbers together with seven circulating libraries and that no Country ever peopled so fast.

Coit and Simon attributed the story to Gideon Granger, who had an interest in the *Gazette*, and to Ephraim Root, who had placed the fantastic price of $100 per acre on his Rootstown land that lay along the presumably important Indian path from the Salt Springs to the Cuyahoga River. According to Coit, the only claims not made in the story were that "the Inhabitants had more Money than they knew what to do with" and that a "Salt Mountain" had been discovered in the country.[12]

But such idylls were what the people often believed, and they came to the Reserve in increasing numbers to make contracts with Simon for land. In spite of the Indian scare in 1800, Simon made contracts that summer for the Erie Company of nearly $15,000 and collected $1,300 [13]—a sizeable increase over his $13 collection in 1798. And Simon, who now charged a commission that ranged from three per cent on contracts for the Erie Company to eight per cent on contracts made for individual proprietors, could give up wearing trousers made by Mrs. Brown and homespun shirts made by Mrs. Young for such clothing as a "Taylor"-made nankeen vest fastened with buttons from his own mold.[14]

Particularly profitable to Simon was his association with Joseph Howland. Simon's opinion on the location of the county buildings having been followed, Howland gave Simon the agency of all his lands not pooled in the Erie Company. Howland proved highly cooperative in following Simon's suggestions about contributing to the courthouse and the jail in Warren, for which Simon was one of the building committee members, and about building roads and bridges in Howland township. Such improvements, coupled with the proximity of the property to the county buildings, resulted in numerous sales in Howland and in an early increase in value of that land when much of the Reserve could not be sold at any price. Their correspondence over the years indicates that Simon and Howland even cooperated in several stock-financed projects aimed at developing the Reserve, one being a road, with signposts painted by the wife of a settler and tollgates for the collection of fees, that Simon later considered the beginning of the country's internal improvement program.

Simon's success in Howland township also served as a guide in developing other townships. "It is of importance," Howland once said bluntly of the settlement process, "to have a beginning & to make some little noise about the business to awake the people to their own interest." [15] One way to awake the people was for the proprietors to encourage the establishment of a town by contributing land for a public square. Also, encouraged by Simon, the Erie Company laid out roads through Town 2 Range 1 [Coitsville], which was adjacent to Youngstown on the east, and through Town 3 Range 2 [Liberty], adjacent to Youngstown on the north. Such improvements, coupled with the location and lower cost of land in those townships, continued to attract settlers to the southeastern corner of the Reserve; but in Cleveland, where the Connecticut Land Company continued to hold out for a high price on lots and where Huntington felt grateful when the Land Company put up street signs, the population scarcely increased.

It was thus in no small part because of Simon's activities that the population of the Reserve continued to increase. By 1802, the population of the area described by the Northwest Ordinance of July 13, 1787, as the eastern state of the Northwest Territory [16] was over 45,000; and on April 30, 1802, Congress approved an "Act to enable the people . . . to form a constitution and State government, and for the admission of such State into the Union, on an equal footing with the original States. . . ." [17] According to the process provided for by the Ordinance, an election of representatives to a convention to form a state constitution was then held. The ballot for the first time succeeded the *viva voce* method of voting used until then on the Reserve; and in Warren on that important election day Simon read the settlers, some of whom were illiterate, the instructions for casting their votes [18] for the two representatives Trumbull County was entitled to.

Had an election in Federalist Norwich resulted, as it did on the Reserve, in the choice of a Jeffersonian like Huntington as representative to the convention, an uprising might have taken place. Since the revolutionary election of 1800 party antagonism had been so strong in Norwich that otherwise peaceful citizens sometimes resorted to brawling. In fact, the gentle Christopher Starr, a Federalist, was later subjected to a "chastisement with his big hickory" by an elderly Jeffersonian neighbor in a well attended conflict on the Chelsea Landing wharf, and the dispute had to be settled by arbitration. [19] But the election of 1802 passed peacefully among even the stanchest Federalists on the "wild" western Reserve. Losing contestant John S. Edwards even rode part way to the Chillicothe convention with winner Samuel Huntington. When they put up at Jonathan Law's along the way, Law said he at first "feared that company," but then sat up with them during their all-night discussion of Federalist and Jeffersonian differences. And although Edwards was "shackled with the errors of Federalism," according to Law, [20] he was beginning to believe that the sun would soon set on its principles.

The constitutional convention Huntington said was "an harmonious session" of "28 Republicans & 7 Federalists." He wrote to Turhand Kirtland from Chillicothe on December 3, 1802, that

though it might not be expected that general politics would have found their way from the Atlantic States across the Allegany, yet the line that divides parties in the States is as distinctly drawn here as there. [However, he added], those politics but seldom were brought up in the debates & never disturbed the calm discussion of any question. Had one of your concieted hot-headed Federalists from Connecticut been here at the session of this Convention, he would have been obliged to unlearn the lesson he has been taught respecting the ignorance and disorganizing spirit of the people in this western Country. . . . Many men of talents & information who emigrated here early from Virginia Maryland and Pennsylvania have acquired immense property & had a seat in the Convention—those men were among the most zealous to secure inviolably the equal rights of the people & to bar the door forever against the admission of slavery. . . . Though our frame of government is not exactly such as to suit any one member of the Convention or perhaps any other person, yet it is the best that could be agreed upon & considering the various opinions entertained by persons meeting in that body from all parts of America, brought up under different Governments, & impressed with [various] habits & prejudices—it is perhaps as worthy of surprise as admiration that they should unite with so much cordiality on those principles which secure the great objects of national freedom to the people & as much energy in the government as is necessary to their protection.[21]

And still other events that stirred or changed the older states passed over the Reserve settlers, who were struggling to clear their land and build their homes, almost without notice. The "in's & out's" as Howland termed it, of relations with England and France kept commerce "perplexed" and the Atlantic states in fear of war. "I sometimes wish myself removed to N Connecticut," said Howland, "with an idea of never returning from thence."[22]

The Louisiana Purchase, which Coit pointed out might prove advantageous to the Reserve, concerned Simon and the settlers less than the price of cartage to Fort McIntosh or the fear that they might be paid for their produce in counterfeit money or paper that would be discounted or defaulted by the eastern banks.

Even the doings of Aaron Burr were taken pretty casually on the Reserve, according to Simon. Daniel Coit wrote excitedly to Simon: "Pray is all the world beyond the Ohio River to be lopped from the Union and erected into a Kingdom for Aaron Burr? Or will the State of Ohio maintain their firmness and resist all the Devil that little man carries about with him?" [23] But while Burr might well have been expected to contact his cousin John S. Edwards in the recruitment of what was by one reported as "troops" and by another as "settlers," Simon reported they had seen nothing of Burr and knew only what they read in the newspapers about the affair.

But underneath this seemingly placid life in "the promised land" there were problems developing that Simon was aware of, even if others were not. There was a growing competition between towns; there was an increasing distrust of the large landholders since their denunciation by St. Clair in 1800; and there were multiplying antagonisms between New England and Pennsylvania settlers, based on both intellectual and political differences.

In 1805 the state decided to divide Trumbull County into smaller counties, and Simon's advice was sought, as it had been and would be in nearly every division of Western Reserve lands, in establishing the county boundaries. "You will perhaps wish to know why I am running to Chillicothe at this time," Simon wrote to Daniel Coit on December 5, 1805, "but to tell you in short we have gotten into a great ferment about County division, and we the inhabitants of this County have generally taken sides and are known by the Warren and Youngstown parties." [24] Of the two divisions proposed, Simon said, "I fancy it would not be uncharitable to say that interest was the principal moving cause to direct." [25]

In the first place, Simon was opposed to the Youngstown party's removal of the county seat from Warren for practical reasons: Ephraim Quinby had donated four acres of his land in Warren for a public square, and a courthouse and jail had been built with money contributed by Joseph Howland and others; but the settlers in Youngstown, who were in a financial tangle and in some cases without deeds to their property because of John Young's removal from the Reserve, were unlikely to donate either land or money for public use. In the second place, Simon believed that a county seat should not be moved once it had been located.

However, said Simon, "The Y.town party have the Representatives in the Legislature." And although he said it was not his intention to secure a division that was prejudicial to Warren, it was felt "necessary that some person from the County who are for the other division should be there and I have very lately agreed to go." [26] Soon after, Simon wrote Joseph Howland that "this county is now divided but not as we at Warren would have wished nor is it in a manner to injure us." [27] A northern county called Geauga, the Indian name of Grand River, had been established—the first of the six county divisions then determined upon for the future.

The division did not satisfy the Youngstown settlers, however, and in October, 1809, they succeeded in electing a Representative, Robert Hughes, who favored the removal of the county seat from Warren to Youngstown. Some of the Warren party then decided that throwing out the alien votes would secure the election of their candidate and prevent removal of the county seat. Consequently, the election was contested under the terms of the Naturalization Act then in effect, that required an alien to have lived in the United States fourteen years in order to vote. And at Youngstown Daniel Sheehy, who had become the leader of the Irish population, held forth in such flaming oratory against the questioning of his people's "rights" that he was finally put in jail.

Contesting the election turned out to be pointless, for the Legislature seated Hughes in December, over all protests. And the Warren residents did not lose the Trumbull County seat, as they had feared; neither did the Youngstown residents gain that coveted title until 1876, when they took the honor away from Canfield to become the county seat of Mahoning County. The only immediate results of the contest were to increase the rivalry between the settlers in the two towns and to bring into the open the prejudice between Irish and "American" settlers—results which Simon might have been well-advised to use his influence to prevent.

There was growing prejudice too, which Simon felt, against the large landholder. By 1802 Simon had made an agreement to buy all or part of the Connecticut Land Company holdings of Nathan Grosvenor, and he had also taken up bonds to Connecticut that had been defaulted by other proprietors. Because the Company had not been successful in selling the six townships set aside to cover the Company expenses, it was decided to partition them among the proprietors. In 1802 Simon served as a member of the committee that arranged this land, which had already been surveyed into lots of two to one hundred acres each, into equalized drafts. It cannot be determined exactly what land fell to Simon after Ephraim Root drew in 1802 for Grosvenor and other proprietors, and through them for Simon, but Simon acquired some lots in Cleveland. Later Simon took over Samuel Huntington's interest in the Erie Company, when Huntington gave up trying to help develop Cleveland and moved to Painesville. By 1813 Simon owned, although not free of debt or unencumbered by mortgages, or had owned and sold land in Town 3 Range 2 [Liberty], Town 2 Range 5 [Milton], Town 1 Range 4 [Elsworth], Town 4 Range 3 [Howland], Town 6 Range 6 [Parkman], Town 4 Range 4 [Warren], Town 9 Range 8 [Chardon], Town 10 Range 8 [Concord], Town 7 Range 12 [Cleveland], Town 1 Range 17 [Homer], and in the Surplus Lands, a gore of land that lay between the east line of the Firelands and the west line of the Reserve, as they were finally surveyed in 1806–1807. He was taxed in 1813, although part of the tax may have covered land he did not himself own but had the agency of, on 3,000 acres in two- and ten-acre lots in Cleveland.[28]

But as early as 1805 Simon felt the impact of being a large landholder. For it was then he wrote: "We have a singular kind of Republicanism in this County, i.e. that no man whose property is above mediocrity (and if so much it is very dangerous) is safe to be trusted." [29]

The third problem in the Reserve that would affect Simon was the antagonism between the New England and the Pennsylvania settlers. Many of the Pennsylvanians had come to the Reserve from Washington County, a county with the heritage of a Republican protest against taxation called the Whisky Rebellion and with a record in 1796 of only 25 Federalist to 1,256 Republican votes.[30] There were marked political differences between the Republican Pennsylvanians and the Federalist New England settlers.

And there were intellectual and social differences too. The Pennsylvanians, according to early settler Caleb Ensign, "had little book learning but were strong, hardy, and otherwise well fitted to become such pioneers. They suffered less than most of the earlier New England settlers as they were nearer their old homes and friends . . . they never wanted for bread, tho' they usually had little to spare." The New England settlers, however, "were separated from 'native land' and friends by long distances— ambitious to secure for themselves and children better inheritances even at the price of great privation." [31]

In the early days the "meetings and greetings" between the "two sorts of immigration . . . were friendly and sincere—the restraints of conventional society and the inequalities of homes . . . did not so much corrupt their neighborly intercourse as the conditions of later times." But there were prejudices on both sides. "The Yankee was mistrusted for his better education and shrewdness—the Pennamites were thought dull and shy." [32]

As far as politics were concerned the Pennamites generally had their way in those early days, for there was "much of the Democracy of Pennsylvania" [33] in his country, according to Simon. And it was true that the Territorial laws had in many cases been adopted from Pennsylvania codes. Also, although Republican Huntington in 1802 felt the constitution was an amalgamation of the different backgrounds of the representatives, the Federalists were outnumbered four-to-one in the convention and the constitution was much like those of Pennsylvania and Kentucky but more liberal in the granting of suffrage to all white males of twenty-one years of age who had lived in the state for a year prior to an election and who had paid, either directly or by road work, a state or county tax; and in providing no check on legislative power.

The democracy or Republicanism of Pennsylvania was a kind of government the Yankees, even a Republican Yankee like Huntington, feared and distrusted. The Yankees, as Simon said of himself, were generally fond of steady government and not too much change. And in 1808 three Republican Yankee judges— Huntington, George Tod, and Calvin Pease—asserted the right of judicial review when they declared invalid an act of the Legislature, directed against lawyers, that gave Justices of the Peace jurisdiction in cases up to fifty dollars. According to their decision, the act violated the United States Constitution, which guaranteed trial by jury in suits involving over twenty dollars; and the Ohio Constitution, which held that the right of trial by jury should be held inviolate.

Then on December 21, 1808, Simon arrived in Chillicothe to petition the Legislature for an adjustment in land appraisals and found the Legislature engaged in impeaching Messrs. Huntington, Tod, and Pease for their decision. The impeachments of Tod and Pease failed by only one vote; and the Legislature then determined not to proceed with Huntington's case—probably because he had been elected Governor of Ohio before the proceedings began and had, in the meantime, taken that office.

But the following year all the judges were swept out of office by the Republican Legislature. And although Simon might say, as he did in 1809 following the impeachment affair, that "as we are mostly Americans by birth we shall never arrive to that pitch of anarchy" [34] he associated with Pennsylvania Republicanism, he would soon feel Republican opposition to his own actions.

As far as Simon's personal life was concerned, Daniel Coit observed in 1803 that he had heard it rumored that Simon, now thirty-two, had decided to "exchange his life of celibacy." The Major, only recently married himself, correctly and somewhat pompously played Standish in choosing Nancy Bishop of Lisbon—a slim, brown-eyed woman of steady habits and determination, according to The Major—for the absent Simon's future wife.

Nancy kept Simon waiting for an answer, however. When Simon arrived on the Reserve in April, 1803, following a visit to Connecticut, he wrote to Nancy asking her to "be so good as to form an opinion and give me an anser on the subject. If your opinion should be favorable to my wishes and you should condescend to honour me with your hand and consent to mygrate to this country," continued Simon, "I shall endeavour before I leave here to make such arrangements and after to do all in my power to make the change not disagreeable to you." [35]

But it was not until June that Nancy agreed to the "transaction," and then Simon wrote: "I proposed going home in December, which will probably be the case. I shall be disposed to go as early as any way correct . . . I think I shall perform the Journey more Chearfully than I have sometimes done." [36]

The following March Simon and Nancy were married at Lisbon, and in June they started for the town of Warren where Simon had bought a lot from Ephraim Quinby and put up a log house, one of only sixteen houses then in the town, for himself and his new wife.

Simon was accustomed to making the journey by horseback, but that year he and Nancy traveled in a carriage bought for the purpose. At Chambersburgh he had to sell the carriage because he knew the roads of the Reserve were not fit for its use, and he and Nancy then continued to Warren on horseback, traveling part of the way with Simon's sister Rebecca, her husband, and their four children, who were moving to a new home in their town of Kinsman.

On July 24, 1804—thirty-one days after they had begun their journey—Simon and Nancy arrived in Warren. "Nancy performed the journey with more ease or less fatigue than she or I expected," said Simon. "She is now in good health and thinks it is good for her to be here." [37]

On March 11, 1805, Simon wrote to The Major that

Your friends Nancy & Simon . . . have (as they think) a fine boy, now between four & five weeks old, is in every respect apparently healthy and is reputed to be something larger than ordinary size; and Nancy so far recovered as to think it a bad job well over.[38]

The boy was named Simon Junior and was said to look just like his father. On February 23, 1807, Simon reported to Daniel Coit that his time had been much taken up with nursing. "Altho I have not been principal in the nursing department I have been a sort of superintendant." [39] A new child, a daughter, had made its appearance on January 24. Simon's first daughter was named Anna Maria; a second daughter, born in 1809, was named Olive Douglass after Simon's mother, who had died in 1806. "We think of them as do all parents," Simon said of his growing family, "that they are all fine children." [40]

During these early years Daniel Coit would often sit in front of the fire in his comfortable house in Norwich, with his wife in her rocker beside him, and write to Simon about their various interests. Sometimes he wrapped seeds—pear, apple, lima bean, white currant—in little papers and enclosed them in his letters for Simon to give to Nancy for her garden. There were discussions of the Merino sheep Simon had brought to the Reserve, and later there was advice from Coit about the mulberry trees Simon was trying in the cultivation of silkworms. Coit even passed on advice about eyewashes being used in the east on children's sore eyes—an affliction which seemed frequently to trouble Simon's children.

But always Simon and Coit were exploring ideas for the development of the Reserve. Coit had traveled in Europe after the Revolution and had been particularly impressed with the canals of Holland. He discussed the possible use of this kind of transportation in his own state and sometimes wrote to Simon, as did Joseph Howland, about the possibility of canals in the Reserve.

Simon could also depend upon Coit to investigate any resources he discovered as he continued to survey and explore. On one of Coit's visits to the Reserve Simon gave him clay found in Canfield to take back to Connecticut to be fired. When Coit found the clay made fine stoneware, he visited New England pottery-makers and wrote Simon details of the salt glazing process. And subsequently pottery-making was established in Canfield. When evidence of salt was found in a stream in Town 4 Range 15, Coit visited Uniontown, Pennsylvania, to observe the drilling for salt being done there. And on the Reserve Simon helped Coit's son Henry set up a salt-drilling operation.

By 1811 Simon was convinced the future of the state lay not in agriculture but in manufacturing. And he contemplated "at some future day . . . entering into some kind of manufacturing employment. . . ." He thought it practicable to make iron in Newton and to establish a water works for future manufacturing use in Elyria, and he tried to interest the proprietors in establishing such works or in selling the property to him for his own development.[41]

Simon also encouraged the proprietors to send preachers and schoolteachers to the Reserve. Late in 1800 the five-dollar bills that proprietors like Daniel Coit had placed regularly in the collection plate for the Connecticut Missionary Society were put to use sending the Reverend Joseph Badger to the Reserve. Mr. Badger put in arduous years riding the circuit of the Reserve homes to bring Congregationalism to the western "heathens" and Indians. Some of the other proprietors also sent preachers: Jonathan Brace and Enoch Perkins, a cousin to Simon, interested the Reverend David Bacon in settling their township of Tallmadge; and Benjamin Gorham sent a minister to live on his land in Cleveland. But it was Simon who saw that the "divine" men were paid for delivering a sermon or for conducting a burial. However, he often found the preachers unable both to tend their "flocks" and keep the weeds out of their crops, and many of the missionaries gave up and went back home.

As far as schoolteachers were concerned, Simon might advise a proprietor that there were a number of children on his land who needed a school, and the proprietor might then try to send an educated man to the western country to settle and teach. But like the preachers, many of these men found the frontier life too hard and did not stay. Occasionally a man Simon thought would make a good teacher appeared on the Reserve, as Samuel Oviatt did, and Simon would see that he got a land bargain in a place which had no school. But since there were no school funds, the settlers had to pay tuition for their children to be educated; and schoolhouses had to be built through public subscription on land donated by an interested proprietor or settler.

Although he was willing to encourage the establishment of grammar schools, Simon still had reservations, even "prejuidices," as The Major told him, about higher education. Simon made some effort to interest proprietors in giving money to the academy that the Reverend Badger finally succeeded in getting built in Burton in 1805. But it was difficult business supporting the school because, as Simon later pointed out, the only kind of endowment most of the proprietors could give was land; and since the school was subjected to land taxes, a gift of land that could not be sold was to make the school poor rather than rich.

And the fact was, Simon's prejudice against classical education was increased during these years by the fact that Bishop continued in a wild, deranged state. Simon experienced sad and anxious days in 1805 when Christopher Starr, who had been appointed Bishop's "Conservator," was called to the home of the man employed to care for Bishop. Bishop, according to his terrified caretaker, had resisted the removal of his beard. Christopher was able to quiet Bishop, but he suspected the caretaker of beating the young man,[42] and so he took Bishop to live with his family. Bishop was less mischievous after that, according to Christopher, but he was always "troublesome about having his beard taken off," [43] and once he turned on the older man when he was being led down the hall at bedtime. Bishop knocked the candle from Christopher's hand and fought against being shut in his room. Christopher blamed the scuffle on the time of the moon; but Simon, who had lost hope for Bishop's recovery, became increasingly hesitant about committing any young man of his acquaintance to the kind of education he thought had caused Bishop's trouble. And he took very little interest in helping the Reverend Mr. Badger with his academy or, for several years, in establishing any form of higher education.

The only kind of higher education Simon thought worthwhile was practical education. And in 1805 he "took to school" with him the three Kinsman boys—John, Joseph, and Frederick—to give them the kind of education he felt they needed. In Simon's land office they copied his almost illegible notes and letters, made out deeds, listed lands for taxes, kept accounts, and learned the ins-and-outs of surveying, arranging postal routes, exchanging money, and bartering produce. In 1807 Simon also took the crippled Leonard Case into his office to copy deeds and maps. Simon's land office was then in its zenith, according to Case,[44] and what he learned at that time enabled Case to serve later as a tax collector. Simon also took young Joshua Henshaw into his land office as a clerk-surveyor, and he even boarded him in his own home. And when John S. Edwards arrived on the Reserve with his new wife, in 1807, Simon and Nancy kept the young couple with them until Edwards could have a house built.[45] And it was no doubt through Simon that Edwards, although an educated man, learned what he needed to know to be County Recorder.

These were years so filled with change on the Reserve and in Simon's life that they seemed almost the "revolution" Hannah Huntington had once talked about. Of course, not everything changed. Moses Cleaveland continued to be slow and careless in handling his land affairs, and after Cleaveland's death in 1806 it fell to Simon, as one of Cleaveland's executors, to help settle the estate; and Uriel Holmes continued to argue about his swamp in Claridon.

But from these years Simon learned that even more changes were needed on the Reserve. To help the settlers and to encourage settlement, additional improvements—particularly roads and bridges—were needed; to save the greater part of the land from reverting to Connecticut, the settlers needed reliable money that could be sent to the heavily indebted proprietors; and to help the many bankrupt proprietors, the state needed to make changes in its land and estate laws.

6.

God in his mercy keep me & mine
from such a Revolution.

Hannah Huntington, Letter to Samuel Huntington, November 1, 1800

$\mathcal{D}$URING THESE YEARS, as a result of the shortage of specie or dependable paper, Simon's account books often looked like those of a general storekeeper rather than those of a land agent. Land-hungry settlers took on contracts, often against Simon's advice, for more than they could pay; and land-poor proprietors agreed to sell land with little or no money down. When interest payments fell due, the settlers were often unable to pay in specie or negotiable paper, both of which continued to be scarce; and Simon persuaded the proprietors to take cows, butter, and even "bare" skins, coonskins, and boots because any sort of payment would increase a settler's stake in his land and make him less apt to give up his contract.

Whatever produce Simon accepted eventually had to be exchanged to establish a credit to a proprietor or to the Erie Company. A dozen yards of cloth that Simon accepted from a settler as an interest payment might eventually net a fifty-cent profit that could be credited to the Erie Company. A settler might also pay his debts in road work, if the proprietor agreed. And in some cases the proprietors accepted land in Connecticut, Massachusetts, or other New England states as payment on Western Reserve contracts. The Major worked out still another kind of ar-

{ 65 }

rangement when he paid in Western Reserve land the carpenters who had built him a new house in Norwich. Eventually the day of reckoning had to come for an indebted settler, but the proprietors were the first to feel the effect of the credit system they followed in settling the Reserve.

By dealing in produce or work, or by swapping or bartering land, Simon was able to raise enough money to pay the Erie Company proprietors a small yearly dividend. In 1802, for example, the fourth Company dividend was two and one-half per cent on a proprietor's original investment.[1] These proprietors still complained of the slowness of land sales and the lack of profit on their investment, but they did not share, except for the early failure of Joseph Williams, the bankruptcy that threatened nearly all the original landowners. And from the tangled Williams estate, which is representative of the difficulties the proprietors and their heirs encountered, Simon managed to salvage a reasonable settlement, although it required securing changes in and additions to the Ohio laws.

Williams was a Brigadier General in the Twentieth Regiment of Connecticut's Militia, a director of the Union Bank of New London and of the Norwich Bank, and a member of the Connecticut General Assembly from 1792 to 1796. He was credited with making the first proposal to devote proceeds from the sale of the western lands to the support of Connecticut schools. And when the Connecticut Land Company proprietors presented security for the purchase of the Western Reserve, Williams obligated himself for about $16,000.

Williams also took an active interest in Norwich affairs: He served on the building committee for the new Congregational meetinghouse built in 1795; he was one of the proprietors of a grammar school established at the Landing in 1797; he was a steady contributor to the Missionary Society for the establishment of religion in the Western Reserve. He was, in short, a "solid" citizen.

He was thought to be, in addition, a citizen of considerable means. Besides being the principal owner of several ships engaged in the West Indies trade, Williams owned a wharf and a warehouse at Chelsea Landing.[2] But by 1800 the Norwich trade had "suffered severely," as Timothy Dwight would later note in his *Travels in New-England and New-York*, "from several causes; particularly from fires and French depredations." In fact, Dwight said that Norwich, in proportion to its trading capital, experienced greater loses from French depredations than any other town.[3]

Williams was among those who lost ships to the French. At one time, with Williams sailing as Captain, the schooner "Fair Lady" was taken by a French vessel. A prize crew was put on board, and "Fair Lady" was taken into a French port. Williams was taken on board the French ship and subsequently was recaptured by a Connecticut vessel and returned to his home. His schooner, however, was lost.[4] Then in 1799 his sloop "Prosperity" was also taken by a belligerent cruiser, was found to have "contraband goods on board," and was condemned and forfeited.[5]

These losses, coupled with the interest payment due on his bond to the state of Connecticut were more than Williams could cover. The first confirmation of disaster was when Williams' brother Isaac, also involved in Williams' indebtedness, was put in debtors' prison in Hartford. The court agreed to release Isaac "upon his paying cost," and he asked "the General to pay and he refus'd." This refusal at first appeared shocking; but the General, who was "thought by the Doctor to be near his end," could not pay for his brother's release, as Hannah Huntington reported, because he had "fail'd."[6] The idea of being confined for life turned Isaac's brain, according to Hannah, and a month later the General was dead "& his family reduc'd almost to beggary & out of the many good things he had posses'd his family have not wherewith to procure them bread."[7]

It was tragic and terrifying to see their once affluent and respected friends suddenly reduced to poverty and disgrace, and Hannah wrote fervently, "God in his mercy keep me & mine from such a revolution."[8]

It would take several years to straighten out the chaos of

General Williams' affairs. The principal difficulty was that the state of Connecticut, as holder of Williams' Reserve bonds and mortgages, claimed to be the privileged creditor; but the administrator of the estate, Joseph Williams Junior, claimed that the widow's dower was the privileged interest. But unless first the Territorial and then the Ohio taxes were kept paid on the land, it would be seized by the state and sold for back taxes.

Simon, acting as agent for the administrator, kept track of Williams' Reserve land and saw that the taxes were paid. Finally the administrator was permitted to sell the encumbered land to satisfy some of the claims against the estate, but Simon found the Ohio laws imperfect for handling the situation. Although much of the land in the state was owned by nonresidents, Simon said, "We have no statute that contemplates the settlement of the estate of any person dying out of the State nor have we any law authorizing the Court to give direction for the sale." [9] By the laws then in effect the land had to pass through another administrator in Ohio, a long and expensive process, particularly for a bankrupt estate. And on November 19, 1806, Simon wrote to the Representatives of the Ohio Legislature seeking a revision in the laws that would permit the court to authorize the sale of the land.[10] Finally, after some additional lobbying, Simon was able to report to Joseph Williams Junior that the desired change in the laws had been effected; and he then petitioned the Court of Common Pleas for the auction of 16,378 acres of Williams' Reserve lands. And in 1809, nine years after General Williams' bankruptcy and death, a notice of the sale was tacked up on courthouse doors on the Reserve.

After that, Simon was able to forward to Williams' son Joseph enough money to relieve the Connecticut demands and eventually to provide Williams' widow with a little over $1,700. A few years later the General's brother Isaac, recovered from his ordeal in debtors' prison, journeyed to the Reserve to settle; and Joseph Williams Junior, expressing obligation to Simon for his prior attentions to the family, asked Simon to write if he heard from Uncle Isaac.[11]

Of additional concern to Simon was the debacle that for a time threatened Joseph Howland. In 1806 Howland's New York ship-ping office suddenly announced a suspension of payments. How-land was not at the time in New York. He was, in fact, on the road to Norwich; and a rider was dispatched from New York to over-take him with the news.

Howland was stunned by the suspension. He wrote Simon at once that he was certain the suspension would be found unneces-sary, but to make certain the Reserve lands were not involved he had deeded some or all of his property to Gardner Greene of Boston.[12] Greene was not as cooperative as Howland in develop-ing the Reserve. He was also reluctant to give Simon a power of attorney to make out deeds for his property, and this acted as a deterrent to the sale of the land because the settlers were still inclined to be suspicious if they could not get a clear title made out by Simon. But Howland was eventually able to straighten out his affairs and to recover much of his Reserve property. By 1811 he was again keeping Simon advised about the development of the Erie Canal and sending him early drawings of the project.[13]

But these were, in reality, the more fortunate proprietors. After 1807, failures were announced almost continuously; the eastern papers were filled with advertisements of lands for sale from bankrupt estates. Even the mighty Phelps, who had once thought he had had to divide the Reserve into "small share, hardly worth holding," was not spared. It has been variously said that Phelps went to debtors' prison and died there,[14] and that he concealed himself to escape debtors' prison but that his reverses preyed on his mind and caused his death.[15] There is no documentary evi-dence in Phelps's papers [16] in support of either statement; and strangely enough, the available letters of other proprietors do not mention Phelps's fate. However, his papers at Western Reserve Historical Society contain letters addressed to him at Canan-daigua in 1808.[17] In any event, the complete settlement of Phelps's affairs extended into the 1870's, through two generations of his heirs. And it can only be imagined how many persons experienced delay or difficulty in obtaining a clear title to land they had purchased from Phelps.

The financial difficulties among the proprietors engaged in

commerce were often related, like the Williams and Howland affairs, to the European wars and to the stagnation or stoppage of trade under the embargo Jefferson obtained from Congress on December 22, 1807. A measure recommended by Jefferson for the protection of American seamen, ships, and cargoes after the U.S.S. "Chesapeake" was fired on by the British "Leopard" and searched for British deserters, this embargo "laid a sudden and complete interdict, indefinite as to time, upon the foreign commerce of the United States." [18] The effect on those engaged in shipping and trade was catastrophic. But the financial difficulties of many other proprietors were the result of the settler's inability, for various reasons, to pay for his land in specie or negotiable paper and of the proprietor's constantly increasing liability for taxes, interest, and land improvements.

Shortly after the Reserve was taken under the government of the Northwest Territory, a tax was placed upon the lands of both residents and nonresidents. The proprietors considered this part of the discriminatory legislation directed against them, and Simon said it was a "degradation" that they were taxed when U. S. lands were not; further, little or none of the tax money was applied to roads or other improvements. Then between 1803, the year in which the state of Ohio was established, and 1810, the tax on land crept from a rate of sixty, forty, and twenty cents per hundred acres on first- second- and third-class lands to a rate of $1.25, $1, and sixty-five cents on the three classes of lands.[19]

The tax was burdensome to both settlers and proprietors, for they were additionally in debt at six per cent interest for their land. Some of the settlers had ninety per cent or more of their land contracted for at this interest rate, and some of the proprietors had eighty-five per cent or more of their land mortgaged at this same rate to Connecticut.[20]

In order to equal a settler's principal, interest, and land taxes, 100 acres bought in 1800 at the minimum price of $1 per acre had to increase in value to over $1.50 per acre by 1810. And for the original proprietors, who had purchased at about forty cents an acre, such an increase in value was still without profit since the cost turned out to be more than forty cents an acre after the total acreage was determined.[21] To their price must also be added the assessments they had paid the Connecticut Land Company for settling Indian claims,[22] making the original surveys, and building roads, bridges, and other improvements. Except for the townships where Simon had encouraged the making of improvements, there was little increase in land value. In fact, sales at any price were sometimes impossible, and the taxed land became a heavy liability to both settlers and proprietors. Settler John Young, the first purchaser from the Connecticut Land Company to settle in the Reserve, had trouble meeting his debts; and he and his wife packed up and returned to Whitestown, New York, in 1802. And for the proprietors the situation became even worse after the 1807 partition of the lands lying west of the Cuyahoga River.

In 1805, Oliver Phelps and some of the other Connecticut Land Company Directors, in combination with representatives from the Firelands Company, negotiated a treaty freeing the lands west of the Cuyahoga River from Indian claims. The Connecticut Land Company then proceeded to ready the land for partition. There was another dispute over the property lines, this time over the south boundary of the Reserve. But this was eventually settled and in January, 1807, the land was partitioned among the proprietors.

Simon objected to bringing this additional land into the market for at least three economic reasons: There was already more land on the market than could be sold; the proprietors' scattered holdings would be further diffused, and this would discourage the making of improvements; and the proprietors would be subjected to still more taxes that would make the state richer, but committed to a relatively small expenditure for improvements, and the proprietors poorer. The land was nevertheless partitioned— largely to satisfy Oliver Phelps, who wanted to put up the new lands as bond on the interest payments for which he was in arrears.

Then in 1809 a final partition was made. This consisted of defaulted notes and the gore of land—called the Surplus

Lands—that was found in the final surveys between the west line run by the Connecticut Land Company and the east line run by the Firelands Company. After this partition, which closed the books of the Company—except as a matter of record and the transfer of deeds—the whole Reserve was up for sale and in competition with United States lands that were priced more favorably.[23]

Simon's objections to the partition proved valid in that the proprietors were made poorer. So much of the land reverted to Connecticut that the School Fund was threatened. And in 1810 James Hillhouse, who, with Uriah Tracy, had presented the Western Reserve Cession Act to Congress, was appointed commissioner of the School Fund with the task of bringing order out of the chaos.[24]

In this task Hillhouse sought Simon's help: Simon knew the land, the proprietors, and the settlers; he also knew and had even helped shape the Ohio land and estate laws while dealing with the Williams estate.

Simon's first concern was to prevent the land from being sold for Ohio taxes. If he could not sell the land on the open market in time to satisfy the most pressing claimants, it was then put up for auction—as had been done in the Williams case—where the price paid had to equal one-half the appraised value of the property. In addition to the advantage of netting a greater amount for the proprietor, the auction system did not devalue the Reserve lands as much as the tax sales. But the success of Simon's agency on behalf of Hillhouse and the state of Connecticut can be seen in the 1820 report that the principal of the School Fund was reported to be $1,700,000 and yielding interest of $60,000.[25] And Connecticut apparently began to think better of her "large white elephant," for Simon's account books show the occasional sale of a tract of his land to that state.

For the Reserve was steadily growing in spite of the financial tangle involved in its settlement. The growth was too slow, however, for proprietors like Williams and Phelps: they died as bankrupts. And Ephraim Root, who was once thought to be the richest man in Hartford, had had land listed since 1814 for nonpayment of taxes.[26] It was said he had become a "notoriously hard drinker," and that

unnerved and unable to raise a glass to his mouth, he would have rum placed in a coffee pot on a table, at which he was bolstered up, and by means of handle & spout of the pot managed to continue his potation to the very end. He died penniless, drink and taxes on his extended estates of wild land in those years of financial depression had dissipated all his property and otherwise ruined a splendid man—and left only a great lesson.[27]

7.

It is of the first importance . . .
that you fall, not by the hands
of each other. You are to each other
friends and not enemies.

Elijah Wadsworth, Address to the Troops, August 27, 1812

*O*N JUNE 16, 1812, the *Trump of Fame*, the first newspaper
in the Western Reserve, began printing an act chartering the
Western Reserve Bank. Simon was one of the commissioners of
this first bank to be founded in the Reserve; and the aim of the
bank was to provide the settlers with the sound money Simon
knew was essential to the continued settlement of the Reserve.

But this same edition of the *Trump of Fame* also announced
"that the militia ordered to Detroit" with General William Hull
"left Dayton on the 1st of the present month." Two days later
—on June 18—Congress declared war on Great Britain, and
before the Western Reserve Bank could be put in operation
Simon, who had been elected a Brigadier General in 1808 and
given command of the Third Brigade, Fourth Division of the Ohio
Militia, was ordered by Elijah Wadsworth, Major General of the
Division, to draft, arm, and equip four of the companies under his
command and hold them in readiness for active service.[1]

Disagreement, confusion, bungling, opposition, and unpopularity mark the War of 1812. There was disagreement, for example —which continues to the present among historians—over the causes of the war. As Warren H. Goodman notes in his "Origins of the War of 1812: A Survey of Changing Interpretations," [2] Madison's war message said the declaration was forced on the United States by British violation of the American flag on the high seas, the harassment of the eastern coast, the impressment of American men, and the plunder of commerce.[3] John Randolph, however, charged that "agrarian cupidity" urged the war.[4]

But if fought for the defense of commerce, it was difficult to explain why the war was voted against by the New England states and why, as Henry Adams observed, "Except beyond the mountains the war party was everywhere a minority." [5] Equally difficult to explain would be a desire on the part of individuals to add more land to either the public domain or to their personal holdings, for those who would presumably speculate in such lands were already deeply in debt. Thus later historians, although not entirely deserting Randolph's claim, have tended to advance other causes that Goodman [6] summarizes as follows:

The desire to defend the national honor; the hunger for agricultural land; the belief that the Indian problem could be settled only by removing the British from the continent; the competition between Americans and Canadians for the fur trade of the Northwest; the South's lust for the Floridas; Anglophobia; the anti-English propaganda activities of political exiles from England and Ireland; the desire to end Spanish interference with the export trade of Mississippi and Alabama; the ideal of manifest destiny; the desire to foster domestic manufacturing by excluding British products; and the West's desire to improve its economic condition by forcing the repeal of the British Orders in Council.[7]

Only Pratt, in his "Western Aims in the War of 1812," [8] attaches much significance to the Indian problem. Indian friction, says Pratt, was the result of American expansion into the Indian lands; [9] and reports of increased Indian hostility were based not on British excitation and propaganda, but simply on increased Indian hostility.[10] Yet documents of the period validate that the principal—indeed, almost the only—concern of the settlers was the Indians and their savagery. And while the Indian friction was definitely caused in part by expansion into the Indian lands, it was also caused by the white man's treatment of the Indians.

As far as the Western Reserve expansion was concerned, Cleaveland's treaty or contract created Indian friction at the very beginning of white settlement in the area. In 1801, Samuel Huntington observed that the Indians looked with "wistful eye" on the lands they had given up.[11] And in 1805, when the surrender of the lands west of the Cuyahoga River was being negotiated, the Indians withdrew from the Cleveland meetings and had to be followed to Fort Industry [Toledo] before they agreed to part with the land. When the treaty was signed, it is said that "many of them wept"; [12] and on July 5, 1805, Simon heard that "the whole town of Detroit has been of late burned to the ground." [13]

Between 1795 and 1812 this same thrust into Indian lands was repeated all along the frontier. As Hacker notes,[14] between 1795 and 1809, the Federal government acquired by treaty from the Indians more than 48,000,000 acres of lands in the Ohio valley alone.[15] And finally, the Indians had organized under the leadership of Tecumseh and his brother, The Prophet.

Then, although Tecumseh camped peacefully in the West Union Shaker colony near the Wabash on the eve of the Battle of Tippecanoe and expressed his people's desire to live peacefully with the white men, the cry all about, as Shaker Elder Issachar Bates said, was for "War! war! war! . . . Alas, Alas." And when Tecumseh withdrew to his settlement at Tippecanoe, Harrison's forces—doing irreparable damage to the Shaker buildings and pilfering freely of Shaker supplies and equipment—followed the Indian chief and his people—who were said by Bates not to have taken "to the value of one cucumber" without the Shakers' permission—[16]and burned the Indians' town and stores of provisions to the ground.[17]

By January, 1812, fear of the Indians was so strong on the Reserve that Calvin Pease remarked that "the few straggling old Indians & Squaws that hunt about the Cuyahoga are magnified into an army of 12,000 men." [18] And on June 24, 1812—only four days before news of the declaration of war reached Cleveland—the citizens of that town gathered in the public square to watch the hanging of O'Mick [Omique], an Indian who had lived peacefully among them for several years, for his presumed participation in the murder of two trappers at Sandusky.[19] All appeals from the Indians to give O'Mick to them for justice had been ignored; and so too was the fact that after the hanging and burial, Dr. David Long and his friends dug up O'Mick's body for dissection—a desecration the settlers would never have permitted on a white man.

After that, the newspapers reported that the Indians were growing more troublesome; and by April, 1813, there were stories of grisly Indian atrocities that the settlers did not seem to see they had in any way provoked:

A force . . . found the bodies . . . cruelly tomahawked and dead. . . . The situation of Mrs. Kennedy was shocking beyond description. She having been pregnant her body was found entirely naked, cut open, and the child taken out and hung upon a peg in the chimney. Her entrails were scattered all about the door, and the hogs were eating them.[20]

Confusion and official blundering also had to be contended with before Simon was able to get his Militia forces organized and established at the war front. There were, first of all, conflicting orders from Washington about the number of men needed, how they were to be raised, whose command they would be under, and when and where they were to march.[21] Wadsworth also found that some companies had not elected their officers, and one company commander reported that one-half his men were "Quakers and will not go if called." [22]

Then those who volunteered or were drafted during the early summer were dismissed, even after the declaration of war, for it was found they could not be equipped for battle.[23] Although it was known that only one out of five men reporting for muster might have a gun, it was not until July that Return Jonathan Meigs, then Governor of Ohio, ordered 350 muskets for Wadsworth's forces. When these guns arrived in August, they were found to need repairs before they could be used.[24] And inquiries in Washington only brought the answer that the government had no arms available for men on the Reserve who were being asked to fight.[25]

Even notifying Hull of the long-expected declaration of war was mishandled. In December, 1807, Simon had received a letter from Gideon Granger, still Postmaster General, saying:

You cannot be ignorant of the unpleasant aspect of public affairs between this Nation and Great Britain, nor of the vigorous preparations making for War in Upper Canada. In this state of things it has become necessary to establish a line of expresses through your Country to Detroit . . . I have to Solicit you (And even more to express my opinion that it is your duty) to depart immediately for Detroit . . . to proceed as far on your way as Cleveland, where you can plan the general arrangements and where . . . you will pass the Cayahoga, and proceed Westward on the line making the best possible arrangements and particularly providing by every possible means for the passage of the Water. . . . Tho' well acquainted in your Village, I know of no other person whose exertions would at this time be as satisfactory to the Government. . . .[26]

Simon left Warren on December 12—Granger's express letter from Washington having reached him in the unprecedented time of three days—and after arranging for carriers at Cleveland he proceeded through almost uninhabited country to the western line of the state. There were no roads or bridges in this area, for it had but that year been partitioned among the proprietors. And Simon traveled by what paths he could make for himself, and crossed streams and rivers by canoe with his horse swimming alongside.[27] But he made the arrangements for the mail Granger had requested.

This express service from Washington to Detroit was not used, however, to send Hull notice of the declaration of war. The notice to Hull was placed in the ordinary mail, and it was not until June 28 that Cleveland Postmaster John Walworth "received a communication from the Post Office Department requesting him to forward dispatches which would be found in the mail to General Hull by express." Walworth then called in Charles Shaler, a Cleveland settler, to take the dispatches to Hull, who was then thought to be "near the rapids of the Maumee." [28]

Shaler and Walworth searched for the dispatches first in the Cleveland mail and then—although Walworth was reluctant to open the mail pouch of another office and consented to do so only because he had received a private letter with news of the declaration of war—in the Detroit mail. Here the dispatches were finally found, and Shaler started his 150-mile ride to the front.

On the night of July 2—two weeks after the declaration of war by Congress—Shaler arrived at Hull's Detroit camp, where "the very sentinels were asleep on their posts." [29] By this time, according to the journal of Miami Rapids settler Lewis Bond, the news had been made known to the British by "an express . . . sent by John J. Aster of New York with private letters giving this information." [30]

In addition to mishandling the notification of Hull, Washington had done nothing about building a road to Detroit that Simon had arranged for when he established the express mail service in 1807. At the time Simon arranged this express mail service, the Indians had made no land cession to the United States from the western line of Ohio to the boundary established by Hull's 1807 Treaty of Detroit except for a twelve-mile-square piece of land at the former British fort at the Miami [Maumee] Rapids and a two-mile-square tract of land at the lower rapids of the Sandusky River. In crossing this part of the proposed route to Detroit Simon "conversed with several distinguished Indians upon the subject of opening and constructing a road to connect the twelve miles grant or reservation with that of two miles and to connect the latter with the Connecticut Western Reserve." [31]

The Indians were amenable to ceding the land needed for Simon's proposed road, and in 1808 Hull negotiated the Treaty of Brownstown on the basis of Simon's prior conversations with the Indians. But it was not until August 27, 1812—nearly four years after the Treaty of Brownstown and more than two months after the declaration of war—that Albert Gallatin, then Secretary of the Treasury, instructed Meigs to make contracts for building this road.[32] Meigs then sent Gallatin's letter on to Simon, in order to make arrangements for cutting the road. But in the meantime, Hull's forces had of necessity slowly hacked out a road from Dayton to Detroit.

The disorganized situation became frantic on August 22, 1812, when word was received at Cleveland that Hull had surrendered Detroit to the British. The Clevelanders believed themselves "in an allarming situation." Several citizens sent Simon an express letter saying,

[The British] are advancing rapidly towards this place. Last evening nine Boats reached the River Huron laden it is stated with 300 regulars and 600 Indians . . . Our situation is deplorable. Your good sence will dictate to you what we stand in need of, therefore we shall expect your aid to the extent of your power.[33]

Simon immediately sent an express letter to Wadsworth that suggested Simon march his Third Brigade to Cleveland's defense. Wadsworth had also received news of Hull's surrender and was already preparing orders to Simon to march one-half his Brigade, "officered & if possible, equipped according to law," to Cleveland. But as far as equipment was concerned, Wadsworth could only say, "I hope you will be able to arm the whole of your detachment, & furnish them with ammunition if possible. I shall take on what little powder & lead we have here, with a few spare Armes." [34]

There were more confusing and contradictory letters from Cleveland on the following day, but by August 26 Wadsworth was in Cleveland and taking a realistic look at the situation. He that day sent Simon orders to dismiss one-half the men ordered into immediate service for the defense of Cleveland.[35] Portions of other Brigades were also dismissed at this time, for Wadsworth had discovered that "the men in camp here are so badly armed that it would be useless to march them to the frontier." [36]

Yet on August 27 Simon was given command of a hodgepodge group of men from the various Brigades—some of whom openly resented being required to serve under officers other than those whom they had elected—and was ordered to march to Huron to defend "that part of the Western frontiers, against an invasion of any hostile power." [37] Simon had to obtain provisions for his troops over his own signature, since Wadsworth had no government money for equipping the Militia forces. [38] As camp equipment Simon had only nine tents, 282 yards of tenting, and five camp kettles. [39] But by September 5 he had established his men at the Huron River.

In the meantime General Reasin Beall had been given command of troops from the First and Second Brigades and ordered to march to Mansfield. Beall had a force of about six-hundred men, and troops from Virginia were to join him. He was to consult with Simon and arrange a line of defense between their forces by building blockhouses along the road from Mansfield to Huron. [40] But "untill the army . . . is furnished with munitions of war," wrote Wadsworth, "we shall not extend ourselves far into the enemy's country but arrange the defence of the frontier in the best manner." [41]

Simon began at once to build a blockhouse at the mouth of the Huron River and to send scouting parties along the lake shore and into the surrounding country. On September 9 he reported to Wadsworth his first loss of men; two men of a party sent to Sandusky peninsula had been killed by Indians. But another party had discovered a British schooner aground on Cunningham's [Kelley's] Island, he noted, and had successfully destroyed her without loss of men. [42]

In the meantime, Wadsworth had learned, as he wrote Simon, that

all the Indians in the N.W. territory are in motion towards our frontier. Fort Wayne is besieged, the British & Indians are fortifying a post at Miami Rapids & we may expect a visit from them. Col. Wells' head is on a post at Chicago, which place hath been taken & the garrison supposed slaughtered. [43]

And on September 9, Wadsworth received word that President Madison had determined to "repair the disaster at Detroit" and that fifteen-hundred men had been requested to march to the frontier.[44] But even though he warned Simon of the additional dangers to the frontier and of the decision to fight for Detroit, Wadsworth ordered Simon to "remove the main body of your troops to a distance of from eight to ten miles from the Lake" because he was "apprehensive that the position you have chosen for your camp . . . is a dangerous one."[45] And the fact was that Beall had not yet marched his troops as ordered, and Simon's forces were in a hopelessly exposed situation without any possibility of immediate reinforcement.

Simon, as ordered, moved his troops and stores back from Lake Erie to establish Camp Avery. Here the men began construction of blockhouses that Wadsworth said, "if supplied with provisions & water & garrisoned by 75 or 100 men will repel 1000 Indians."[46]

Just how Simon was to provision and garrison the three or four such blockhouses he was supposed to build Wadsworth did not make clear. For Simon had only about 250 men with him. "You will no doubt recollect," Simon protested to Wadsworth, "that when I came here my expectation was to have with me a full Regiment & those well provided." In fact, Simon's situation was so alarming that he had felt it necessary to obtain the actual number of his force "cautiously" and to lead his men to believe they numbered four hundred. "You will no doubt be able to judge," Simon continued, "wheather I can protect this part of the Country with a detachment of about 250 effective men, on the frontier of a powerfull & numerous enemy, at least 45 or 50 miles in advance of any aid or succour."[47]

On September 16 Major Elisha Whittlesey, Aide-de-camp to Wadsworth, advised Simon that Wadsworth had decided to send two companies to Simon's assistance. But in the interim Simon was ordered to leave his forces under the direction of Colonel Richard Hayes and return to Cleveland to receive orders for raising his quota of the 1,500 men Wadsworth had now been asked to organize to join the Northwest Army. From Cleveland Simon was directed to return to Warren to arrange his affairs, which he had left so hurriedly to go to Cleveland's defense, and prepare for a winter campaign.

Simon had no sooner reached Warren than he received a letter from Hayes telling him of difficulties at the Huron camp: Indians had killed three men and wounded two of a scouting party; Beall had reportedly gone home; the men had plundered property they had been sent to Sandusky to recover; there were new cases of the ague every day; the men were not equipped for a winter campaign; three men had deserted; and he had had to organize the men into companies of less than twenty because "that is as many as one officer can controll of such beings as they are." [48]

Hayes's troubled letter was followed by another express from Wadsworth that directed Simon to return to Huron as fast as possible. "I expect before this," wrote Wadsworth, "Fort Wayne has been attacked by a force of 2000 Indians & 300 Regulars & Militia from Detroit & Malden." [49] What Wadsworth feared was an attack on the Huron camp as the enemy forces returned from Fort Wayne. And only Simon and his meager forces protected the Reserve, for Beall had still not marched and the Cleveland troops still lacked the equipment needed for the front.

Simon arranged with Joshua Henshaw to handle his land correspondence, said good-by to the visiting Daniel Coit, and on the morning of September 28 he left Nancy and their four children—a second son, Alfred, had been born in 1811—and returned to Huron to lead men who had been cautioned by Wadsworth, on the eve of their departure for Huron: "It is of the first importance that friendship prevails among the troops and that you fall, not by the hands of each other. You are to each other friends and not enemies, embarked in the same common cause and the same interest in jeopardy." [50]

Organizing the Militia had been from its beginning in 1804 a difficult affair in which Yankee-Pennsylvanian differences were often evident. The Yankees were particularly eager not only to be elected officers but to fill the Militia posts with their own men. In fact, the desire to elect Yankee officers over the Pennsylvanians at times led to unethical behavior; Caleb Ensign tells the story of the educated Yankees who offered to write out ballots for some illiterate Pennsylvanians and cast the votes for a Yankee candidate rather than for the Pennsylvanians' man.[51]

The Yankees were also anxious to establish the military discipline they felt was essential to the proper functioning of the Militia. But the soldiers objected to taking orders and sometimes appeared on muster days without their arms, contrary to orders. When they brought guns, it was difficult to keep them from firing without cause. Neither did the soldiers want to salute the officers. As a consequence, orders were steadily handed down about maintaining discipline among the troops and keeping any men but the sentries from firing their guns in camp.

All these differences made it difficult to raise men for service. If the men did not object to serving under certain officers or to the principle of the war, they did object to leaving their families unprotected against the Indians. The correspondence of Simon and Elijah Wadsworth indicates that rarely were the ranks filled by volunteers, although settlers reminiscing after the event liked to think the westerners flocked eagerly to the flag. And our "drum and trumpet histories of the War of 1812," as Clauder calls them, gloss over ". . . the poor showing of our officers and militia on the battlefields. . . ." [52]

Moreover, Simon's troops were still short of equipment; they even lacked flints for their guns. More men had been killed by Indians while he was away, and Beall's troops had still not appeared when Simon reached Huron on October 2.

Beall's letters during this period indicate he was more occupied with making suggestions for action to Wadsworth than he was with marching according to Wadsworth's orders.[53] And on October 2, 1812, Wadsworth put Beall under arrest to await court-martial.

Wadsworth named Simon president of the general court-martial of Beall and charged Beall with disobedience of orders in not consulting with Simon, not informing Simon about the forces, not marching to join Simon, and with unsoldier-like conduct in not going "to the assistance of the troops at Huron after being repeatedly informed of their perilous situation." [54]

Beall pleaded not guilty at his court-martial, which began November 11 at what were then the headquarters of both Simon and Wadsworth at Huron. And on November 16 Major Benjamin Tappan, Aide-de-camp to Wadsworth, reported that the court found Beall not guilty.

The verdict was obviously a generous one. But after Wadsworth had ordered Beall released and his sword returned to him, Beall resigned. On November 29 Wadsworth also resigned. The Beall verdict no doubt negated his authority; but in addition Wadsworth had indebted himself to the point of jeopardy in equipping the Militia. And so, in a General Order dated November 29, Wadsworth placed his three Regiments under Simon's command.

Simon immediately reorganized the Division into two Regiments and proceeded to establish the discipline and order that would put an end to the kind of disagreement that had greeted him on his return to Huron on October 2. On that day the soldiers who had gone on a scouting party to Sandusky Bay accused their commanding officer of cowardice, failure to keep order, and un-gentleman-like conduct. On his part, the officer denounced the soldiers as cowards and stated that he had to drive them to the charge at the point of the bayonet.[55]

While these Ohio Militia events and changes were taking place, Harrison had successfully held Fort Wayne against an attack by the British and their Indian allies. The British had been highly optimistic about taking Fort Wayne. Lewis Bond, who had been taken prisoner by the British and was living with a British family in Detroit, heard their "boastings and national insulting language" that had accompanied preparations for the attack.[56] And on their retreat to Detroit the disappointed forces burned fields of grain and houses, and shot cattle and hogs until they "lay in such quantity as to create an intollerable stench. . . ."[57] over the country.

In December, in the wake of this retreat of the enemy, the American line of defense was moved forward: Simon was ordered to Lower Sandusky with some of his men; Harrison established himself at Upper Sandusky; and General James Winchester, commanding the left wing of the Northwest Army, encamped at Fort Defiance on the Maumee River.

At his Sandusky camp Simon continued his efforts to organize his men. He kept them occupied building huts for themselves and sleds for the transportation of baggage and stores. With the help of Whittlesey, who was now his Aide-de-camp, records of fatigue and guard duty were kept. The men were again specifically forbidden to fire guns in camp because of the danger and because of the waste of precious ammunition. Then, as a result of complaints about the soldiers' intoxication, Simon ordered the settlers at Lower Sandusky not to sell any liquor to the men without a permit signed by him. Such orders were not calculated to make Simon popular with the soldiers, but he was credited by Whittlesey with finally achieving "good order" among the raw and undisciplined Militia men.[58]

By January 15, 1813, Winchester had moved his forces on down the Maumee to the Rapids. On January 16 Simon received an express from Winchester advising him of this move and requesting provisions and a Battalion of infantry to reinforce a proposed march to the River Raisin. Simon sent Harrison notice of Winchester's location and ordered the Battalion of Major William Cotgreave to report to Winchester at the Rapids. On January 17 Harrison arrived at the Lower Sandusky camp to discuss Winchester's move with Simon; on January 18 Harrison inspected Simon's forces, and Cotgreave's Battalion moved out with "a piece of artillery and . . . baggage sleds" that the men would have to haul "through mud to their waistbands" across the Miami [Maumee or Black] Swamp.[59]

In the meantime Winchester had received word "from the River Raisin informing that 400 Indians had assembled there and that Col. Elliott with a detachment from Malden was expected there with a view to attack this camp this day." He asked to be reinforced with all the "disposable troops" that could be mustered.[60]

Simon and Harrison were in Simon's quarters, a small log hut previously made by Indians, when this express from Winchester

arrived. Harrison remarked that "he did not think the move ju-
dicious" and that he feared the information "was communicated
too late," but it was decided that Winchester's plan to march to
the River Raisin must be given "every assistance." [61]

On the morning of January 19 Simon and Harrison left camp
in a sleigh. At the Miami or Black Swamp they took to their
horses; "but when their horses sank so deep in the mud that they
could not raise their feet under the weight of their riders," they
had to dismount and lead their horses, "jumping from bog to bog
or from one cake of broken ice to another or wading through mud
partly frozen." [62]

Simon and Harrison arrived at the Rapids on January 20,
shortly ahead of Cotgreave's slower moving Battalion and a day
ahead of the Regiment of Colonel John Andrews, also ordered to
the Rapids after Winchester's appeal for all disposable troops. At
the Rapids the Generals discovered that Winchester had already
moved on toward the River Raisin, and on January 22 Harrison
ordered Simon's troops to "march to unite the right with the left
wing of the army at the River Raisin." [63]

Winchester's forces had arrived, in the meantime, about a mile
from the British camp at River Raisin, and Winchester established his headquarters in the house of a Mr. Navarre. The
British at first thought the American troops were an advance
guard of Harrison's army and that an attack on Malden was
planned. But

some traitors at River Raisin . . . sent privately to Malden, giving a
full account of the number of Americans, how they were camped, and
the very spot where the Genl. quartered, that they had no cannon, etc.
On the receipt of this intelligence Proctor collected the militia and
Indians manning the forts of Detroit and Malden [and] taking all or
nearly all his regulars and sailors . . . determined to attack the
American . . . camp at French Town . . . at daybreak on the 22d of
Jany. 1813.[64]

Winchester's expedition against the British was "ill-
conducted," according to Lewis Bond. When the British attacked:

The Americans reserved their fire until the enemy were within a short distance of the palisadoes, [but] Genl. Winchester being roused by the firing came to the scene of action and ordered a retreat. About 300 men did retreat with him across the River some distance, but a party of Indians had taken post in a position so as to cut off his retreat which the Genl. discovering ordered his men to ground their arms, which was no sooner done than a massacre commenced and the greater part of these unfortunate men were murdered. While this horrid transaction took place . . . the gallant fellows in the camp had repulsed the British . . . but when it was known that the Genl . . . and a number of other officers were prisoners and most of the 300 men who retreated killed, they in the camp were induced to capitulate.

In Bond's opinion, the debacle was the fault of Winchester.[65]

The troops under Simon had proceeded that day only a few miles from the Rapids when they met men coming from the battle. Cotgreave's advance Battalion turned about, and the troops again encamped at the Rapids. That evening Simon and Harrison held a council of war to decide whether to try to fortify at the Rapids or to go back across the Maumee and Portage rivers while they were frozen. The troops had brought no tools with them for building any sort of fortification; and since they had no boats they could move provisions and equipment across the rivers only when they were frozen. It was therefore decided to fall back to the Portage or Carrying River. The storehouse and provisions which could not be transported were set on fire, and at "2 o'clock on the morning of Saturday the 23rd the troops crossed on the ice from the west to the east side of the Miami [Maumee] River. . . ."[66] It was a move that Simon and Harrison would be criticized for making.

In the meantime, British General Proctor beat a hasty return to Malden, for he feared an attack by Harrison. He left the American wounded behind, and the following day [January 23] a party of Indians murdered all who were not able to walk and burned the village of Frenchtown.[67]

The savages then returned to Detroit to celebrate their victory.

They danced from door to door to show the scalps they had taken and which they had prepared by tearing the scalp from the head, scraping it of its flesh, stretching it on a hoop, and roasting or drying it before a fire. "The flesh side of the scalp," according to Bond's description of the gruesome trophies, was "painted vermillion and sometimes decorated with feathers or coloured hair . . . then tied to a small pole or rod which they carry in such a manner that they may be exhibited most to view." The prisoners were then offered for sale, amid much shouting and waving of the scalp-poles by the Indians. And the fearful people of Detroit—both American prisoners and British citizens—watched silently because, like the doctor who had watched the Indians tomahawk the wounded at Frenchtown and not resisted even when he felt the brains of one man splatter in his face, they were afraid their resistance might make them share the same fate.[68]

Unaware of these grisly events to the north that would go down in history as the River Raisin Massacre, Harrison and Simon set up camp at the Portage or Carrying River. The following week they received reinforcements and supplies of war, and on February 1 they again advanced to the Rapids to prepare for the expected enemy attack by building Fort Meigs.

The Militia forces were subject to only six months' service, and Simon's term had now nearly expired. After Fort Meigs was completed, he performed but one other service at the front. Several companies were put under his command, and they marched between thirty-five and forty miles on the ice of the Maumee River in search of Indians that scouts had reported were camped on an island in Maumee Bay. But like so many of the American troop movements during the early months of the war, this march was too late; when they arrived at the island, Simon and his men found that the Indians had gone.

On February 25, 1813, Simon dismissed the men who had served their six-month tour and also prepared to return to his Warren home. He and Harrison had by this time become friends, and Harrison asked Simon to remember him to Jonathan Brace.[69] Officially, Harrison wrote to Simon: "I cannot avoid expressing my high sense of the zeal and ability with which you have performed your duty since you have been under my orders and I beg you to believe that upon all occasions and in every situation I shall be with great truth Your friend. . . ." [70]

Simon was by this time disgusted with the government's conduct of the war. And although in the past his correspondence had been politically noncommittal, after his return to Warren he did not hesitate to express his views. He wrote to Daniel Coit on March 14:

I fancy that you have with others been much surprised at the loss of the brave Kentuckians at the River Raisin, and perhaps thought that if they had been better soldiers they would have had beter fortune, but being myself acquainted personally with some and with the Characters of many, I am induced to believe that they were chargeable with no other fault than that of depreciating too much the strength of their enemy—and for that no man can be less blameable than the citizens of Kentucky, for whatever is said by our Government is orthodox there, and they had been so frequently told that Canada was to be conquered by a proclamation, that they had worked themselves into a belief that a few men with the promise of a Republican Government could certainly do it; but they found themselves mistaken, and left Kentucky to mourn the loss of many of her most valuable men. . . . But so long as it is calculated on that the Province of Upper Canada and all the Western Indians are to be conquered by one, two, or three thousand men, I fear we shall be disappointed. [71]

Two days later he wrote to his cousin Elias Perkins of New London, Connecticut:

I hope that if our government are intending to prosecute the war they will not do it at the halves, the business of conquering a province with a population of 80 or 100 thousand people is no trifling job, and so long as the most efficient means to be made use of is to decry the strength of the enemy and send out a force not sufficient to take New London, we may expect to hear unpleasant news. [72]

Simon soon discovered that on the Republican Reserve disbelief of that party's conviction that Canada wanted to join the United States and talk of the lack of troop strength were equated with the New England opposition to the administration and the war. On September 12, 1812, Daniel Coit had told Simon of a secret delegation from Connecticut and other northern states that was meeting with delegates from the south about changing the administration.[73] And in October a Connecticut resident wrote to his brother on the Reserve that he feared their hands might yet mingle in each other's blood.[74] That some of the settlers believed Simon shared the New England view became evident after a meeting was held on April 7, 1813, in the Warren courthouse, to nominate Simon as a candidate for Representative from Ohio's Sixth Congressional District.[75]

On April 12, five days after Simon's nomination, a committee that included Simon's Battalion Commander William Cotgreave met in answer to a report being circulated that "Gen. Simon Perkins, while in the service of his country . . . endeavored to influence the officers and soldiers under his command not to go beyond the bounds of the United States." This story, wrote the committee:

Is without foundation, as we have been under the command of said Gen. and with him the principal part of the time of our and his tour of duty . . . and we know that he did endeavor to inculcate better on the minds of officers and men the necessity of obedience to orders, to ensure honor to ourselves and to enable us to render service to our country.

This announcement was followed by a letter to Simon asking whether, if he were elected a member of Congress, he "would support the administration in the stand they have taken against Great Britain." [76]

Simon answered:

My opinion in regard to the proper mode of conducting the war is, that while it continues, to prosecute it with vigor and energy, and to enable the government to bring it to an honorable and speedy termination my exertions and influence will be to support the administration. Knowing, as I think I do, the political sentiments of the citizens of this district, I would not suffer myself to be run as a candidate if I did not think I should acquit myself to their satisfaction.[77]

The committee at Warren then voted unanimously to support Simon as a candidate for Congress, but that did not end the affair. On April 15, "At a meeting of a large and respectable number of the Republican electors of the county of Cuyahoga," it was "Resolved: That we view with sentiments of approbation and concern, the nomination of Gen. Simon Perkins." And the strongly worded Cuyahoga resolve continued:

That we consider Gen. Perkins an enemy to the Administration and opposed to the war, and that a statement made by him was intended to deceive the electors of this district with respect to his political sentiments and intentions, as evidence of his intentions to desert and betray his political faith to purchase his election, both of which motives we consider as equally base and dishonorable.[78]

The curiosity of this matter, as the Cleveland *Leader* later noted, was that:

Upon the surrender of Gen. Hull . . . Gen. Perkins forthwith marched out his Brigade and took position at Huron . . . no Brigade was ever better officered, had better men, or was better disciplined . . . and no officer in camp was more to be relied upon for the general purposes of war than Gen. Perkins. [The] very men who passed these dununciatory resolutions retained their scalps on their heads by his protection.[79]

The explanation of the Clevelanders' "boiling over patriotism" was "that certain citizens of Cuyahoga county failed to shave the Government while Gen. Perkins was in camp," and, continued the *Leader* article, "a certain individual who probably drew these resolutions wanted a place in Congress himself at the next term, and did not want a neighbor in the way." [80]

And strange as it seems, the Cuyahoga electors in their defamatory April 15 meeting additionally resolved to support none other than the slow-to-march Reasin Beall, whom they called "a friend of the Administration, and [of] the vigorous prosecution of the war . . ." and "the most probable means of preventing the election of Gen. Perkins, whom we believe an enemy to both." [81]

Simon or any one of several of his supporters—such as Cotgreave, who had been on the court-martial board—could have revealed the information about Beall's court-martial. But nothing was said of the affair; and Simon, true to his Connecticut Federalist heritage, did no campaigning.[82] Instead, he occupied himself writing letters to Paymaster Samuel Huntington regarding pay for his soldiers and to the Secretary of the Treasury to defend Wadsworth's claims for the money he had spent in equipping the Militia.

According to the *Trump of Fame* for April 21, 1813, Simon carried the election against Beall, 456 to 307, in the southeastern part of the Reserve, but lost the election in other parts of the Sixth Congressional District. And he wrote to his cousin Elias Perkins, "I spend the summer at home, the want of votes keep me from Congress." [83]

Simon had "cherished a fondness for the military life," according to Whittlesey, and President Madison had offered Simon a commission as Colonel in the United States Army. Prior to the election, Simon had accepted the commission. But on May 28, following the election, Simon wrote to John Armstrong, Secretary of War, and declined it.[84] Simon's refusal created a stir among his acquaintances in Washington, not only because of his prior acceptance but because a new war push was then in the offing. "It is new for an officer to decline after a previous acceptance on the eve of a campaign," wrote General Lewis Coss to Simon.[85] Simon then decided to accept the commission after all.[86] But in the meantime, his refusal had been made public. And that refusal was allowed to stand.

Just after his return from the front Simon had said to cousin Elias Perkins:

The business in which I have been engaged was a new one to me, and neither very splendid to myself or profitable to the government, but I have the satisfaction to think that I was not deemed a cypher among my brother officers and that the men whom I had the honour to command were not thought inferior to the best in the N. West Army.[87]

The election affair of 1813 deprived Simon, however, of even the small satisfaction he had felt over his command. As a result, he would never again agree to run for a public office; and although it would be many years before he would again express his political opinions openly, he would set himself against the democratic forces that had turned the majority of the settlers against him.

But he turned again to his business of settling his country and building the Reserve for its people. As Wadsworth had said, "It is of the first importance . . . that you fall, not by the hands of each other. You are to each other friends and not enemies." [88]

8.

Good as a Western Reserve Bank bill.

Newspaper clipping (n.p., n.d.), Joseph Perkins' Scrapbook

*S*IMON'S FIRST CONCERN that summer of 1813 was the completion of the new house he had begun before going to the front. It was a modest frame house of simple New England lines, conveniently located—on a site very like that of Simon's old Lisbon home—on a gentle rise of land near the Warren public square and overlooking the winding Mahoning River. Near the house Simon also built an office, and here he transacted land business, took care of the mail, and held meetings.

In October, 1813, Simon, Nancy, the four children, and Simon's clerk, Joshua Henshaw, moved into the new house. Following his usual reticence about personal affairs, Simon had not told his friend Daniel Coit about the move, and for that reason Coit said to him, ". . . you do not deserve it." But to Nancy, who had now lived in a log cabin for seven years, he wished "much joy on the subject" of the new house.[1]

During those log-cabin years Nancy had often managed their household alone. Simon might be gone to explore or survey a piece of land, to pay taxes at the different county seats, or to discuss land and financial affairs with the state legislators at Chillicothe. And during their early years on the Reserve, Simon made frequent trips back east. Traveling alone on horseback, he could reach Connecticut in twenty days, a laborious exercise he was later to insist his own sons must imitate because he thought it might make them as healthy as he had been. But the eastern trips meant Simon was gone for at least two months. At such times, Henshaw took care of any urgent land business and looked after the affairs of Simon's farm; and for several years Asael Adams Junior, who had come to the Reserve with his father and Dr. Jabez Adams, his uncle, carried the mail between Warren and Pittsburgh. But it was left to Nancy, whom The Major once described as a "sincere honest woman" with a "fine distinguishing mind," [2] to care for the children and to manage the garden that provided them with food.

Between 1815 and 1824, Simon and Nancy had five more children: Martha, born in 1815; Charles, 1817; Joseph, 1819; Jacob, 1821; and Henry Bishop, 1824. They had been more fortunate than many frontier families in the health of their children, but they were unable to save Martha, who suffered from some unnamed illness and died in 1817.

Nancy did not complain about her frontier life, but it is evident that she missed her Connecticut home and was determined her family would not live in the rough way some westerners did. When Leonard Case visited one Reserve family, he was

furnished with hot heavy cakes for bread or pone, sausage meat preserved in an iron kettle of about 12 or 14 gallons, from which what was wanted each meal was taken & the residue shoved under the bed and a large house dog went in & helped himself out of it when he pleased. Tea drawn in an old tin cup, no teacups nor much of any table furniture.[3]

But in Simon's house there were knives and forks, tumblers and wine glasses. The children and Nancy had shoes that Simon bought in Pittsburgh; their clothes were made of calico, linen, or flannel; and Nancy had bonnets which at times might cost Simon seventy-two bushels of wheat. And in their new home Nancy and Simon firmly taught the children manners, morality, religion, family loyalty, and a sense of duty and responsibility to their country.

But the new house was also to be a place, as Simon wrote one of the proprietors, "in which to entertain you & my friends generally when they call."[4] For in the years just before the War of 1812, immigration from New England had shown an increase, and Simon expected this trend to resume after the war ended.

One of the largest settlement groups to journey from Norwich just before the war was the one organized by Amos and Miner Spicer. In 1810 the Spicers built a house in Norwich for The Major; and after a journey to the Reserve to look at The Major's lands, they agreed to accept land in payment of their bill. At the end of July, 1811, the Spicers, Paul Williams, and "three or four other families . . . near 50 (6 Waggons)" left Norwich for Ohio, "most of them bound for Portage"[5] in Town 2 Range 11.[6]

The Major, to Simon's displeasure, agreed to a price of less than $2 per acre for the land. It was worth more, said Simon. But The Major had been anxious to settle his bill, and he pointed out that the Spicers "have beaten the Bush & have been at expence in effecting the settlement. Their removal and settlement will doubtless affect the value of the land somewhat" in the rest of the township.[7]

Then The Major also told Simon: "From what I can learn there must be many emigrants with you this season. There has certainly been many gone from this State & Massachusetts this season & many are proposing to go this fall."[8] And on February 7, 1812, he observed:

The spirit of emigration seems to increase. . . . People begin to look forward to the weight of representation on the West side of the Mountains. We don't know how soon the seat of Government may be there. . . . The time will come perhaps not so far distant as we may imagine when the Great Ridge will be a dividing line between Two Vast Nations speaking the same language.[9]

This westward migration ceased, of course, during the war. Simon observed in March, 1813, that "the population of the Country has not increased for the last twelve months."[10] He predicted, however, that "at the close of the War, sales will be more frequent than they ever have been, and . . . lands will command a better price than formerly."[11] Then on October 10, 1813—following Captain Oliver H. Perry's September 10 defeat of the British fleet at Put-in-Bay Island on Lake Erie [12]—Simon wrote to one of the proprietors:

The success of our little fleet on Lake Erie will, I think, have the effect to remove the seat of war so far from us as to induce people from the old states to come and settle with us. We have heretofore been in such an exposed situation as to render our Country uninteresting to people who were seeking a place for a family.[13]

And as Simon expected, the migration of New Englanders soon resumed; for Perry's victory was followed by Harrison's reoccupation of Detroit and the defeat of the British and Indians at Moravian Town, and once more the frontier appeared safe.

But this wave of westward migration was not influenced, as the early wave had been, as much by the romance of the west and the hope of political leadership as by adverse conditions in New England. On December 25, 1813, Daniel Coit wrote that

produce and almost every other article are excessively high with us. Corn $1. . . . Sugar 30 Dolls. pr. barrel. . . . Cotton has risen from 10 to 34 cents, and other things are going on much in the same way. Another embargo has taken place, and the seacoast is greatly distressed. How patriotic we must be to be willing to suffer so much ourselves in order to inflict perhaps the tenth part of the evil on our offending enemy.[14]

Two years later, The Major told Simon:

Things look rather gloomy . . . *Trade*—the thing or the Nothing—on which N England have relied or counted upon is—to use a trodden expression—quite cut up. Our Country have fought for the Rights of Commerce 'till we have few Rights left & but little Commerce. I don't know but we shall all be under the necessity of moving to the Western Country or live in a pretty humble sphere.[15]

In addition to high prices and the stagnation of trade, the victories of Perry and Harrison removed the war front from the western to the eastern states. On August 11, 1814, The Major said that an incident involving the British Consul at New London had caused the British to fire on Stonington, Connecticut.[16] The following month Daniel Coit told Simon: "All our sea coast is in constant alarm and the greatest anxiety prevails. We are in constant expectation that the National ships in our river will occasion us a visit—you had the first of the burthen but we seem to be destined now to take our full share." [17] And two weeks later, Coit said it was a "day of much perplexity & dispondence," [18] with residents of New London and Chelsea moving away from the coastal areas.

Still another event influenced the westward migration: As John S. Edwards had predicted in 1802, the sun was setting on Federalism. In 1812 Daniel Coit had told Simon about the small group of dissenters that met to discuss impeaching Madison, [19] and by 1814 this New England opposition to the administration was so strong [20] that a convention was held in Hartford to discuss the issues of protection of commerce, the conscription law then pending, and the appropriation of state taxes for the payment of state troops. Led by Timothy Pickering, the "extremists" of the group even advocated the secession of the New England states from the Union. [21]

The possible secession caused particular anxiety among the Federalists on the Reserve, who already thought themselves at the mercy of the Republican settlers.

Those who are really your friends tremble in anticipation of the consequences [said Elisha Whittlesey to a Connecticut friend]. Even if you should secede from the Union without blood being shed, what would be our situation? We could not fall down and worship the beast, which would be required if we intended to live here and eat our jonnycakes in peace. [22]

And when moderation and steadiness prevailed at Hartford and secession talk ended, the Federalists on the Reserve were relieved. But the convention, which alarmed the nation and created a schism in the party, marked the decline if not the end of Federalism. [23]

During these same years many of the proprietors' sons were coming of age. They could no longer look to trade for a profitable vocation, their political party was out of power, and manufacturing, although on the rise, was not yet well established or protected. Sent west to view the country, the young men toured the Reserve from the southern plain-lands to the rolling country in the north. They stared at tall trees, as Daniel Coit pictured them, of oak, beach, maple, hickory, black walnut, and ash; and they looked at the clogged, polluted, but potentially good harbors along Lake Erie. Compared to the Reserve, their homeland looked hilly and rough, and filled with rocks and stones. And on May 13, 1817, Daniel Coit wrote to Simon: "Emigrations from this part of the Country are increasing. Business generally is much depressed since the peace and many think of changing their situation without knowing whether they will benefit themselves or not by the change." [24]

Many of the New England emigrants settled on their family lands. But even those who did not own Reserve property chose to buy land from Simon at three to four dollars an acre—even though they might have bought equally good Congress lands south of the Reserve for two dollars an acre—because they found, for one thing, that the schools, churches, and other institutions they valued were being established on the Reserve. The schools might meet only in the settlers' houses or in log cabins built for the purpose, but in 1807 Asael Adams had a school in Hubbard, a Mr. Dunlap a school at Cannonsburgh, and the Reverend Mr. Badger his Academy at Burton. At Tallmadge a Congregational Church, later considered a perfect example of New England architecture,[25] would be built on land Simon insisted the proprietors deed to the people for that purpose, even though the sale of the township to the Reverend Mr. Bacon had had to be voided. At Parkman and Chardon there were public squares on land that Simon had obtained from the proprietors or had bought and donated himself; and in Warren there was a courthouse, built by Isaac Ladd in 1815, for which Simon had subscribed $200—the largest amount given by any individual.

But still another factor attracted the New Englanders to the more expensive Reserve lands. The settlers on the United States lands were then "almost exclusively from Pennsylvania, Virginia and Maryland and were the natives of those states or Germans,

Irish & Scotch or their descendants. They formed such a motley society," said Whittlesey, "that few or no persons from New England would settle among them." [26] Since this "society" had spilled over into the southern part of the Reserve, the New Englanders followed the advice that Calvin Pease gave to a Vermont acquaintance in 1801: "I fancy your people will be best suited in the north part of the purchase, as a great proportion of the settlers on the south part are Pennsylvanians . . . while the northern part is settling entirely by Yankees." [27] And so it was that the New Englanders not only added to the settlement of the Reserve, but moved settlement north and, eventually, west over the Reserve.

But wherever they settled on the Reserve, the New Englanders—particularly those from Connecticut—were apt to leave their impress. Simon told James Pumpelly in 1816 that letters addressed to "New Connecticut" would no longer reach him, because it was "a place not known, generally, to our Post Masters." [28] Nevertheless, its Connecticut heritage was left on the Reserve not only in the institutions that were established but in the architecture of the early homes built by men like Simon, Whittlesey, and Wadsworth; [29] and in town and township names: Lisbon, New Haven, Hartford, Litchfield.

This new group of settlers, like those who had come before them, sought Simon's advice on land matters and on their other affairs too. Daniel Coit depended upon Simon to advise his son Henry about drilling for salt in Town 4 Range 15 and to admonish Henry for his too free spending habits. To those who came to farm, Simon provided crop and stock information. In fact, Simon was honored in 1816 by the Massachusetts Institute for Agriculture for his contribution to agriculture in the United States.[30] And some of the young men were even taken into Simon's home and trained by him. In 1818, for example, Simon assured Zephaniah Swift: "Your son I will expect to live with me as you propose, & I think I may be of service to him, & in my absence he may be of use to me . . . & in many other respects we may be mutually beneficial." [31]

But whether they came to the Reserve to be manufacturers,

farmers, or businessmen, Simon offered his advice and friendship, saying, as he did to Swift, that he would be as good a friend to a young man as he merited. And his general counsel was that the young settlers would find in the new country "a very different kind of business and employment from that which they have been habituated to; but if they should not become discouraged they will no doubt do well." [32]

As far as the Reserve and the state were concerned, the most significant area in which Simon's advice was now sought was in money and banking. In November, 1813, the Western Reserve Bank went into operation with Simon as its president.[33] It was a time when wildcat banks were multiplying, but the terms of the Western Reserve Bank charter were meant to set it aside, from its beginning, from such operations. The stock of other banks could be paid for by the subscribers not only on the installment plan but also in cattle or other produce.[34] The stock of the Western Reserve Bank, at $25 per share, could be paid for in installments, but the installments were subject to thirty days' call and payment in specie or in currently negotiable paper. Another important provision of the charter was that the officers were personally liable for the debts of the bank.[35]

It seemed a favorable time for Simon to start in the banking business. Because of his proximity to Pittsburgh, Simon had already established banking connections there. Then the war brought a variety of money—previously so scarce that nearly all transactions had been carried on with either produce, work, or property as the medium of exchange—into the Reserve. When the troops from Kentucky and Virginia crossed the Reserve to join the Northwest Army, they no doubt left some southern paper in their wake; and when supplies were sought for the Army, government promises to pay were left with the farmers and storekeepers on the Reserve to serve as money. In July, 1813, Simon said, "Money is more plenty in this Country this season than usual." [36] Then after the war ended, the increase in immigration from New England brought eastern paper to the Reserve.

Much of this money passed through Simon's hands in his

capacity as land agent for either the payment of debts or the purchase of land. Since he paid in 1815, on his own land and on land for which he was the agent, one-seventh of the total land taxes in Ohio,[37] a large amount of what Simon collected went to the state for its expenses. But the balance went to the eastern proprietors as payment on land contracts. And in Norwich, New Haven, Boston, and New York Simon built up personal accounts due him from proprietors for the 3–8 per cent commission he charged on collections and sales and for the $1 fee he charged for paying an owner's land taxes. Additional money sometimes came to Simon in these years on sales of his Reserve land, his Tioga-Owega land, and of Nancy's land in Delaware County, New York, that she inherited from her father. By 1818 Simon also owned land in Gros Isle, Michigan, and eventually realized some profit from this land. But this growing personal wealth was now pledged, under the terms of its charter, to the redemption of the paper issued by the Western Reserve Bank.

Then in 1814 Daniel Coit began to warn Simon that financial affairs in the United States were fast approaching a crisis. On August 11, 1814, The Major wrote to Simon that he was having trouble collecting a check on the Pennsylvania Bank for more than $3,000. "Have enduced our Bank to undertake the collection of it," he said. "It is, however, on Condition that they be not liable to pay their own paper for it. At this time," which was when secession talk was beginning to run high in New England and the Hartford convention was approaching, "exchange is in favor of N England," said The Major. "N York's paper & that of other Banks South are not easily negotiated here in large sum." [38] The following month he told Simon the Pennsylvania check would not pass. "There is great distrust," [39] he said.

By the following year the New York banks had stopped paying specie, and in December The Major told Simon that "the fair exchange here at this time between N York money & that of the N England Banks is 10 pr Cent. Those banks further south are much worse." [40] In the meantime banks had further multiplied in the west. Like the eastern banks, they stopped paying specie in

1816 and 1817. Benjamin Gorham then complained about the "confounded country drafts" Simon had sent him and that he had had difficulty in exchanging. And in February, 1817, Simon wrote: "Ohio paper is discredited abroad, as we have many un-chartered Banks whose paper is good for nothing at home & which is sent away for a market where no difference is known and the good & bad all sold alike." [41]

It was in this climate of distrust that the Second Bank of the United States was established. An event that Bray Hammond says was due to "extreme fiscal needs of the federal government, the disorder of an unregulated currency, and the promotional ambitions of businessmen," [42] the creation of the bank should have been greeted with enthusiasm in financial circles. But instead, it only climaxed the economic crisis because its establishment was coupled with government demands for the resumption of specie payments and the recall of Treasury funds from state banks. In these banks, the Treasury funds had served, unfortunately, as the basis for the issue of additional paper and the increase of loans. The recall of the funds would make it impossible for some banks and difficult for others to resume specie payments on their own paper.

But by the fall of 1817 the chartered banks in Ohio had generally resumed specie payments. And now an additional difficulty plagued them. Shrewd opportunists, called specie runners, bought up discounted western paper from eastern banks and rode west to demand its redemption at the bank of origin; and agents of the United States Bank were also sent out to claim specie for the paper of western banks.

In May, 1818, two agents appeared at Cleveland's Commercial Bank of Lake Erie, which had been established in 1816, with a bundle of notes for redemption. Simon's friend Leonard Case was then Cashier of the Commercial Bank, and he insisted the two men were agents of the United States Bank, employed to buy up western paper for the purpose of breaking the banks. The two men "made it known in the Bar Room at the Tavern as soon as they arrived," said Case, "that they intended to break the Bank, they intended to draw from all the Banks in the State all their Specie, that the U.S. Bank was able to do it & intended to break them all." [43]

On Monday morning the two men were "pretty well how came you," according to Case. They staggered into the Commercial Bank, threw down their bundle of bank paper, and demanded United States paper or coin. While Case and a helper counted out the money, the two men went back to the tavern for another drink. [44]

For three days the "agents" were on the streets of Cleveland in "a perfect spree," and did not come to collect the money. By that time the directors of the Commercial Bank were "so wrathy at the conduct of the agents" that they decided to put the money back in the vault and give the men a post note, payable "to John Smith cash U. S. Bank at ten days date," for the nearly $11,000 they had demanded. [45]

The two men finally came back to the Commercial Bank on Thursday morning. They at first refused the note and again demanded the specie; then, "after stupidly blustering about for a time," they finally took the note and left town. But the event caused a run on the bank for specie, and in November the "door was closed from necessity." [46]

Many similar bank failures followed in the state, for as historian Samuel Reznick has observed, the Second Bank of the United States decided upon a policy of contraction in August, 1818, and the "resulting pressure upon specie brought about a suspension of payments in many places and by many banks." [47] But at Warren, when agents of the United States Bank appeared at Simon's Western Reserve Bank, he paid out $40,000 in specie on his own paper. [48] In addition, he continued to pay specie not only on his own paper but also on that of other specie-paying banks.

It required a constant correspondence with his clients in Connecticut, Massachusetts, and New York for Simon to keep up to date on specie-paying banks and rates of discount on the variety of paper in circulation. The many failures among eastern banks eventually made it necessary, however, for Simon to stop redemption for other banks. He found that during the time it took to transport paper east, a supposedly sound bank might have closed its doors. But even though he wrote Daniel Coit that large sums of specie had been carried out of the country, Western Reserve Bank notes were steadily redeemed.

The money panic spread and distrust of bank notes grew, but Daniel Coit wrote Simon: "I will accept only eastern paper and yours." [49] And on the Reserve and in Ohio the name of the Western Reserve Bank became "synonymous with safety. 'Good as a Western Reserve Bank bill' became a proverb and the citizens . . . would be more startled by an earthquake than by the failure of this Bank." [50]

9.

*Permit me to congratulate you
on your great popularity . . . you were
appointed Commissioner of the C. Fund
without a dissenting voice.*

Samuel MacCracken, Letter to Simon Perkins, February 26, 1833

*H*ARD TIMES AGAIN settled over the country. In Montgomery County, Pennsylvania, one speaker blamed the country's financial woes on people being

too fond of shewing out in our families. . . . Our daughters must be dressed off in their silks and crapes instead of their linsey-woolsey. . . . We must get back the good old simplicity of former times if we expect to see more prosperous days. . . . Teach your sons [said Judge Ross], to be too proud to ride a hackney which their fathers cannot pay for.[1]

Much later, Reznick would see the depression as caused by the extravagant speculation and apparent prosperity of the prior period, coupled with the crisis in the affairs of the Second Bank of the United States, which precipitated and signaled the "distress and mental attitudes characteristic of depression."[2] But those persons who lived through the depression of 1819–1825 increasingly blamed the hard times on either the banks or "the estated gentlemen [who] hold in subjection, oppression and bondage, the most virtuous part of our community." [3]

Simon quietly continued his policy of redeeming Western Reserve Bank paper, which for a time withdrew most of it from circulation; and by January, 1821, he was able to say to cousin Elias Perkins, "I was never so free of Debts, since I was a man of business, as at the present time." [4] He was left, however, as he told Jonathan Brace, with "no money of my own to make purchases with." [5]

Convinced that banking reform would benefit the banks and the financial condition of his country, Simon also agitated during these years for greater limitation of the amount of paper a bank might issue, personal liability of a bank's directors, and repeal of the Bonus Law that was passed in 1816 and under which the Western Reserve Bank had received a new charter extending to December, 1842. This law stipulated that banks chartered by the state must give one of every twenty-five shares of the bank's capital stock to the state—up to one-sixth of the total number of shares—and that the state would thereafter receive dividends on its stock. [6] In return, the state granted what the legislators thought were important privileges of exemption from state taxes, and charters that extended to 1843, at which time the "Bonus" was to be paid.

This law was passed, as Simon said, without the application of the banks and without regard for actual banking conditions. Instead of the Bonus Law Simon wanted an annual tax placed upon the banks:

Why I would prefer to pay an annual tax [he told Cyrus Bosworth of the Ohio Legislature], is that I would choose to pay my taxes on bank stock as well as on all other property . . . when I received the protection of government; which is annually & constantly; it being for that protection only that a tax on bank stock is paid. . . . The state would be benefited by receiving the money now when it is wanted, in small sums which the banks will be willing to pay, & which the state can collect, & which if left until 1843 will become so large as to invite litigation. . . . [And then he added], I will close this with the old adage, a bird in the hand is worth two in the bush.[7]

But Simon did not petition the Legislature for the change; nor did he lobby personally in the state's capital, as he sometimes did for measures he desired. Public sentiment was running against bankers, and so Simon chose to work behind the scenes through men like Bosworth. He felt a move had been made toward proper banking controls, however, when the Bonus Law was repealed in 1825.[8]

As for the "oppression" of the "most virtuous part of our community" by the "estated gentlemen," Simon continued to discourage the proprietors from suing the settlers. "It will have more the effect," he told Jonathan Brace, "to cause them to leave their farms than to collect money." [9] But this good-intentioned policy solved nothing, in the long run, for interest on a settler's debt continued to be compounded at six per cent and payment of the resultant interest and principal became indeed "oppressive." Yet Simon failed to see that the financial system he followed in selling land—which involved granting extensive credit and imposing compound interest—needed to be changed. It is true he tried to reduce the amount of credit extended; and, feeling it was better to hold land than poor men's notes, he even declined selling land unless a more sizable down payment was made than had been in the past. But he did not see—even though the system had ruined wealthy men like Oliver Phelps and Ephraim Root—that the banking reform needed by the settlers and the rest of the country was greater restriction of credit and the end of compound interest.

And then the land declined drastically in value. In 1820 Simon had to admit that land on long credit might sell for "2, 4, 5 dollars an acre," but "what it would sell for prompt pay is . . . doubtful." [10] The low price of produce, the scarcity of money, and the abundance of United States land in market at $1.25 per acre [11] affected the value of Reserve land; and in 1825 Elisha Whittlesey wrote, "There is not any certain cash value to any land in this section of the country. There have but few emigrants purchased on this side [east] of the Cuyahoga River for several years past and the emigration into the counties on the Reserve to the west has been extremely limited." [12] And when sales were made, pay might again be in the stock or produce of the country.

Again the proprietors expressed their discouragement with the venture and their desire to sell their land at almost any price. The Major began to complain because Miner Spicer could not pay him for the additional land Spicer had agreed to purchase in Town 2 Range 11. He became impatient, too, because no buyers could be found for his Cunningham's [Kelley's] Island property. Even patient Daniel Coit began to lose hope for "the promised land" when he had to submit his argument with Uriel Holmes, over the division of Claridon township, to the Geauga County Court.

In 1798, Holmes had spent a day with Simon and agreed to the division of the township as made by the Connecticut Land Company. Then before this agreement was put into writing, Holmes changed his mind. At some point it appears that he bought out Nathaniel Patch and Martain Smith, the other two proprietors involved in the draft of this township. Coit's share was to be pooled in the Erie Company; and Simon, in an effort to satisfy Holmes and free the land for sale, offered him many alternate partition plans. One, for example, was to survey the township into mile-square lots for which Coit and Holmes would draw to the amount of their interests. This was not the kind of partition Simon favored, because it scattered holdings. But it would have been an equitable solution to the dispute over the quality of the land. Holmes, however, turned it down. In fact, he wanted any evaluation of the land decided without Simon, for he thought Simon was ingenious and persuasive. Next it was decided to make east and west surveys of the township. And finally— possibly by drawing lots—Coit received the east part of the township and Holmes the west. [13] Oddly enough, this was nearly the same division as had originally been made of the property.

Then Holmes said that the quality of the land he had received in Ashtabula as equalizing land was not just compensation for the swamp land in the west survey of Claridon. The case was finally taken to the Geauga County Court and there Coit submitted, rather than carry the dispute any further, to a decision he thought was unfair.

After that, Coit's discouragement increased. He was, he admitted, growing old, "and perhaps on that account have more doubts and apprehensions than I should from the same circumstances in earlier life." [14] On September 17, 1818, just three days before his sixty-fourth birthday, he had fallen from a ladder while picking grapes in his garden and had broken his right thigh.[15] The accident had given him considerable pain, and he thereafter had a series of colds and eye infections. He and The Major became increasingly concerned about the Erie Company affairs, which had become more and more difficult to handle. As the proprietors died or sold out their interests, dividends that had once been paid to a single proprietor had to be split among several heirs; there had also been disputes over the distribution of some of the estates, and partitions of jointly held interests had had to be settled in court. On February 19, 1821, Coit wrote to Simon:

The Erie Company have been called together for the purpose of appointing another trustee, and have made choice, unanimously (so far as represented, which was more than nine-tenths of the Interest) of William C. Gilman. This is a circumstance which while Major P. and myself continue to act that is not very important, but in case of our deaths, may save considerable trouble.[16]

And in 1825, as the country still floundered in depression, he said, "The whole of this business has been unfortunate from various unforeseen causes; I would have done much better with the property that I have had invested in it." [17]

But Simon had not lost his optimism, and whenever possible he was again buying land. Although he did not see the settlers' need for a change in the country's financial system, he tried to help them solve their problem of transporting their produce to market and selling it for reliable money. He wrote to an eastern correspondent, for example, "Please give me your opinion as to future prospects of any foreign market for the produce of our Country, which might give a spur to Industry and regard for labour above what we now have." [18] And even though Gardner Greene advised him in 1810 that "new settlements are unpropritious to Manufactories, as the culture of the earth, enclosures & Buildings require all the hands to be employed in the primary calls of nature," [19] Simon continued to encourage manufacturing ventures: mills and a water power business along the Black River; [20] iron works in Newton township.[21] Not all of his ideas were realized but his interest continued and in turn spurred other persons to undertake manufacturing.

He continued too his interest in internal improvement projects. The development of the country still depended upon the individual and the companies he might organize, and Simon invested in the Trumbull-Ashtabula Turnpike Company; the Big Beaver Bridge Company; and with Huntington and others, in a company to develop a harbor at Fairport.

By 1824, other newly settled parts of the West were experiencing the same problems Simon had faced in settling the Reserve. Like the Reserve, these areas needed sound money, roads, bridges, and other improvements. And the New England states, still struggling to make the transition from commerce to manufacturing, sought protection for their new industries. Simon and the eastern proprietors thus hoped for the eventual success of their western venture and for economic relief in the election of a president who would favor both Henry Clay's "American System" of internal improvements and a protective tariff.

When John Quincy Adams was finally elected, they felt they had such a president. Since none of the presidential candidates of 1824—Andrew Jackson, John Quincy Adams, William Crawford, and Henry Clay—had received a majority in the electoral college, the election of the president had to be made by the House of Representatives under the terms of the Twelfth Amendment to the Constitution. Clay, having run fourth in the election, was no longer a candidate. Neither was Crawford, who had had a stroke. Clay, in what has been called the "corrupt bargain" of 1825, threw his votes to Adams and helped assure him of election. Adams, in turn, named Clay to the post of Secretary of State.

Such a combination indicated an administration favorable to federally financed internal improvements and, because of Adams' New England heritage, to protection of manufacturing.

Consequently, following the Adams victory of 1825, Simon looked for national aid in the reforms and projects he felt would help the Reserve and his state. Working through his friend and former Aide-de-camp Elisha Whittlesey, who had recently been elected to the House of Representatives, Simon first sought a new postal system for the state. The early routes, as he told Whittlesey, had been established as they were in all new countries—piecemeal. Simon worked out an improved postal plan based on the location of the population and sent it to Whittlesey, who secured its acceptance by the postal department.

Simon also encouraged Whittlesey to obtain United States grants of school lands and sent him careful lists of the total acreage in the Reserve and the Firelands as a basis for requests for public lands equal to the amount set aside in townships of the public domain for the benefit of the schools.[22] Next, Simon discussed appropriations for dredging some of the harbors of Lake Erie; for he now anticipated—as did the other leading men of Ohio and the proprietors in the east—that the northern part of Ohio would benefit from the long-awaited opening of New York's Erie Canal.

In fact Simon, who had probably been the first man in the state to have a plan of the Erie Canal, was often in Columbus, now the capital, to discuss a similar canal to connect Lake Erie with the Ohio River. Such a canal, according to Simon and the legislators, would make it possible to ship produce economically to eastern markets rather than to the unhealthy and often glutted New Orleans market. The farmers might then again realize some profit on their produce, and manufacturers of other goods might also gain from their labor.

The idea of a canal was by no means new to men like Simon. In 1807 he had even engaged, with others, in a plan called the Cuyahoga and Muskingum Navigational Lottery to connect the Cuyahoga and Muskingum rivers by a waterway across the Portage Path. The venture had failed because there were not enough lottery tickets sold to make the project possible, and the money raised had had to be refunded.[23] But it was a plan Simon did not forget; and in 1811, when he and Howland were frequently discussing the Erie Canal, he said:

I think it important that people generally be informed on the Subject. The value of land in this country would rise at once an Hundred per cent if the fancied Canall could be effected; and the land nigh the Lake would rise 5–10–20 fold . . . I once thought the location of [Town 2 Range 12] very good. It was then conjectured that across the Portage would be a road of great travel and at the Rivers each a Town. . . .[24]

On his part, Howland had advised Simon:

The means which must be resorted to for a considerable part, are immense. Viz a contribution of lands in the vicinity of the route of the canal—these contributions will be a credit on which cash may be borrowed to great amount & sales of said contribution lands—from this source I think much may be calculated on—this having a deep interest in the thing will do much. . . .[25]

It was against this background that Simon had his first official connection with building a canal across Ohio. On February 25, 1820, in a joint session of the Ohio Senate and House of Representatives, he was elected one of three commissioners to "survey and locate the route for a Canal, between Lake Erie and the Ohio River, agreeably to an Act, passed for that purpose."[26] This canal survey had depended, however, on Congress agreeing to the General Assembly's proposal to purchase United States lands in the southern part of the state; and when Congress "manifested . . . an indisposition to make the proposed sale to this state,"[27] the survey was not made.

Simon's next connection with the canal was to accompany James Geddes, a New York engineer employed by the state of Ohio, on a survey of some of the possible routes for the canal. He and Geddes—as Simon wrote in an article for the *Western Reserve Chronicle* of May 25, 1822—journeyed along the dividing ridge that crossed the state and from which the rivers and streams flowed either north into Lake Erie or south toward the Ohio River. Along this ridge Simon and Geddes searched for the place or places where the summit or ridge could most conveniently be passed or breached by a canal and also have enough water to feed the canal until it could again be supplied by streams along its lower levels. It was in Town 1 Range 11 that they found a pond whose waters might be made use of either to flow north toward the Cuyahoga River and Lake Erie or to flow south to the Tuscarawas branch of the Muskingum River. It was Geddes' opinion, as Simon reported in the *Chronicle*, that the streams to the east that they had passed in their excursion along the ridge could be carried into the summit pond.

In addition to this Cuyahoga-Muskingum route, four other possible canal routes were examined by Geddes that summer: a Mahoning-Grand River route, a Black-Killbuck River route, a Maumee-Great Miami route, and a Scioto-Sandusky route.[28] And naturally considerable competition and rivalry developed in the various parts of the state as to which should be chosen for the canal location. Simon's Warren friends and neighbors of course favored the Mahoning-Grand River route.

But on February 8, 1825, the Ohio Legislature passed an act that would permit the state to borrow money and build two canals:

The one commencing at the mouth of the Scioto River, and terminating at Lake Erie, either at the confluence of the Cuyahoga or Black River, as may be found most eligible. The other line of canal commencing at the city of Cincinnati, and terminating at the foot of the rapids of the Miami of the Lake.[29]

This act eliminated the Mahoning-Grand River route from consideration; and on March 9, 1825, a meeting of Trumbull County residents was held at Warren to protest the levy of taxes against them for payment of interest on the canal loans. It was inequitable taxation, in the view of the Warren residents, since the canals were so situated as to be no benefit to them. The citizens appointed a committee to protest the taxation,[30] but Simon declined to take any part in the affair. He knew the Mahoning-Grand River route had ben bypassed because, for one thing, it was "considered as forming a part of the contemplated national canal, from the waters of the Atlantic to the Lakes." [31]

Simon had, in fact, provided Whittlesey with data to use in promoting this canal. In addition, Simon and the legislators felt that the stagnating central and western portions of the state needed the canals more than the south and eastern sections.[32] And so, although it made him unpopular, Simon would not take part in the tax protest; and Alfred Kelley, one of the canal commissioners, then said to him: "It gave me great pleasure to learn that you took no part in those proceedings & I hope to hear that this was the case with the more substantial & reflecting part of your citizens generally." [33]

In the meantime it was left to Kelley and the other commissioners to decide upon the terminal location for the central canal. That is, whether the Lake Erie end of the canal would be at the Cuyahoga or the Black River. It would obviously be of great benefit to the state if land were contributed for this part of the canal; and Simon was asked by Kelley, for the canal commissioners and in response to an act of the Legislature, to contribute land he either owned or had the agency of along the canal routes.[34] Simon then owned some land in Town 4 Range 18, possibly near or on the proposed Black River route; but he, The Major, and Paul Williams owned land in Town 2 Range 11 [Portage] on the Cuyahoga-Muskingum route that had been discussed since 1807 for a waterway.

In his letter soliciting land, Kelley also expressed the hope that Simon would meet with him to discuss "some other subjects connected with the Canal policy"; and on April 18, 1825, Kelley eagerly agreed to a suggestion evidently made by Simon that he meet with the commissioners on May 5 in Wooster. "It will certainly not be an intrusion," said Kelley. "On the contrary your attendance will give me & I presume all the members of the board much pleasure—and as you suggest 'may do some good.' " [35]

Then sometime between May 5 and June 7, 1825, Simon rode

{116}

over the Cuyahoga-Muskingum route with Kelley and Paul Williams. As Kelley later recalled, the route of the canal was then concluded upon.[36] It was a route—as Kelley and the canal commissioners reported to the Legislature—that was abundantly supplied with water, as James Geddes had earlier verified, to operate the locks needed across the dividing or summit ridge; and it would, along with the planned western canal, benefit the greater part of the state.[37]

Following their exploration of the route the men rode "along the road . . . to the place where" Kelley felt a town might be laid out.[38] It must have seemed to Simon that history was repeating itself, for Kelley's suggestion was very like the one Simon had outlined to Howland in 1811: ". . . across the Portage would be a road of great travel, and at the Rivers each a Town. . . ."[39]

Kelley then solicited Simon and Williams for permission to plat the ground and asked that Simon "give to the state a share of the lots." After some discussion, Simon agreed to give the state a third of the town building lots. Kelley, it was further agreed, was to make the "location of the ground," to advise on laying out the town plat, and to plat and select the lots for the state. Simon's only condition to the gift, according to Kelley, was that "Lock No. 1 & the basins should be located in a certain way."[40]

During these years Simon had also discussed the canal and its proposed route with The Major, who still owned land in Town 2 Range 11. But in spite of the possible increase in land values along the route, The Major was anxious to sell the property. He had recently suffered losses in the failures of the Eagle and Derby banks in Connecticut; and he was committed to the purchase of the stock of a newly chartered bank. He told Simon he needed money, and he was willing to sell Simon his land in the township at $3.50 per acre,[41] a considerably better price than he had agreed to only a few years before when he traded land to the Spicers to pay his debt to them for carpenter work. And this land Simon now included in that he would give to the state.

Also involved, according to *A Centennial History of Akron*, were 1,003 acres of land Simon had bought in 1807 for $4,012 at a tax sale.[42] No validation of this purchase has been found in Simon's papers, but if such a purchase was made, the taxes paid by 1825 would have made the cost of the land to Simon about $2.39 per acre. In addition, Simon exchanged some land with Paul Williams and included that land, also, in property given to the state.[43]

In June and July, Joshua Henshaw laid out the town that would be named Akron because of its summit location, and Simon then deeded to the state seventy-two town lots, that for the most part surrounded the public square and the land set aside for public buildings—a plat of ground through which a tailrace had to be run for the canal—and additional lots bordering on the canal itself.[44] The gift, coupled with Williams' deed of land for canal use, assured the state not only of the land needed for canal construction but also of additional income from the sale of Akron town lots. But Simon's unpopularity even spread to Sandusky, another area bypassed as a canal location, and the Sandusky *Clarion*, according to William D. Ellis, said of Simon, "He's as selfish a man as exists, which will account for the liberality of this weathercock." [45]

The construction of the Ohio Canal began that year, and it acted as an immediate boost to the economy of the state. Canal workers swarmed into the area and poured their wages back into the state in the purchase of land and produce. But by 1826 the Canal Fund commissioners were meeting difficulty in borrowing additional construction money in New York. Money was again tight and interest rates had jumped to seven per cent.[46] It was feared that construction would have to be halted or that the cost of the canal would soar beyond all expectations.

At this point one of the Canal Fund commissioners resigned, and Simon was appointed to the vacancy on the board [47] which had the responsibility of handling the financing of the canals. In October Simon went to New York to aid Ethan Brown in securing the badly needed loans. According to John Still, Simon showed "temperamental tendencies" toward the other board members, but there is little doubt that it was Simon's financial reputation that enabled the state to secure the money they needed at six per cent interest. And the construction of the Ohio Canal continued.

Finally—on July 4, 1827—that portion of the Ohio Canal from Akron to Cleveland was opened. It was a day of great celebration. On July 3 Simon and other dignitaries boarded a boat, the "State of Ohio," that had been built for the occasion in a newly established Akron boatyard and were towed slowly down the canal toward Cleveland for the opening day celebration.

"The morning of the fourth was wet and unpleasant until about nine o'clock, when the clouds were dispersed and the sun broke forth with apparently more than ordinary splendor. . . . About eight o'clock the 'Pioneer' " put out from Cleveland "with a full load of passengers, accompanied by a band of music." About six miles up the canal the "Pioneer" met the "State of Ohio" and other boats that were coming down the canal, and the boats returned to Cleveland.

The scene, on approaching [Cleveland] was truly exhilirating. The banks of the canal and the neighboring eminences were lined with spectators—the boats with the flags and decorations presented an imposing appearance—the flags with appropriate inscriptions and the standards of the State and Union, displayed from Belden's Tavern and the Franklin House, the alternate discharges of cannon in quick succession from the shore and the boats, mingling their thunders with the lofty strains of the band and the merry windings of the horn and bugle. . . . These were the effects and evidences of the enterprise and spirit of 'Young Ohio'. . . .[48]

And in the opinion of the majority of legislators then in the General Assembly, no one better represented this enterprise and spirit than Simon, who then marched with other dignitaries from the boats to the public square and then to a banquet at Belden's Tavern. His donation of land and his unremunerated service as a Canal Fund commissioner had helped make the canal dream a reality.

And the completion of the Ohio Canal marked a turning point in the economy of the state, much as Simon had anticipated. Farming became a profitable venture because transportation of produce to eastern markets was inexpensive, and settlers were again attracted to the land. Even Cleveland at last came to life; and the land did increase in value, as Simon had once predicted, by "5–10–20." Moreover, the founding of Akron marked the beginning of the state's industrial development. For Simon had every intention of making Akron a manufacturing town. In the next few years he gave more land to the state, retaining the right to use the water from the locks in the Akron area. His 1831 agreement to build a flouring mill, in connection with receiving water rights at three of the locks,[49] may mark the beginning of the city's cereal industry. Eventually, too, he was involved in a plan to utilize the waters of the Little Cuyahoga River to furnish Akron with an excellent power system for manufacturing use.

And in 1833, although the legislators would soon turn critical of Simon and the other men who had built the canals, the members of the predominantly Jacksonian General Assembly reappointed Simon to the position of Canal Fund Commissioner, "without a dissenting voice." And his friend Samuel MacCracken added, "I think now Sir *if you have a price*, that you must join the *Jackson ranks. . . .*"[50]

Once again the tide of immigration to the Reserve increased. Akron, at the junction of both the Ohio Canal and, after it was opened in 1840, the Pennsylvania and Ohio Canal, became a boom town. Cleveland's population also leaped from 606 in 1820, to 1,076 by 1830, and to 6,071 by 1840.[51] And William C. Gilman wrote Simon, "New England is almost exhausted of funds to supply the purchasers of Western lands."[52]

10.

Pitch of anarchy.

Simon Perkins, Letter to Elias Perkins, February 20, 1809

*D*URING THESE same years Simon was concerned with the problem of educating his children and establishing them in life. His four older children had been educated under a Lorrin Andrews, and Simon Junior had attended classes in the log schoolhouse that was located near the Warren courthouse. The four younger children were at first taught at home by a Miss Converse, and then went to a school held by a Mrs. Lathrop. Jacob later remembered that he had cried "lustily for the privilege of attending" Miss Converse's school, but that "Charles was almost obliged to use force to induce me to go to Mrs. Lathrop's." [1]

But Nancy wanted the children to have additional education. And Simon yielded to her wishes and sent Anna Maria and Olive to a Miss Pierce's school in Litchfield, Connecticut, where they were drilled extensively in geography, music, and the arts and manners thought suitable for young ladies of good families.

Then in 1826 fifteen-year-old Alfred was also sent to Connecticut to school. He was enrolled in the newly established American Literary, Scientific, and Military Academy operated by Captain Alden Partridge at Middletown. Like Simon, Partridge was a critic of contemporary education. He felt young men should be given a practical education that would prepare them for either peace or war. The Academy consequently offered mathematics, engineering, surveying, and military training. [2] It was a curriculum that obviously fitted Simon's ideas of what a young man needed for life—particularly for a western life; but it did not satisfy Nancy or, more emphatically, The Major, who now fancied himself the patriarch of the Perkins family.

On a "dreadful cold Christmas Day" in 1826, The Major wrote to Simon:

Feeling no disposition to go abroad, I have concluded that I could not satisfy myself better than by calling cousin Simon into my room & have a little conversation with him. Presuming no subject will be more acceptable than the boys, I will commence with yours first.

Alfred seems pleased with his school & I have no doubt he has done well . . . but I feel bound to say . . . it is not the place to lay the foundation for a man of Science. I mean not the best place to prepare a lad for great acquirements.

General Simon Perkins is a great man in Ohio. He has become very rich. He came from where the wise men come & his name is Perkins. Now Sir, permit me to say that you are bound I think in justice to yourself & in justice to your family to give as many of your children a first rate education as shall discover a taste for science.[3]

The school The Major would choose for a first-rate education was, of course, Yale. Perkins boys had then gone to the college at New Haven for over one hundred years: Simon and The Major's grandfather, Dr. Joseph Perkins, had graduated in 1727 and become a physician and surgeon of distinction in Lisbon and Norwich;[4] and in 1825 The Major's youngest son, also named Alfred, had begun his studies there. He was doing well, and The Major obviously thought Simon could do no better for his son Alfred than to send him also to Yale.

But it was a difficult decision for Simon to make. What concerned him first was the health of his sons. Bishop was evidently not going to recover; and in 1819 Simon's nephew Joseph Kinsman, who had received his early education in Simon's home and office, had died of consumption. Again Simon felt that the disease was brought on, as Bishop's trouble had been, by excessive study. And "health with young men," he insisted, "is at least as important as books."[5]

{122}

The Major anticipated Simon's fears, however, when he wrote him on that cold Christmas Day.

I am aware that you have apprehentions & I will not say prejudices to combat. I know your mind is alive to the lads being injured by too close application. I have, I believe, a just sense of all the danger (if it is worth while so to speak) in giving a lad an education. The cases which are most likely to rest painfully on your mind would not operate with me as any stumbling blocks in your case were it mine.[6]

If Alfred now "commences sitting," continued The Major, he could enter college two years from the coming fall. At eighteen he would still be young enough, according to the "men of Science" The Major had consulted.

It no doubt may seem a frightful distance of time to look ahead before he will be good for anything [said The Major], but the time will arrive as soon as your young orchard of fruit trees will reward you with fruit . . . and as abundantly repay for your care & watchfulness.[7]

But it was probably The Major's final argument that Simon found most convincing.

One thing I will mention which you may think may have been omitted. You are a new country & it will be many years before your State will be flooded by men of Science of your own creating & men of first rate talent & acquirements will generally remain & find suitable encouragement at home.[8]

What Simon wanted most was for his sons to continue to live in the state that he had now had such a significant role in shaping.

And so on January 20, 1827, Simon wrote to The Major that he might visit Connecticut the coming summer and would "then do with Alfred as you and my other friends and good policy may seem to direct." He granted Alfred permission to study Latin—a *de facto* act, since The Major had already provided Alfred with a Latin book for the purpose—and closed by saying, "My only wish is to do that which may be best for the lad." [9]

Simon was subsequently "induced" by The Major, as he put it, to enroll Alfred in the Plainfield Academy to prepare for Yale. In

January, 1828, The Major wrote that Alfred, working at the rate of 250 lines a day, was almost through Virgil. He was in want of books, however, "say Cicero and Greek grammer." [10] Then in May, The Major wrote delightedly that a letter from Alfred had given him reason to hope "he has made up his mind to be a man of science." [11]

In the meantime Simon's concern for the health of his children had been renewed by the illness of Anna Maria. Maria was now married to John W. Allen, a young Connecticut lawyer who had come to the Reserve in 1825 and, with Simon's help, established a practice in Cleveland. In 1828, in spite of all the care the devoted Allen and Simon and Nancy could give her, Maria died of consumption.

But The Major, presuming on his twelve-year seniority over Simon, continued to press him about the children. During The Major's journey to the Reserve in 1827 for the opening of the Ohio Canal he had discovered, in spite of the progress being made, that there was much still wanting in the country.

My mind is impressed [he wrote Simon], with the importance of the rising generation having a better chance of improvement or education than they at present enjoy. I was made (excuse me Sir) quite ashamed when passing through the State of New York to find the united exertions of so great a portion of *every body* there exerting themselves in establishing Academies & Colleges & education societies when compared with anything I saw in Ohio. Agree they are older & ahead—but the further Ohio is astern the greater the necessity of exertion.[12]

His visit had also raised The Major's concern for the moral training of the young men of the West. They should be "made to understand," said The Major, "the importance of strict morality at least & that 'Righteousness exalteth a nation but that sin is a reproach to any people.' "

He condemned the apathy of the West toward moral and Christian education and wrote:

If due attention should be paid to these things you would soon see a great change in the conduct of the inhabitants. There is growing up in our country or rather in many parts of it a generation that will never be led by a few honest individuals . . . such inhabitants will always be under the control of unprincipalled demagoges. Nothing in an elective government can stop it but educating many of your young men & teaching them correct principles . . . & there is not time to be lost.[13]

The Major did not say what he had seen or heard during his visit that so alarmed him. As far as Simon's sons were concerned perhaps he heard the tale that twenty-two-year-old Simon Junior sometimes drank too much on the sleighing parties he and his friends had when the Mahoning River was frozen; perhaps he heard that young Simon and a friend once leaped onto a dining table and kicked the china in every direction to dance along the table's length.[14] But The Major was quite concerned that Simon and Nancy were not only "shiftless or negligent about a suitable instructer for your sons," but also "easy about moral instruction." [15]

Certainly Nancy left little moral instruction unattended, as one of her letters to Alfred shows:

I do hope you do make a practice of daily reading your Bible . . . and form your rule of conduct from it. I hope you are very choice of your time, for he who waists his time in the morning of life may repent it all the evening of his days. . . . Make choice of good companions, avoid those who are in principle heinious, vicious, immoral and infidel. They will poison you. Remember the old adage a man is known by the company he keeps. [And finally], My son, I would again caution you about your spelling.[16]

And on his part Simon had set his sons an example of integrity and hard work. Although he professed no formal religion, he went with Nancy to church each Sunday. And when The Major talked about joining a temperance society, Simon could remind him that he had always set his sons the moral example of temperance.

But in October, 1829—although he remained anxious about Alfred's health and still wanted the young man to work with him in his office—Simon permitted his son to enter Yale, where The

Major thought he would receive the scientific and moral education he needed. And in 1832 Jacob and Charles were also assured of a moral if not a very scientific education when they were sent to Kinsman to a church school "where Mr. McIlvain preached . . . and read from a sermon 'The finger of God in the Asiatick Cholera,' " and where "A temperance meeting was also held in the evening as that cause was held as being the principal invitation to the Cholera." [17]

Had The Major lived to learn about the letter Simon received in February, 1833, from Jeremiah Day, president of Yale, he would no doubt have said, in spite of Simon's compliance with his suggestion for the education of Alfred, that Simon had been too easy about guarding "all the passes to vice." For Alfred, wrote President Day, had been "found in a state of intoxication in front of the college yard. He had, a short time before, proceeded from one of the rooms in the college, in a very boisterous manner, and in the use of very profane language." [18]

As punishment Alfred was expelled from school until the last week in June. "During this time," wrote Day, "he should be absent from New Haven; and that he may be prepared for the final examination of his class, on the first week in July, it will be important that he still prosecute his studies in reference to that occasion." [19]

The same mail brought a hasty letter from Alfred. "I think they have been unpardonably severe to me . . . I do not think that you will consider it a very strange thing that a young person, although of temperate habits . . . once in a long time should drink more than is proper." [20]

But Simon was not interested in excuses, and he wrote his son a firmly disapproving letter.

I can say . . . that the offence seems to have been committed, and there is no help for it now, but hope you may refrain from falling into errors again of a similar character . . . a man may be restored to the estimation & love of his friends, when they are convinced that his merits deserve their kind & good feelings.

I hope I may learn that this admonition . . . may be salutary, and that you will submit to it without too much complaining . . . I should be mortified to hear that you sunk down under this discipline . . . that you was foolishly stubborn & disregarded it, but I hope you may find someplace to study & let all your acquaintances know that you may be a man, even in adversity . . . remember that there must be a government every where, that nullifications is not the order of the day with wise or good men . . . you will do honour to yourself to submit & try to mind & set an example for good men to follow . . . convince the world, that instead of a crime you have only been guilty of a foible . . . now is the time to begin to establish a good reputation.

[And then Simon concluded,] I forgive all that has taken place if we are permitted to hear no more of it . . . & that you will assume the high moral & exemplary station which we did suppose that you occupied.[21]

A chastened Alfred went into temporary seclusion. Where—apparently no one knew. But he evidently used the rustication well, for he passed his Yale examinations and was graduated with his class. Then following his graduation, Alfred returned to Warren and began to work in Simon's land office. He gained a reputation in Warren for his fine manners, and he no doubt influenced Simon to permit the other boys further education.

Jacob and Charles were then sent to the Burton Academy. Here they witnessed the camp meetings of a religious revival that was sweeping the Reserve in 1834. Only the year before, the Mormons had laid the cornerstone for their temple at Kirtland; and on the heights southeast of Cleveland, the Shakers of the North Union colony were experiencing visits from departed members and the gift of songs to their young members. At Burton, the revival made many of the students converts to Congregationalism; and Jacob was so impressed that he wrote to his mother, "Ma tell Pa to spend his few remaining days in the service of God, tell him now before the days of life are past to make his peace with God." [22]

That fall Jacob was permitted to journey to Connecticut to study at Isaac Webb's school in Middletown. And here he became as enthusiastic about his studies as he had been about the religious experience at Burton. He filled copybooks with French and English exercises, and soon he pressed Simon for permission to prepare for college:

I am now a little more than fourteen years old, and as yet I have studied with no definite ideas or plans respecting my going to college, or even what institution I should enter. . . . Were I to consult my own wishes at present I should enter Yale College next fall . . . I should thus graduate (provided I was not helped out before my time) just as I completed my nineteenth year. If you have no reason to the contrary I should be gratified to know what college I shall enter and at what time.[23]

Simon would not yet commit himself to a college education for Jacob, however, because a winter of fever and ague in Warren and the death from consumption of his nephew Alfred had renewed his concern for his family's health. He planned a visit to Connecticut the summer of 1836; and he had written to John Arnold Rockwell, husband of The Major's daughter, Mary,

I might bring [Jacob home] with me, keep him one year & then let him return. . . . I have thought that if he should come home & spend one year & then return to compleat his education, he would eventually be a little more of a western man than if he was to remain with Mr. Webb, and if he should spend one year now with me it might be much more important to him than at some future period, or perhaps by declining it now, a few years hence might be too late . . . it is very well for boys to be schollars, but still necessary I presume you will say that they should know something about men & things, which books do not touch. . . .[24]

But Simon did not bring Jacob home. Acceding to the scholarly Jacob's eager pleas, he permitted him to study another year at Webb's school and in October, 1837, reluctantly allowed Jacob to enter Yale.

During these years there had been increased agitation among the Reserve settlers for the establishment of schools. The Legislature had been almost as occupied with new school laws as with canal legislation. Motivated by his twofold desire to provide the

{ 128 }

settlers with the institutions they valued and to keep his own college-age children near home, Simon finally took an active part in helping colleges as they were chartered.

In 1825, although The Major evidently never knew it, Simon had offered land in the proposed town of Akron to the newly chartered Western Reserve College. But since the town had not yet been platted, the trustees decided to locate the college in Hudson instead. Simon then "contributed largely" to build what was "at first called the natural science building and . . . eventually . . . the Athenaeum," but which "might properly have been named Perkins Hall," had buildings then been named after their contributors.[25]

Simon also made contributions to Oberlin, Granville Literary and Theological Institute [later Denison University], and to Allegheny College in Pennsylvania; but it was the young Western Reserve College at Hudson that interested him most, and in addition to his contribution for the science building Simon gave the college land in Parkman, in Town 4 Range 18 [Pittsfield], and in other parts of the Reserve.

As for establishing the older children, it had been decided that Olive and her husband Frederick Kinsman, who worked with Simon in his land business, would live in Warren; and Simon built them a large brick house only a few steps from his own home.

Simon Junior, who had married Grace Tod in 1832, moved to Akron to farm and oversee Simon's land interests there. And in 1834–1835, on a hill west of the town plat, Simon built his eldest son a large stone house that overlooked, from the rear windows, the Portage Path, and from its great, columned front porch, the Ohio Canal. It was a much grander house than Simon had built or would ever build for himself. And in time, eleven children— whose names he had trouble remembering—filled the spacious rooms of Simon Junior's house. The young man soon gained prominence in his own right as first a Senator and then a Representative in the Ohio Legislature. And in Akron he carried on his father's efforts to establish schools when he joined with others to obtain a charter for a high school, unique in its day, that was to teach no particular system of religion.[26]

But Simon's land contributions were not limited to schools. In 1834 he gave the Akron & Middlebury Baptist Church and Society the lots on which they would build their meetinghouse; and in 1840 he made a similar donation to the First Congregational Society. He gave the people of Parkman their public square, meetinghouse and lot, and graveyard; and he also contributed toward the Akron courthouse, jail, and cemetery. Moreover, he encouraged his friends in the Legislature to establish a mental institution. Except for a county hospital in Cincinnati, there were no separate hospitals for the mentally ill on the Reserve. They simply roamed the streets, existed by begging, or were committed to prisons or jails along with the criminals.[27] And although Simon knew it would not help Bishop, who was now considered incurable, he encouraged the establishment of a mental hospital in Columbus in 1838.

But in spite of these advances and the increase in land prices that followed the building of the canals, the proprietors of the Erie Company now decided that they wanted to liquidate the Company. Daniel Coit, seventy-six years old in 1830, had remained quite lame from the 1818 injury to his right thigh; and on October 10 he fell over the rockers of his wife's chair and broke the thigh again.[28] He now realized that all his western land would not be sold in his lifetime, and he wanted to bring his affairs into as much order as possible for the sake of his heirs. The Major, seventy-one and approaching death, had long been impatient to end his land affairs.

It was at first planned by the Trustees that the remaining land and contracts would be divided among the proprietors, or their heirs, or both. Simon objected to such fragmentation of ownership and to the division of Erie Company land contracts among individuals who would no doubt press for payment of the debts. So, in 1831, Simon himself bought the remaining assets of the Erie Company. For $10,000 he purchased about 2,000 acres of land—most of which lay in the long disputed Claridon town-ship—and about $12,000 in land contracts.[29]

Eventually, in Claridon township, a reservoir was dredged out that fed into the Little Cuyahoga River and the Cascade Mill Race—a mighty source of water power that is usually credited to the hydraulic genius of Dr. Eliakiam Crosby. Coupled with Si-mon's rights to the surplus water from the Ohio Canal, Akron was supplied with a superior water power for manufacturing use.[30] And although the Coit-Holmes dispute that had occupied Simon from his first days on the Reserve was finally ended, this ingenious water system involved Simon in another conflict that brought his name before an investigating committee of the Ohio Legislature.

For it was during these years, 1825–1840, that democracy reached, in the opinion of Simon and his friends, the "pitch of anarchy" he had once thought impossible. On February 22, 1828, with Jackson's election indicated, Whittlesey wrote Simon of "the perils which threaten us." And when Jackson's followers invaded the White House after his inauguration, men like Whittlesey were sure the civil institutions of the country were indeed threat-ened. As Morison has said, "Glasses were broken and trodden under foot, punch was spilled, and damask chairs soiled by muddy boots." [31]

And Simon was among the first to feel the effects of the new era. For twenty-eight years he had served, under both Republican and Federalist regimes, as Postmaster at Warren. But in 1829 he was notified of his removal as Postmaster on the charge that he was not always present to receive the mail but sometimes dele-gated the task to a deputy.

Simon was at first inclined to question the action, but on Janu-ary 24, 1830, Whittlesey wrote him from Washington that it would be a hopeless effort.

The affairs of the [post] office are in a most wretched and disorgan-ized condition. The number of clerks has been increased, some say six and others twelve, and an answer cannot be obtained on common ordinary business . . . short of a week or ten days. . . . If the truth could be made public, there would be a tremendous day of retribution.[32]

That September, Simon was asked to run for Governor of Ohio on the Anti-Masonic ticket.[33] He was highly concerned with the condition of the country, but still he refused to run for a public office. "I am under the necessity of declining to do any act," said Simon, "which should at this time divide the anti-Jackson votes." [34]

A few months later, Whittlesey wrote anxiously to Simon:

I cannot in the compass of a letter point out to you all the dangers to which this nation is exposed, by its government being committed to those who are alike incompetent and knavish. You must both see and feel the danger. It is near at hand, and unless averted will enter the dwelling of every one of us. Some of us here think a vigorous effort should be made to place those in power who are more competent and honest and who will administer the government on national principles and for national purposes.

This can only be done by disseminated intelligence among the people and arousing them to action. . . . Will you have the goodness to confer with our friends at Warren and endeavor to make some organization among yourselves for the purpose mentioned, and urge upon others to do the same in other townships, as you shall have an opportunity of conferring with them on this subject.[35]

And finally, as Simon found even his honesty being questioned, he began openly to lend his strength to organizing and supporting the political party that would be called the Whigs.

11.

The poor against the rich.

Simon Perkins, Letter to Elisha Whittlesey, February 24, 1834

*I*T MUST HAVE SEEMED to Simon that between 1829 and 1842 he was doubted, criticized, and investigated from every side. Certainly he felt that all the once-accepted ways of doing business and of running the country were being overthrown. That which had once been praised as a great benefit to the country was now investigated in terms of its possible profit to an individual or a company. Of course there was some justification for the fact that legislators—especially the followers of Andrew Jackson—were taking a closer look at the way profits were being made, for "The spirit of speculation," as a correspondent said to Martin Van Buren, was "rife throughout the West. . . ." Land offices were doing an immense business; and Van Buren's correspondent, John Law, observed that the value of property had in some instances risen from 500 to 1,000 per cent.[1] But as the investigations continued, it seemed that making a profit, once thought praiseworthy, became suspect.

In 1836 Alfred Kelley was quizzed on the possibility of any personal financial benefit he might have received from the location of the canals. The accusation was that he had an interest in the Akron land and that this had determined the location of the Ohio Canal. Simon, as a result, came to Kelley's defense with an account of their tour of the canal site and of Kelley's careful refusal to take any interest in Akron land for the very reason that it might be construed as a persuasive factor in locating the canals.[2]

In addition there was growing agitation for greater control over the Canal Fund commissioners' use of the canal moneys. In 1836, the Ohio House of Representatives adopted a resolution to appoint a committee to examine and audit the books of the canal commissioners and the Canal Fund commissioners.[3] Simon was already concerned because the Legislature, passing from the development of canals even before the system was entirely completed to what Simon felt was a reckless chartering of railroads, decided to loan canal funds to private companies organized to build railroads. As far as his personal integrity was concerned, Simon was offended that he might be doubted when he had accepted only his traveling expenses on Canal Fund business and declined the $3 per day pay that Canal Fund commissioners were entitled to. And on February 13, 1838, he resigned as a Canal Fund commissioner.[4]

But the ugliest affair in which Simon was involved was allied to providing Akron with its water power system. As early as 1823, at a tax sale, Simon had bought some land that had belonged to a Jacob Welsh, who had died. Welsh's son and heir, John Welsh, claimed he had attempted to pay the taxes on this land and wanted Simon to return the property to him.[5] Then on August 23, 1828, John Welsh advised Simon that ninety acres of his father's land were to be sold at the September term of Common Pleas Court in Ravenna,[6] and on October 30, 1829, Welsh again offered Simon ninety acres of land in Portage County at $4 per acre. It was worth more, said Welsh, but he needed the money to pay his debts.[7]

Whether Simon bought this Portage County land cannot be determined, but at some time before 1834 Welsh needed money to pay taxes on his father's land in Portage and Geauga counties to prevent its being sold for taxes. What Welsh planned was to keep the taxes paid until he could obtain a court order for the auction of the property. And Thomas Webb, a Warren neighbor of Simon and editor of the *Trump of Fame*, came to Simon, acting in his capacity of administrator of the Jacob Welsh estate, to borrow the money John Welsh needed for taxes. According to his own deposition,[8] Simon agreed to loan Webb the money Welsh needed, on the provision that Webb would include land owned by Welsh in the neighborhood of Akron in that which was to be auctioned.

Because of inadequate identification of the property in the documents available, it cannot be determined whether it was the land Welsh offered Simon in 1828 and 1829 or a different tract of land that was involved in the subsequent suit of John Welsh vs. Simon Perkins *et al*. But in any event, Jacob Welsh's heirs brought suit against Simon, Eliakiam Crosby and others in relation to a tract of land in Portage County. Then, according to the later testimony of Leicester King, "in the summer of 1834 he became the purchaser of an equal interest with Simon Perkins and Eliakiam Crosby, of certain lands, lying in Portage County, including a tract purchased by Crosby at administrators' sale, made by Thomas D. Webb, administrator of Jacob Welch, deceased," but that there was a "suit pending between Welch's heirs and Perkins, Crosby and others, in relation to the title to that tract. . . ." [9] Evidently King, Crosby, and Simon—all involved in the development of Akron's water system—wanted or needed the tract of land enough to purchase it again rather than risk the outcome of the suit over the land.

This suit eventually reached the Ohio Supreme Court, where Peter Hitchcock sat in judgment on the case and decided in favor of Simon and Crosby's title to the land. Dissatisfied with this decision, Jacob Welsh's heirs occasioned an investigation of Hitchcock's conduct by the Ohio Judiciary Committee and charged that Hitchcock had been employed by Simon and the defendants as attorney prior to sitting on the decision of the case as a judge in the Supreme Court.[10]

And as the Hitchcock investigation indicates, both sides acted questionably in the Welsh land affair. Simon admittedly wielded his financial influence to have included in the Welsh auction land that lay along the route of the Akron water system. At the time,

Welsh's heirs were willing to submit to his demands in order to assure the sale of the land at auction rather than at a tax sale. They wanted to renege on the bargain, however, when the property increased in value because of the Akron water system.

But of greatest significance, as far as Simon was concerned, were the effects of the Jackson-Biddle Bank War of 1830–1836. Simon had long agreed that banking reform was needed. He still supported the payment of specie for a bank's notes, the taxation of state banks in return for the protection afforded them by the state, and the personal liability of bankers for the notes of their banks. But being conservative, Simon wanted banking reform made within the existing system rather than by the overthrow of the system itself. He therefore favored the recharter of the Second Bank of the United States, under fire from Jackson as being both unconstitutional and inexpedient, but he wanted restrictions as to the number of officers and branches and its functions.

That the Bank should be permitted to continue to do business [said Simon], I think there can be no doubt; and that it should be suitably restricted is, as I conclude, equally evident; and my plan, in the absence of a better, would be to recharter for a period of time, from ten to twenty years, with permission to place the Bank or one office of Discount etc. in each state in the Union, and perhaps in the states of N York and Pennsylvania permit two, and no more, except in the District of Columbia, & what should be done there I would not attempt to suggest.

In favor of rechartering it may as I think be said that it is necessary to aid the financial operations of the Government, and that it is not unconstitutional; therefore it is both expedient and proper that something of the kind should be allowed. But if it should be rechartered, without any restrictions as to its number of officers or branches, it may and no doubt will establish them in every place where a good banking business can be done and in twenty years cause all the local banks to close their concerns and decline their business.[11]

As far as its functions were concerned, Simon evidently thought the bank should provide a central banking service. "I cannot discover that the friends of the bank or the officers of

Government can urge the renewal of the charter as an auxiliary to the Government," he said, "except as a place of deposit for their funds, and then to place those funds in convenient places to be disbursed." [12]

Furthermore—differing from state bankers such as Leonard Case, who had an intense dislike for the United States Bank that dated from its demands in 1817–1819 for specie payment of state bank notes [13]—Simon felt both the United States Bank and state banks could and should operate together for the good of the country. He envisioned a checks-and-balance system or a regulatory relationship between the two.

If the USB has been an important check on the state banks [he said], those banks will also be a check on the USB, if that is suitably restricted; and it may be well not to dispense with either, but to keep each within proper bounds, when both no doubt will be well managed and continue to be useful to the country and profitable to the stockholders and the state banks an important source of revenue to the states. [14]

Simon thus suggested, as does Bray Hammond,[15] that the significant contributions of the bank lay in regulatory and central banking functions. The development of these functions could have been assured by the terms of a new charter, but Jackson, according to Whittlesey, was bent on destruction, not reform of the United States Bank. The President rejected, as Commager has observed, "the finality or binding character of the opinion of the Supreme Court on a question of constitutionality," and vetoed—on July 10, 1832—the bill for the recharter of the Second Bank of the United States.[16]

The veto was followed by the removal of public funds from the bank and their deposit in Jackson's "pet" banks. After that, the financial situation went from bad to worse; for the funds in Jackson's "pet" banks increased speculation and the extension of credit unexpectedly.

Moreover, Jackson's animosity against the bank continued and anti-banking sentiment became widespread. On February 18, 1836, Whittlesey wrote Simon about Jackson's efforts to prevent the bank from operating under a Pennsylvania charter: "The President is encouraging the elements of a mob in Philadelphia to organize and tear down the Bank of the United States. . . ." [17] And only two days later: "The Globe, the mouthpiece if not the thinking machine of the President breathes death and destruction to the bank of the United States. . . . This paper has attacked the Ohio Life & Trust Company. The President wants to be the only *Monster* in the United States." [18]

The attack against the Ohio Life Insurance and Trust Company again touched Simon personally, as would the anti-banking sentiment that resulted from the bank war, for he was one of the original incorporators and held stock in this company. Chartered on February 12, 1834, the company had expected to take over the role of the Chillicothe and Cincinnati branches of the Second Bank and had established numerous branches and agencies throughout the state. The company was first charged, as Jackson had charged the Second Bank, with being unconstitutional and later with engaging in practices of taking and issuing bonds that were not provided for in its charter.[19] On this score, the principle involved was if an incorporated company possessed the rights of an individual, unless such rights were restricted. But the issue of whether the charter of the company should be repealed was a political one that threatened to involve Martin Van Buren after the Cincinnati *Republican* published a letter—in March, 1834—that purported to give Van Buren's views upon repeal. In a note written for Van Buren from Washington on April 5, 1834, Van Buren denied taking any part in or expressing any opinion on the question,[20] but in 1836, with his election approaching, Cincinnati friends to Van Buren felt they must caution him about becoming involved in the affair.

Some of our ultra friends are for making the Trust Co a test in our next elections [wrote John H. Groesbeck], and if this is done you will certainly suffer by it, because it must be born in mind that this Bank dispenses its favours all through the State and is owned by both parties, and many of our best and most influential men own Stock and are interested in this institution, and regard it as one of the most usefull institutions in our country and cannot therefore be influenced to prejudice the institution in any way, and it is a very unauspicious time to agitate the Subject . . . whether constitutional or unconstitutional. . . .[21]

And another correspondent cautioned Van Buren: "it is very impolitick at least to have you identified in the vexed question. . . ."[22]

The subsequent Supreme Court investigation of the company absolved it of any breach of its charter. In fact, the report issued in December, 1836, by P. B. Wilcox, Master Commissioner, stated: "this institution has entitled itself to no small credit, in withstanding the temptations by which it has been surrounded. It is the more conspicuous for standing comparatively alone. It is an evidence of its integrity, and therefore of its stability."[23] But Simon and his friend Whittlesey, who also held an interest in the company, found some of the company's practices objectionable.

It seems to me companies err in supposing they were incorporated to make money [said Whittlesey] and that the end justified the means. Monied men should pause, and not be driven by speculators, mere gamblers, and black legs into these new fangled notions. . . . We have an irritable and exciting population and can any one be so blind as not to see that monied men and corporations will become odious by the means they use to obtain wealth. Money men should reflect that the whole energies of the Government are brought to bear on them by moving the lower ranks in society against them.[24]

Simon was even more specific and emphatic in his disapproval. He wrote to J. N. Perkins, a relative and the treasurer of the company in New York:

Our family, and I consider yours and my own the same, I think I know the history of for at least 150 years and is as yet untarnished. This is about all the patrimoney that I have had in life & to me it has been of value that I cannot estimate, and your good fortune it has not prejudiced.

I came into this country to do business for others, and I have done more and a better business than any other man of my acquaintance in the State, and if there is any one thing that I view as a more important auxiliary than any other it is the fair reputation of our family.

When I first heard [the] statements [about the Ohio Life Insurance and Trust Company], I could not but reflect that however good intentions may be, that a man may be so far embarrassed as to be tempted to do that which he would not do under different circumstances, when a small deviation from the true course may be fatal; and young men, I find, have a great anxiety to possess wealth when one ounce of character is worth a waggon load of it.

A man should be industrious [concluded Simon], and that well applied will give to any one all that is required to make him happy and his family respectable. But give him all Broadway with a vile character, and all honorable men would shew him and his.[25]

In the meantime, Jackson's removal of public funds from the "pet" banks and his specie circular [26] had created financial havoc. Banks all over the country stopped specie payment; but again Simon, as was his policy, almost immediately resumed payment on Western Reserve Bank notes.[27] Although he was sure his own bank could survive the storm,[28] Simon viewed the possible election of Van Buren—whom he called either "Matty," "the little Dutchman," or the "Sourcrout of Kinderhook"—with great alarm. There had been, as he said, too much "setting 'the poor against the rich' & 'breaking down the aristocracy of the Country' . . . harped all over the nation." [29] Like other members of the growing Whig party, he now thought only his friend Harrison could save the nation.

On February 12, 1835, Harrison had written Simon:

I have most unexpectedly to myself been brought out for the Presidency. I most solemnly assure you that I had as little expectation of being a candidate for that exalted station when the movement was first made in Pennsylvania as I had of being called on to fill the office of Prime Minister of England, and I am not a little astonished at the favourable reception it has met with, seeing that there was scarcely a man who had not formed a predilection in favour of some one else.

What will be the result God only knows. There are men infinitely better qualified for the Presidency than I am. But the people some-

times take it in their heads to indulge their fancies. Without dispar-
agement to the present rulers of the nation, however, I think with
good *"help"* I might manage matters as well as they do.[30]

On March 9, 1835, Simon answered Harrison:

In regard to the successor to Genl. Jackson, I feel myself justified in
saying that any Gentleman who could be thought to be faithful to the
Constitution and have an honest heart & most likely to run down the
heir apparent would be the man on whom the major part of the votes
of this region would be most likely to unite, and your name would be
very satisfactory if it could succeed, or hold out the best prospect.[31]

But there had been criticism of Harrison's actions in the War
of 1812; and Simon and Whittlesey, who would be called one of
the founders of the Whig party, conferred on this problem. They
had, of course, firsthand knowledge of Harrison's handling of the
troops in the River Raisin affair, a disaster for which Harrison
was frequently criticized. And although he felt it was too late to
contradict the charges that year,[32] Simon gave his military papers
to Whittlesey to use in Washington to combat the criticism.

It did prove to be too late, but Harrison still made a good
showing. Moreover, his popularity continued. Then, as the "poor
against the rich" and the "breaking down the aristocracy of the
country" cries continued, Simon said he felt "distressed . . . to
see what our Locofoco [33] have brought us to, driven all honest
men from places of publick trust and confidence. . . ." [34] And
finally, Simon once again openly took part in politics: "At a
meeting of Electors of Trumbull County friendly to the election
of William Henry Harrison . . . held pursuant to notice given by
the Whig Central Committee . . . at the Court House in Warren," Simon was appointed president of the meeting; [35] and in
what was apparently a letter to the delegates to the nominating
convention, Simon said, "If we can place Gen. Harrison in the
Presidency we shall, as all good men must acknowledge, effect a
more glorious political revolution than has been performed since
the close of the Revolutionary War." [36]

It was, as Morison has observed, "the jolliest and most idiotic
presidential election in our history." [37] For the old Federalist res-

ervation against campaigning was now cast aside—even by Simon. Tippecanoe Clubs were organized throughout the country, and in Cleveland the "Log Cabin and Hard Cider" slogan was carried out when the club built a log headquarters building on Superior Street, next to the American House.

Flags flanked the doorway [of the cabin], a large stump served as a speaker's rostrum inside, and campaign insignia and implements hung on the walls. Van Buren was represented by the drawing of an eagle holding a writhing fox in its talons. A little, black bear paced restlessly at the end of a chain fastened to a crossbeam. In a corner stood a cider barrel complete with a tin cup.[38]

On July 22, 1840, Simon wrote Harrison that a Fort Meigs celebration the Whigs had held was a "good thing. Many Locofoco went there but few came away as such"; [39] on September 3, at a meeting of an estimated 12,000 people at New Lisbon, Ohio, Simon presided. "On taking the chair," reported the *Chronicle*, "Gen. P made a short address in the course of which he took occasion to refute from facts within his own knowledge, and original letters in his possession, some of the calumnies set afloat against Gen. Harrison's military conduct." [40]

There were cries of dishonesty, "foul," and corruption made by both sides. "I believe that the enemy now have thrown off all regard for truth and now intend to try the virtue of falsehood," said Simon.[41] On the other hand, one correspondent wrote to Andrew Jackson: "Doubtless the Federalists and Harrison make secret pledges to the South that they will abandon the abolition cause which they now court for support. . . ." [42] And Jackson himself wrote to Martin Van Buren: "Corruption, bribery and fraud has been resorted to over the whole Union." [43]

Then, on November 17, the *Chronicle* posted the election returns. In Ohio, Harrison had received 24,512 votes and Van Buren 13,028. The Log Cabin and Hard Cider campaign had paid off. It was, as the *Chronicle* noted, the "largest electoral vote ever conferred on a candidate for the presidency of the Union." [44]

The victory, however, was brief. A month after his inauguration Harrison was dead, and Whittlesey wrote forlornly to Simon:

If we shall live to meet again, I shall have much to communicate of the strange events that have taken place here since the death of Gen. Harrison. What will be the result no mortal can tell. The history of parties does not furnish an instance of a party coming into power with the like triumph and its defeat so sudden and unexpected.[45]

And the "poor against the rich" doctrine that Simon had experienced since 1805, when he first noted the settlers' distrust of a man whose property was above "mediocrity," continued. Another lawsuit Simon had pending over a tract of land invoked an ugly letter from "one interrested." The writer threatened Simon: "Being fully in the belief as i am that you have no buisness with [the land] Therefore if you obtain judgment, i am determined that you shal be the looser of your ——." [46]

The old story of town rivalry also cropped up again in the three-year fight between Akron and Cuyahoga Falls over being named the county seat. Akron finally won the honor, and celebrated with the "burning [of] tar Barrels—firing of cannon" and "all rejoicing." [47] But for the three years Simon had been beset from both sides to pledge his subscription to the public buildings to one side or the other in order to influence the choice.

During these years, 1829–1842, the state Legislature continued to debate banking reform. Paradoxically, both the Whigs and the Locofocos wanted changes in the banking laws. But as Simon Junior, a Senator in the Legislature from 1839–1840, wrote his father, "The most of those who assume the responsibility would be willing to set things right if they knew how . . . I would be glad of your opinion as to the course best to be pursued to get us out of trouble in money matters—all agree that something must be done but the trouble is, how shall we do it." [48]

The difficulty was to devise a course that would eliminate the unreliable banks without destroying the good ones as well. But no one saw a way. And when Locofoco talk of repealing bank charters was not opposed by the Whigs, Simon Junior thought the

Locofocos became alarmed. "They expected the Whigs would defend those institutions & give them a chance to back out," he wrote. "In this they are disappointed, but they wish to back out & are now consulting as to the manner. What they will do to provide funds for the state is also unsettled—scrip to be used as a circulating medium is spoken of. . . ." [49]

As various bank measures were introduced, Simon's advice was sought by other legislators. On January 9, 1841, John Crowell asked for Simon's view of the bank bill then in the Legislature: "We have theory enough in all conscience, and I feel desirous for my part to have the opinions of a practical banker." [50] It was the opportune moment for Simon to suggest changes or reforms. But he offered no plan, for he had decided to let the people see how they got along without the banks they had so bitterly criticized. Finally, in 1842, the Legislature let all the bank charters lapse, among them, that of the Western Reserve Bank. [51]

Simon, who had recently written Whittlesey to say, "But so it is I am getting old," [52] now wrote to his friend Judge Lane:

There is such a hostile feeling in the community against Banks that I had rather have funds almost anywhere else that I deemed safe than in those institutions in Ohio. I have been largely interested in them and thought that it was more important for the citizens to be able to obtain money to aid them in their business at six pr cent than to have it locked up in the hands of brokers and shavers and three or four times that sum be required for the use of it. But times are now quite changed—brokers and shavers are patriots and bankers are rogues. [53]

Simon had had enough of politics and the banking war. The Western Reserve Bank then began winding up its affairs.

12.

A melancholy tale.

Simon Perkins, Letter to Mrs. Marsh, April 11, 1841

*D*URING THESE turbulent years Simon had again suffered great family losses. An epidemic of fever and ague in 1834 had touched all the family, and Alfred did not recover his health as Simon hoped. In 1835, in an effort to improve his strength, Alfred journeyed west with Elisha Whittlesey to select United States lands for Simon. But the outdoor life did not help Alfred, and Simon became increasingly anxious about him.

At the same time, Olive began to show signs of the family weakness toward consumption, and in 1838 she died. Simon was then advised to send Alfred to a different climate; and the young man, with his brother Charles to keep him company, went on a year's tour of southern France and Italy. The tour, however, did Alfred no good. For after his return to Warren in October, 1839, he became, as Simon said, "an invalid."

Simon now felt, and Alfred and Charles agreed, that the travel or voyages then recommended by medical men were of no help to health and were possibly even debilitating. Simon sought other ways of curing Alfred—such as a breathing tube that was supposed to strengthen the lungs—of what Simon first described as bronchitis.

Simon's anxiety also extended to Jacob, who was studying diligently at Yale. And although Jacob wrote that "the studies will never make any body sick, I think," Simon wrote to Professor James Kingsley:

Keep a watchful eye over him . . . I feel [more] solicitude about his exercise than any thing else. He has or had a good constitution but a deficiency of exercise may ruin it. If he [were] situated where he could do one-fourth of a reasonable day's work every day on a farm, I would think it worth more to him than all the land he could till and all the crops he could raise.[1]

Because of his concern over Jacob's exercise, Simon decided that Jacob should spend his August-September vacation of 1839 in a walking tour to Vermont. But when Jacob's six-week vacation and more than another month passed with no word from Jacob about his health, Simon became angry and scolded his son:

The last letter received from you was I think dated August 9th . . . a time for boys to make their acknowledgement to their friends for the liberality with which a kind parent bestows favours, and with some assurance of good conduct on the part of the receiver, for funds & favours received. [And then Simon's old prejudice against the kind of education Jacob was receiving cropped out]. This is I suppose to be a way that rude & common-sense boys treat their parents, but your reading may have taught you a different lesson & that parents are but of secondary consideration & like worn out garments thrown by as useless; but if you have found books which teach you this—I hope you will cast them off & read such as will teach you that obedience to parents & suitable acknowledgements for favours received is no mark of a blockhead.[2]

But Simon's anger turned to alarm when he learned that Jacob had had the mumps during the first weeks of his vacation and typhus following his return to Yale. He had taken sick with the mumps at Middletown when he began his walking tour. Here he had been cared for by his old schoolmaster, Isaac Webb; and when he recovered he had continued the tour Simon had prescribed for exercise. He had nowhere traveled "rod & tie," he told Simon; and since he had walked fifteen to twenty miles each day for nearly three weeks, lack of exercise could not have been the cause of his illness.

"I think there is no necessity of my leaving college," Jacob wrote, anticipating Simon's reaction. "I can get the lessons so as to recite very tolerably in about 3 hours a day." [3]

And Simon again let Jacob have his way and stay at Yale, where Jacob assured him he lived comfortably in his room, "a tight caboose in the garret of the chapel, about as far removed from earth as its etherial inhabitant, and affording as snug a retreat as a full pension in a good old age." [4]

Then on March 31, 1840, in spite of any cures or medicines the frantic Simon had been able to find, Alfred died. Charles too was unwell with an undiagnosed ailment that afflicted his eyes. And Simon reacted by withdrawing Jacob from Yale and bringing him home to Warren.

Simon now set an exercise program for Jacob and Joseph, who had that year graduated from Marietta College.

I have a high opinion of exercise of riding on horse back for young men [he wrote]. I cannot think but our boys might be as good as their Fathers if they could take the same laborious exercise. When first I came to this country and for many years after it took me 20 days to make the journey, but now with railroads, steam boats, etc. it may be performed in less than four and as is said with no fatigue. But I would rather have my boys ride the colts. [5]

And then—on April 11, 1841—Simon again wrote "a melancholy tale" about his family.

My son Charles, a very valuable young man 23 years old last November died one week ago this day. He has had a lingering complaint, but we did not feel [it] was very dangerous until recently, but he is now gone.

We have had nine children, and 5 are now in their graves and 4 in good health. Simon was here this day, Joseph and Jacob are now at home and Henry is at Marietta. We think of these we have as of those we have lost, that they promise well, if they can be permitted to live. But as Providence directs, we must submit. [6]

Jacob, however, grew impatient to return to Yale and insisted he was well. Again Simon gave in to his pleas and let him complete his studies in 1841–1842. Somewhat wearily, he also gave

Henry permission to study the "dead languages" while he was at Marietta. But finally, following Jacob's return to Warren in 1842, Simon had his four sons near him and the expectation that they would carry on his affairs.

He now lived quietly, writing his letters and occasionally what he called a "political essay" to his few old friends who still lived. Daniel Coit and The Major, once his frequent correspondents, were both gone. But Simon still exchanged letters and views with Elisha Whittlesey. Whittlesey asked Simon to write the history of his time, and said, "I hope you will not fail to do it. . . . You have done much good in your day, and I beg of you not to cease your good offices so long as you are blessed with health and the exercise of your physical and mental powers." [7]

But Simon, typically reticent about himself, did not write the history; and in 1843 he suffered a slight paralytic stroke that affected his right side. His boys, now bearded young men, took over the journeys to other parts of the Reserve where Simon still had lands, contracts, or taxes to be attended to, but they also took over writing his business letters. Even had he wanted to write the history of his times, it was now impossible for Simon to do so.

He remained in somewhat feeble health, but by November, 1844, he had again taken to the exercise he loved and frequently rode out alone on his horse.

He could ride, if he chose, around Warren's public square and remember the days when he had successfully sought to have the first county seat in the Reserve located there. He could remember, too, his part in the first court session that met nearby, between Ephraim Quinby's corncribs. He had then participated in laying out the legal districts of the Reserve and in determining that a white man should be tried for the murder of an Indian. And if he looked upon Warren's courthouse or jail, as he rode past, Simon could know he had had a hand in building them both.

If he rode east from his old frame house, he could tour his farm where he had successfully raised cattle, sheep, and a variety of crops. If he rode west, he could follow the Pennsylvania and Ohio Canal, which wound close by his house, to its junction with the

Ohio Canal, a project to which he had contributed. And here too, he could look upon a town that he had founded, now burst out of its original boundaries. Even if he followed the canal to Cleveland, where the citizens had once violently rejected his leadership, Simon could look there upon lands his sons would soon develop. If he rode, in fact, to the four corners of the Reserve, he could see roads, bridges, harbors, churches and schools that he had had a part in building.

Back home in Warren, he might pass the place on the east side of Main Street where the Western Reserve Bank first began its business in an old store; and then he might pass the building where it had since 1816 carried on its business. The bank's only sign probably hung on the door, those days in 1844, with the "Bank Shut" side showing and marking, in Simon's view, the tragic end of that phase of his career.

But on the morning of November 18 Simon could not take his ride. He was sick and faint. The children were sent for, but Jacob, who had gone to the county seats to pay taxes, did not reach home in time. On "Tuesday evening about 10 o'clock," November 19, 1844, Simon died, "with his reason unbeclouded & his mind entirely calm." [8]

This was the end of Simon's Western Reserve venture. It was the end, in fact, of an era. No more would men band together in those private colonizing efforts that had built the United States. No more would men band together in a private enterprise that had as its fabulous dream the carving of a new state out of 3,000,000 acres of wilderness.

Afterword

"My rule through life," said Simon in his will, "has been to avoid lawsuits as far as practicable . . . and also to decline any and all commerce with men of reputed dishonesty or of suspicious integrity in their dealings, and I advise my executors to observe these rules in all their negotiations so far as my estate is concerned."[1]

To Nancy, Simon left their house and sixty acres, woodland within the distance of one mile for fencing and fuel for the house and farm, and the income from $22,000 worth of Hartford Bank, United States six per cent, and Ohio state stocks.

The rest of his estate—valued a year after his death at $140,000—was equally divided among his four sons. The bulk of this property was in notes, mortgages, and land contracts due him. Of these debts Simon said, "I wish my executors to extend a considerable indulgence to my debtors if they will make their debts secure, pay their interest when due and discharge the principal in a reasonable time."

Although Simon said he was "not disposed to dictate" where

the children should settle, "it would give me pleasure if I could know that some one of them would occupy and possess the farm where I now live and where I have spent the most and best of my days." [2]

And so it was that Henry Bishop, who had liked farming better than the other boys, stayed in Warren. Here he had two farms of 600 acres each on either side of the Warren-Howland road. One farm was devoted to cheese-making, the other to fattening steers and raising colts. A kind-faced man, Henry—as his nephew Jacob Bishop Perkins recalled—never drank, disliked revivals and revivalists, and almost never agreed with his brother Joseph. Eventually Henry built a new home for himself and moved Simon's old house out to one of the Howland farms. He tore down Simon's old office, where most of the land business of the Reserve had been carried on, and built a "new and handsome one" in its place.[3]

One of the earliest business acts in which Simon's sons participated was the reorganization of the Western Reserve Bank under the Independent Banking Act of 1845.[4] In 1852 Henry became a director of this bank.

As far as his other activities were concerned, in 1871 Henry served on a committee to settle a Pennsylvania-Ohio boundary dispute; in 1880 he was a presidential elector for Benjamin Harrison; in 1895 he was a member of a committee for a new Trumbull County courthouse. He was, in addition, a trustee of the Cleveland State Hospital; president of the Trumbull County Agricultural Society; a trustee of the Ohio Agricultural and Mechanical College; member of the Warren school board. And with his brothers, he endowed a professorship at Western Reserve University.[5]

Jacob moved to Cleveland. With Joseph, he promoted the Cleveland-Mahoning Railroad and became its president. In 1850 he was a delegate to Ohio's Constitutional Convention, and in 1856 he was a presidential elector. He was an ardent abolitionist and a popular speaker, but his death in 1859 brought his career to an early end.[6]

Joseph, a "handsome man" who "wore a full beard, Prince Albert coat, a boiled shirt, silk hat, and dress boots," was remembered by his nephew as being fond of horses and immensely conscientious.[7] He moved to Cleveland in 1852 and built a handsome Italian villa style house on fashionable Euclid Avenue.[8]

He became a director of the Western Reserve Bank in 1845, a director and vice-president of Society for Savings, a director of Citizens Savings, and a director of the Bank of Geauga. With Jacob, he promoted the Cleveland-Mahoning Railroad on the right-of-way of the Pennsylvania-Ohio Canal. He was a member of the Ohio Board of Charities and a contributor to Oberlin and Berea [Kentucky] colleges. He received honorary M.A. and Doctor of Laws degrees from Marietta College.[9] For thirty-nine years, he served as a trustee of Western Reserve University, giving generously to that institution and establishing, with Henry and Jacob, the Perkins Professorship of Mathematics and Natural Philosophy, renamed in 1882 the Perkins Professorship of Physics and Astronomy.[10]

Simon Junior continued living in Akron. His nephew remembered him as a "large man with a head and beard that resembled Michaelangelo's Moses. He had a deep, gruff voice that struck terror in us kids whenever he spoke to us." He was not, said Jacob Bishop, "religious or straight-laced," but he was the "soul of honor." [11]

In 1842 Simon started a wool-raising business with John Brown, later of Harper's Ferry fame, as his partner. Brown lived in a cottage or small frame house on Simon's property, located just across the Portage Path from Simon Junior's big house. The partnership was not particularly successful, although Simon Junior exhibited his wool in the Crystal Palace. Simon Junior's children hated Brown because he had buried one of his children without ceremony in a plain wooden box in his backyard and because he had shot his own sheepdog when it would not follow him as he left the farm.[12] But Simon Junior was patient and generous with Brown.

Simon Junior promoted and became president of the Cleveland,

Zanesville & Cincinnati Railroad. He gave Grace Park, Union Park, and Perkins Park to the city of Akron.[13]

And so it was that Simon's sons followed his final words: "I hope my family will continue their present habits of care, kindness, attention and integrity." [14]

Notes

Chapter One

1. Simon Perkins, Surveying Book, 1795, MS., Simon Perkins Papers, Container 79, Folder 2 (Repository: Western Reserve Historical Society), no pagination.
2. Letter Amzi Atwater to John Barr, January 5, 1846, "Bound MSS. of the Western Reserve," Volume 22, Book 7 (Repository: Western Reserve Historical Society), no pagination.
3. No early records of the Erie Company that might have validated the exact total acreage pooled in the Company have yet been discovered. Indications are that if any such records were kept in Norwich or were recorded in Trumbull County they were burned in the fires that destroyed the early courthouses at both locations. A search of the papers of the three Trustees and of their heirs has failed to produce such records. Acreage figures for the Company have therefore been conservatively calculated by comparing the amount of land which was aparted to the members in the January 30, 1798, Connecticut Land Company partition and the land the Company listed for sale in an advertisement catalogued as of 1798. A record of the partition of January 30, 1798, may be found in Book of Drafts, Connecticut Land Company, Ephraim Root Papers, MS. 3235, Container 3 (Repository: Western Reserve Historical Society), no pagination. The Erie Company advertisement is also on file at the Western Reserve Historical Society, Broadside 0.73.

4. [New London] *Connecticut Gazette*, March 14, 1798 (Repository: Connecticut Historical Society), p. 3.
5. Mary E. Perkins, *Old Houses of the Antient Town of Norwich, 1660–1800* (Norwich: Press of the Bulletin Company, 1895), photo, p. 161.
6. Thomas H. Webb, "A Partial Sketch of the History of the . . . Connecticut Western Reserve" (n.d.), Joseph Perkins' Scrapbook, MS. 907 (Repository: Western Reserve Historical Society), p. 16.
7. Deed to Trustees of the Erie Company, January 17, 1798 (MS. copy), Joseph Perkins' Scrapbook, MS. 907 (Repository: Western Reserve Historical Society), pp. 252–255.
8. Mary E. Perkins, *Old Houses of the Antient Town of Norwich*, pp. 399–400.
9. Account Books of Andrew and Joseph Perkins of Norwich, Connecticut, 1783–1825, MSS., "Account Books of grocers (general storekeepers) in New England, 1685–1904" (Repository: Baker Library, Harvard Business School, Harvard University), *passim*.
10. George A. Perkins, *The Family of John Perkins of Ipswich*, Book III (Salem: Salem Press Publishing and Printing Company, 1889), p. 12.
11. Letter Daniel L. Coit to Simon Perkins, March 22, 1830, Simon Perkins Papers, Letterbox 9 (Repository: Western Reserve Historical Society).
12. *Charter of the Colony of Connecticut, 1662* (Hartford: Case Lockwood & Brainard Company, 1900), p. 18.
13. According to Alfred N. Chandler's *Land Title Origins, A Tale of Force and Fraud* (New York: Robert Schalkenbach Foundation, 1945), pp. 135–136, the Connecticut-Rhode Island controversy was terminated in 1663 by an agreement between John Winthrop, Governor of Connecticut, and John Clarke of Newport; the Connecticut-New Haven controversy was terminated in 1665 by the uniting of the colonies.
14. In addition, as Chandler observed in his *Land Title Origins*, p. 50, Virginia had a claim to land north of the Ohio River under the second charter granted to the Virginia [London] Company in May, 1609. Virginia's claim was settled in 1784, as James A. Rhodes notes in *A Short History of Ohio Land Grants* (n.p., n.d.), pp. 5–6, by Congressional acquiescence in Virginia's retention of 4,000,204 acres of land—located north of the Ohio River, between the Scioto and Little Miami rivers, and extending northward in a triangular shape into the future state of Ohio. These lands were called the Virginia Military Lands and were used by that state to pay her soldiers who were in the Continental Army during the Revolution.
15. Harlan Hatcher, *The Western Reserve* (Revised edition; Cleveland and New York: World Publishing Company, 1966), p. 9.
16. Journals of the Continental Congress, 1774–1889, Volume XXX, 1786, January 2–July 31, edited from original records in the Library

of Congress by John C. Fitzpatrick (Washington: United States Government Printing Office, 1934), p. 310.

17. *Ibid.*, p. 296, *et passim.*

18. *A History of the Courts and Lawyers of Ohio*, Volume I, editor-in-chief Carrington E. Marshall (New York: American Historical Society, Inc., 1934), p. 33.

19. William C. Gilman, paper read to the New London County Historical Society, September 1, 1905, printed in *Norwich Bulletin*, September 4, 1905 (Repository: Western Reserve Historical Society), no pagination.

20. Charles S. Hall, *Life and Letters of Samuel Holden Parsons* (Binghamton: Otseningo Publishing Company, 1905), pp. 550–570.

21. Harlan Hatcher, *The Western Reserve*, p. 40.

22. Letter Oliver Phelps to William Walker, October 31, 1795, MS. 747 (Repository: Western Reserve Historical Society).

23. *Ibid.*

24. *Ibid.*

25. Orsamus Turner, *History of the Pioneer Settlement of Phelps and Gorham's Purchase* (Rochester: William Alling, 1851), pp. 135–141.

26. Report of the Committee of the General Assembly on the Sale of Western Lands to the General Assembly, convened at New Haven, 2d Thursday October, 1795, "Bound MSS. of the Western Reserve," Volume 18, Book 1 (Repository: Western Reserve Historical Society), p. 35.

27. Excess Company Agreement, September 5, 1795, MS. 2525 (Repository: Western Reserve Historical Society), no pagination. There would be no excess land in the Reserve because the shore line of Lake Erie dipped further south than originally anticipated. Before this was determined, however, Livingston had sold his agreement to William Hull, later Governor of Michigan Territory, who surrendered Detroit to the British in the War of 1812. By April, 1796, the Company had decided that it was unlikely that any excess land existed; and before Cleaveland left for the Reserve he negotiated an agreement with Hull and Livingston that permitted Hull to participate in the Western Reserve lands to the purchase amount of his excess agreement. Data concerning the appointment of Cleaveland and the agreement made with Hull may be found in Minutes of Meetings of the Connecticut Land Company for April 8, 1796, "Bound MSS. of the Western Reserve," Volume 17, Book 2 and Book 3 (Repository: Western Reserve Historical Society), no pagination.

28. Report of the Committee of General Assembly on the Sale of Western Lands to the General Assembly, convened at New Haven, 2d Thursday October, 1795, "Bound MSS. of the Western Reserve," Volume 18, Book 1 (Repository: Western Reserve Historical Society), pp. 37–38.

29. *Ibid.*, pp. 38–39.

30. Figure compiled from Book of Drafts, Connecticut Land Company, Ephraim Root Papers, MS. 3235, Container 3 (Repository: Western Reserve Historical Society), no pagination.
31. Richard J. Purcell, "Zephaniah Swift," *Dictionary of American Biography*, Volume XVII, edited by Dumas Malone (New York: Charles Scribner's Sons, 1936), p. 250.
32. Letter Zephaniah Swift to Oliver Phelps, December 21, 1795, Phelps Family Land Papers, MS. 3236, Container 1, Folder 1 (Repository: Western Reserve Historical Society).
33. *Ibid.*
34. *Ibid.*
35. Minutes of Proceedings from 1796 to 1800, minutes of January 27 and 28, 1797, "Bound MSS. of the Western Reserve," Volume 17, Book 2 (Repository: Western Reserve Historical Society), no pagination.
36. The mode of partition of the Western Reserve is best explained in Thomas D. Webb, "A Partial Sketch of the History of the . . . Connecticut Western Reserve" (n.d.), Joseph Perkins' Scrapbook, MS. 907 (Repository: Western Reserve Historical Society), pp. 1–131.
37. Erie Company Preliminary Agreement (n.d.), MS., Simon Perkins Papers, Container 94, Folder 1 (Repository: Western Reserve Historical Society), no pagination.
38. Book of Drafts, Connecticut Land Company, Ephraim Root Papers, MS. 3235, Container 3 (Repository: Western Reserve Historical Society), partition of January 30, 1798, no pagination.

Chapter Two

1. Francis Manwaring Caulkins, *History of Norwich, Connecticut* (Hartford: Case, Lockwood and Company, 1866), pp. 398–399.
2. Daniel Coit Gilman, "Historical Discourse," *The Norwich Jubilee* (Norwich: John W. Stedman, 1859), p. 79, and Mary E. Perkins, *Old Houses of the Antient Town of Norwich, 1660–1800* (Norwich: press of the Bulletin Company, 1895), illustration, p. 72.
3. Daniel Coit Gilman, "Historical Discourse," *The Norwich Jubilee*, p. 80, *et passim;* Mary E. Perkins, *Old Houses of the Antient Town of Norwich*, p. 71, *et passim;* Francis Manwaring Caulkins, *History of Norwich*, p. 367, p. 607, *et passim.*
4. George S. Howland, "Trade and Manufactures of Norwich about 1800," *The Norwich Jubilee*, p. 297.
5. Francis Manwaring Caulkins, *History of Norwich*, p. 476 and pp. 478–479.
6. *Ibid.*, p. 397.

7. Lucy W. Stickney, *The Kinsman Family* (Boston: Alfred Mudge & Son, 1876), p. 88.
8. Mary E. Perkins, *Old Houses of the Antient Town of Norwich*, p. 109.
9. Richard J. Purcell, "Uriah Tracy," *Dictionary of American Biography*, Volume XVIII, edited by Dumas Malone (New York: Charles Scribner's Sons, 1936), p. 624.
10. Mary E. Perkins, *Old Houses of the Antient Town of Norwich*, p. 135, p. 242, *et passim*, and Francis Manwaring Caulkins, *History of Norwich*, p. 518, p. 630, *et passim*.
11. Articles of Association, December 11, 1797, MS., Simon Perkins Papers, Container 72, Folder 2 (Repository: Western Reserve Historical Society), no pagination, and Deed to the Trustees of the Erie Company, January 17, 1798 (MS. copy), Joseph Perkins' Scrapbook, MS. 907 (Repository: Western Reserve Historical Society), pp. 252–255. It should be noted, in connection with these documents, that Joseph Perkins did not sign the Articles of Association as one of the proprietors, presumably because he did not hold land in his own name at this time but through his interest in John Kinsman's proprietorship in the Connecticut Land Company. Also, one William Hubbard signed the December 11, 1797, Articles of Association but apparently changed his mind about becoming a member of the Company, for he did not sign the January 17, 1798, Deed to the Trustees of the Erie Company and did not draw in common with the Company in the January 30, 1798, partition, according to the Book of Drafts, Connecticut Land Company, which may be found in the Ephraim Root Papers, MS. 3235, Container 3 (Repository: Western Reserve Historical Society), no pagination.
12. Memorandum of an Agreement between the Trustees of the Erie Company and Simon Perkins, April 14, 1798, MS., Simon Perkins Papers, Container 94, Folder 1 (Repository: Western Reserve Historical Society), no pagination.
13. *Ibid.*
14. Erie Company Agreement with William Wheeler Williams, April 14, 1798, MS., Simon Perkins Papers, Container 94, Folder 1 (Repository: Western Reserve Historical Society), no pagination.
15. Letter to Moses Cleaveland, Joseph Perkins, Daniel L. Coit to Simon Perkins, April 14, 1798, Simon Perkins Papers, Container 94, Folder 1 (Repository: Western Reserve Historical Society).
16. *Ibid.*
17. *Ibid.*
18. Inventory of the Estate both Real and Personal of Simon Perkins of Norwich, Deceased, November 28, 1778, recorded in Estate Records, Norwich District, Book 6, MS. 8632 (Repository: Connecticut State Library), pp. 305–306.
19. *Ibid.*

20. Norwich Land Records, Volume 21 (Repository: Connecticut State Library), pp. 435–437.
21. George E. Perkins, *The Family of John Perkins of Ipswich*, Book III (Salem: Salem Press Publishing and Printing Company, 1889), pp. 28–29.
22. Catalogue of the Sophomore Class of Yale College, 1795, Broadside 0. 49 (Repository: Western Reserve Historical Society).
23. Quoted in Jeannette Mirsky and Allan Nevins, *The World of Eli Whitney* (New York: Collier Books, 1962), p. 50, source not clarified.
24. Letter Christopher Starr to Simon Perkins, January 20, 1823, Simon Perkins Papers, Letterbox 33 (Repository: Western Reserve Historical Society).
25. Letter Moses Cleaveland, Joseph Perkins, and Daniel L. Coit to Simon Perkins, April 14, 1798, Simon Perkins Papers, Container 94, Folder 1 (Repository: Western Reserve Historical Society).
26. Mode of Division of Township No. 8 in the 7th Range, New Connecticut, Moses Cleaveland Papers, MS. 3233, Container 1, Folder 9 (Repository: Western Reserve Historical Society), no pagination.
27. Book of Drafts, Connecticut Land Company, Ephraim Root Papers, MS. 3235, Container 3 (Repository: Western Reserve Historical Society), partition of January 30, 1798, no pagination.
28. Simon Perkins, Account with the Erie Company, 1798, MS., Simon Perkins Papers, Container 94, Folder 1 (Repository: Western Reserve Historical Society), no pagination.
29. Elisha Whittlesey, "Simon Perkins," August 8, 1860, MS., Simon Perkins Papers, Container 75, Folder 2 (Repository: Western Reserve Historical Society), p. 4.
30. Simon Perkins, Surveying Book, 1795, MS., Simon Perkins Papers, Container 79, Folder 2 (Repository: Western Reserve Historical Society), no pagination.
31. Moses Cleaveland, Extract from Journal, July, 1796 (MS. copy), Moses Cleaveland Papers, MS. 3233, Container 1, Folder 5 (Repository: Western Reserve Historical Society), no pagination. It is interesting to note that Cleaveland expected the Reserve to become the sixteenth state in the Union but that during the period of his journey Tennessee had been admitted to statehood. Thus Ohio became the seventeenth rather than the sixteenth state.

Chapter Three

1. Turhand Kirtland, Diary 1798–1800 (MS. copy), MS. 737 (Repository: Western Reserve Historical Society), entry of May 28, 1798, p. 3.
2. Connecticut Land Company Agreements to Build Roads, March 10, 1798, MSS. (not catalogued), Connecticut Land Company miscellaneous papers (Repository: Western Reserve Historical Society), no pagination.
3. Abraham Tappan, "Biographical Sketches of the Surveyors," 1850, "Bound MSS. of the Western Reserve," Volume 23, Book 7 (Repository: Western Reserve Historical Society), p. 52.
4. Turhand Kirtland, Diary 1798–1800 (MS. copy), MS. 737 (Repository: Western Reserve Historical Society), entry of July 4, 1798, p. 18.
5. Connecticut Land Company Agreement with John Young to Build Road, March 10, 1798, MS. (not catalogued), Connecticut Land Company miscellaneous papers (Repository: Western Reserve Historical Society), no pagination.
6. Simon Perkins, Account with the Erie Company, 1798, MS., Simon Perkins Papers, Container 94, Folder 1 (Repository: Western Reserve Historical Society), no pagination.
7. Simon Perkins, Field Notes, October 9, 1798, quoted in Letter Daniel L. Coit to Simon Perkins, September 24, 1816, Simon Perkins Papers, Letterbox 9 (Repository: Western Reserve Historical Society).
8. Margaret Manor Butler, *Pictorial History of the Western Reserve* (Cleveland: Western Reserve Historical Society and Early Settlers Association of the Western Reserve, 1963), p. 136.
9. Description of Fort McIntosh taken from Henry Knox, Letters on Harman Expedition, 1790 (MS. copy), MS. 2404 (Repository: Western Reserve Historical Society).
10. Simon Perkins, Survey of Coitsville, Ohio, 1798, MS. 707 (Repository: Western Reserve Historical Society), no pagination.
11. Simon Perkins, Surveying Book, 1795, MS., Simon Perkins Papers, Container 79, Folder 2 (Repository: Western Reserve Historical Society), no pagination.
12. Simon Perkins, Account with the Erie Company, 1798, MS., Simon Perkins Papers, Container 94, Folder 1 (Repository: Western Reserve Historical Society), no pagination.
13. Minutes of Proceedings from 1796 to 1800, minutes of January 27 and 28, 1797, "Bound MSS. of the Western Reserve," Volume 17, Book 2 (Repository: Western Reserve Historical Society), no pagination.
14. Letter Augustus Porter to John Barr, January 10, 1843, "Bound MSS. of the Western Reserve," Volume 22, Book 3 (Repository: Western Reserve Historical Society), p. 4.

15. Swift had been advised that Washington was opposed to purchasing any more land from the Indians or to making any additional treaties with them following upon the Treaty of Greenville and he had advised the Company of this in a Letter to Oliver Phelps, December 21, 1795, which may be found in the Phelps Family Land Papers, MS. 3236, Container 1, Folder 1 (Repository: Western Reserve Historical Society).

16. This Act was entitled "An Act to regulate trade and intercourse with the Indian tribes, and to preserve peace on the frontiers." The Act may be found in *The Debates and Proceedings in the Congress of the United States, Annals of Congress*, December 5, 1796, to March 3, 1797, Fourth Congress, Second Session (Washington: Gales and Seaton, 1849), pp. 2909–2916.

17. Letter Augustus Porter to John Barr, January 10, 1843, "Bound MSS. of the Western Reserve," Volume 22, Book 3 (Repository: Western Reserve Historical Society), p. 3.

18. Letter Israel Chapin to Moses Cleaveland, February 6, 1797, Moses Cleaveland Papers, MS. 3233. Container 1, Folder 2, and Letter Moses Cleaveland to Israel Chapin, February 8, 1797, Moses Cleaveland Papers, MS. 3233, Container 1, Folder 4 (Repository: Western Reserve Historical Society).

19. Harlan Hatcher, *The Western Reserve* (Revised edition; Cleveland and New York: World Publishing Company, 1966), p. 18. See also footnote 23 below in reference to the terms of Cleaveland's contract.

20. Letter Israel Chapin to Moses Cleaveland, February 6, 1797, Moses Cleaveland Papers, MS. 3233, Container 1, Folder 2 (Repository: Western Reserve Historical Society).

21. *Ibid.* See also Letter Moses Cleaveland to Israel Chapin, February 8, 1797, Moses Cleaveland Papers, MS. 3233, Container 1, Folder 4 (Repository: Western Reserve Historical Society).

22. Letter Joseph Brant to unidentified friend, July 2, 1797, quoted by William L. Stone in his *Life of Joseph Brant, Thayendanegea*, Volume II (Albany: Mumsell, 1865), p. 454. It should be noted, however, that Stone observes, p. 455, that Brant was entertained during his Philadelphia visit by Timothy Burr [a Connecticut Land Company proprietor].

23. Votes and Proceedings, January 30, 1798, available on Reel 1 of Western Reserve Historical Society's microfilm publication of the records of the Connecticut Land Company originally at Connecticut State Library (Repository: Western Reserve Historical Society). It should be noted that the money was not deposited with Chapin, who may have refused agency in the affair, and that Phelps took over negotiations with Brant for settling Cleaveland's treaty or contract. Brant made several trips to see Phelps at Canandaigua and collected on the contract and for his expenses in making the journeys. Finally Phelps states in Letter Oliver Phelps to Ephraim Root, August 17, 1803, Ephraim Root Papers, MS. 3235, Container 2, Folder 3 (Re-

pository: Western Reserve Historical Society) that he has taken up Cleaveland's contract and is enclosing it in the letter. The contract, however, is not with the letter, in Phelps's papers, or in any of the other relevant manuscript collections of the period. The exact terms, therefore, cannot be determined and may be interpreted only through letters of the period pertinent to the subject.

24. Letter Moses Cleaveland to Daniel L. Coit, July 15, 1799, Moses Cleaveland Papers, MS. 3233, Container 1, Folder 4 (Repository: Western Reserve Historical Society).

25. Minutes of the Connecticut Land Company, May 13, 1800, "Bound MSS. of the Western Reserve," Volume 17, Book 2 (Repository: Western Reserve Historical Society), no pagination.

26. *The Debates and Proceedings in the Congress of the United States*, May 15, 1797, to March 3, 1799, Fifth Congress, Volume I (Washington: Gales and Seaton, 1849), p. 618.

27. Letter Simon Perkins to the Trustees, Erie Company, June 10, 1799, Moses Cleaveland Papers, MS. 3233, Container 1, Folder 9 (Repository: Western Reserve Historical Society).

28. Letter Simon Perkins to the Trustees, Erie Company, June 25, 1799, Moses Cleaveland Papers, MS. 3233, Container 1, Folder 9 (Repository: Western Reserve Historical Society).

29. Letter Simon Perkins to the Trustees, Erie Company, August 11, 1799, Moses Cleaveland Papers, MS. 3233, Container 1, Folder 9 (Repository: Western Reserve Historical Society).

30. William Law, Journal [1799], MS. 596 (Repository: Western Reserve Historical Society), entry of June 6 [1799], no pagination.

31. Simon Perkins, Account with the Erie Company, 1799, MS., Simon Perkins Papers, Container 94, Folder 1 (Repository: Western Reserve Historical Society), no pagination.

32. Simon Perkins, Surveying Book, 1795, MS., Simon Perkins Papers, Container 79, Folder 2 (Repository: Western Reserve Historical Society), no pagination.

33. Turhand Kirtland, Diary 1798–1800 (MS. copy), MS. 737 (Repository: Western Reserve Historical Society), entry of September 13, 1799, p. 49.

34. Simon Perkins, Surveying Book, 1795, MS., Simon Perkins Papers, Container 79, Folder 2 (Repository: Western Reserve Historical Society), no pagination.

35. *Ibid.*

36. Letter Simon Perkins to Joseph Perkins, August 4, 1799, John Arnold Rockwell Papers HM–RO 1016 (Repository: Henry Huntington Library).

37. Letter Simon Perkins to the Trustees, Erie Company, September 12, 1799, Moses Cleaveland Papers, MS. 3233, Container 1, Folder 9 (Repository: Western Reserve Historical Society).

38. Letter Simon Perkins to the Trustees, Erie Company, October 5, 1799, Moses Cleaveland Papers, MS. 3233, Container 1, Folder 9 (Repository: Western Reserve Historical Society).

39. Samuel Eliot Morison, *The Oxford History of the American People* (New York: Oxford University Press, 1965), pp. 323–331.

40. Claude G. Bowers, *Jefferson and Hamilton, The Struggle for Democracy in America* (Boston and New York: Houghton Mifflin Company, 1925), p. 29.

41. *Ibid.*, p. 96, quoting from William E. Dodd, *Statesmen of the Old South, or Radicalism to Conservative Revolt* (New York: Macmillan Company, 1921), p. 23.

42. *Celebration of the Two Hundred and Fiftieth Anniversary of the Settlement of Suffield, Connecticut* (Suffield: n.p., 1921), pp. 118–119.

43. Letters Samuel Huntington to Moses Cleaveland, November 15, 1801, and February 10, 1802, Moses Cleaveland Papers, MS. 3233, Container 1, Folder 3 (Repository: Western Reserve Historical Society).

44. Letter Gideon Granger to Ephraim Root, March 20, 1800, available on Reel 3 of Western Reserve Historical Society's microfilm publication of the records of the Connecticut Land Company originally at Connecticut State Library (Repository: Western Reserve Historical Society).

45. Letters Gideon Granger to Ephraim Root, March 7, 1800, and March 11, 1800, available on Reel 3 of Western Reserve Historical Society's microfilm publication of the records of the Connecticut Land Company originally at Connecticut State Library (Repository: Western Reserve Historical Society).

46. Letter Jonathan Brace to Ephraim Root, January 16, 1800, Ephraim Root Papers, MS. 3235, Container 1, Folder 2 (Repository: Western Reserve Historical Society).

47. Letter Joseph Perkins to Ephraim Root, March 1, 1800, Ephraim Root Papers, MS. 3235, Container 2, Folder 3 (Repository: Western Reserve Historical Society).

48. Letter Jonathan Brace to Ephraim Root, February 1, 1800, Ephraim Root Papers, MS. 3235, Container 1, Folder 2 (Repository: Western Reserve Historical Society).

49. *American State Papers, Public Lands*, Volume I, selected and edited by Asbury Dickins and John W. Fortney (Washington: Gales and Seaton, 1834), pp. 83–88.

50. Letter Gideon Granger to Ephraim Root, March 20, 1800, available on Reel 3 of Western Reserve Historical Society's microfilm publication of the records of the Connecticut Land Company originally at Connecticut State Library (Repository: Western Reserve Historical Society).

51. Letter Uriel Holmes to Ephraim Root, March 17, 1800, Ephraim Root Papers, MS. 3235, Container 1, Folder 5 (Repository: Western Reserve Historical Society).

52. Letter Jonathan Brace to Ephraim Root, March 15, 1800, Ephraim Root Papers, MS. 3235, Container 1, Folder 2 (Repository: Western Reserve Historical Society).

53. Albert C. Bates, "The Connecticut Gore Land Company," *Annual Report of the American Historical Association for the Year 1898* (Washington: Government Printing Office, 1899), pp. 156–158.

54. *American State Papers, Public Lands*, Volume I, p. 88.

55. *The Debates and Proceedings in the Congress of the United States*, December 2, 1799, to March 3, 1801, Sixth Congress (Washington: Gales and Seaton, 1851), p. 661, *et passim*.

56. *Ibid.*, p. 662.

57. *Ibid.*, p. 165.

58. *Ibid.*, pp. 1495–1496.

59. Letter Henry Champion to Moses Cleaveland, May 18, 1800, Moses Cleaveland Papers, MS. 3233, Container 1, Folder 3 (Repository: Western Reserve Historical Society).

60. Abraham Tappan, "Sketch of the Surveys West of the Cuyahoga River in 1806–1807," October, 1850, "Bound MSS. of the Western Reserve," Volume 23, Book 8 (Repository: Western Reserve Historical Society), p. 37.

61. It is indicative of the political turbulence of the 1800 period that Pierpont Edwards was affiliated with the Republican party—making him, like Samuel Huntington Junior, something of a prodigal son to his father Jonathan Edwards—and that John Stark Edwards was a Federalist. References to Pierpont Edwards as a Republican leader may be found in Noble E. Cunningham Junior, *The Jeffersonian Republicans in Power, Party Operations, 1801–1809*, published for the Institute of Early American History and Culture at Williamsburg, Virginia (Chapel Hill: University of North Carolina Press, 1963), p. 19, pp. 22–23, p. 208, pp. 227–228. For references to John Stark Edwards as a Federalist see page 53, this book.

62. Petition of the Proprietors of Erie Land Company to Trustees, May 1, 1800, MS., Moses Cleaveland Papers, MS. 3233, Container 1, Folder 9 (Repository: Western Reserve Historical Society), no pagination.

63. Turhand Kirtland, Diary 1798–1800 (MS. copy), MS. 737 (Repository: Western Reserve Historical Society), entries of June 17 and June 19, 1800, p. 55.

64. Letter Simon Perkins to Joseph Howland, August 1, 1800 (typescript copy, not catalogued), Howland Correspondence (Repository: Western Reserve Historical Society).

65. Letter Samuel Huntington to Daniel L. Coit, August 8, 1800, Coit-Huntington Correspondence (Repository: Connecticut Historical Society).

66. Letter Uriel Holmes to Ephraim Root, April 17, 1800, Ephraim Root Papers, MS. 3235, Container 1, Folder 5 (Repository: Western Reserve Historical Society).

67. Letter Samuel Huntington to Daniel L. Coit, August 8, 1800, Coit-Huntington Correspondence (Repository: Connecticut Historical Society).

68. Letter Simon Perkins to the Trustees, Erie Company, June 18, 1800, Moses Cleaveland Papers, MS. 3233, Container 1, Folder 9 (Repository: Western Reserve Historical Society).
69. Letter Simon Perkins to Moses Cleaveland, September 23, 1800, Moses Cleaveland Papers, MS. 3233, Container 1, Folder 3 (Repository: Western Reserve Historical Society).
70. Letter Simon Perkins to Trustees, Erie Company, August 2, 1800, Moses Cleaveland Papers, MS. 3233, Container 1, Folder 9 (Repository: Western Reserve Historical Society).

Chapter Four

1. Seth Pease, Extracts from Field Notes, 1797, "Bound MSS. of the Western Reserve," Volume 23, Book 5 (Repository: Western Reserve Historical Society), entry of June 30, 1797, p. 18.
2. By the following year Samuel Huntington would observe that there was some uneasiness in the Indian-settler relationship. In a letter to Moses Cleaveland, November 15, 1801, Moses Cleaveland Papers, MS. 3233, Container 1, Folder 3 (Repository: Western Reserve Historical Society) Huntington observed:
We have now here about 200 Indians just going up the Cuyahoga . . . they look with a wistful eye on their ancient possessions, a little whiskey however quiets them—they have a jealousy of my coming here—owing to a story that has been propagated among them that I am raising soldiers to drive them out of the country. I have had a great number of workmen here, who they think are soldiers in disguise—I take all pains to undeceive them, not however, without informing them that I can do it, in case they misbehave, whenever I please.
3. The following account of the Indian murder at the Salt Springs is taken from Leonard Case, Local History of the Western Reserve, 1863, MS. 1014 (Repository: Western Reserve Historical Society), no pagination.
4. Turhand Kirtland, Diary 1798–1800 (MS. copy), MS. 737 (Repository: Western Reserve Historical Society), entry of July 28, 1800, p. 58.
5. Letter Samuel Huntington to Daniel L. Coit, August 8, 1800, Coit-Huntington Correspondence (Repository: Connecticut Historical Society).
6. Turhand Kirtland, Diary 1798–1800 (MS. copy), MS. 737 (Repository: Western Reserve Historical Society), entries of July 28 and 29, 1800, p. 58.
7. Letter Samuel Huntington to Daniel L. Coit, August 8, 1800, Coit-Huntington Correspondence (Repository: Connecticut Historical Society).

8. Letter Simon Perkins to Trustees, Erie Company, August 2, 1800, Moses Cleaveland Papers, MS. 3233, Container 1, Folder 9 (Repository: Western Reserve Historical Society).

9. Letter Samuel Huntington to Daniel L. Coit, August 8, 1800, Coit-Huntington Correspondence (Repository: Connecticut Historical Society).

10. Orrin Harmon, "Historical Facts Appertaining to the Township of Mantua" [1866], Copies of Historical Manuscripts, Harmon Family Papers, Container 1, Folder 11 (Repository: Western Reserve Historical Society), p. 61.

11. Letter Samuel Huntington to Joseph Howland, August 10, 1800 (typescript copy, not catalogued), Howland Correspondence (Repository: Western Reserve Historical Society).

12. Letter Simon Perkins to Joseph Howland, August 1, 1800 (typescript copy, not catalogued), Howland Correspondence (Repository: Western Reserve Historical Society).

13. *Ibid.*

14. Turhand Kirtland, Diary 1798–1800 (MS. copy), MS. 737 (Repository: Western Reserve Historical Society), entries of August 27, 28, and 29, 1800, pp. 62–63.

15. *Ibid.*, entries of August 25 and 26, 1800, p. 62.

16. *Ibid.*, entry of September 14, 1800, p. 64.

17. *Ibid.*, entries of September 17 and 18, 1800, pp. 64–65.

18. Letter Simon Perkins to Moses Cleaveland, September 23, 1800, Moses Cleaveland Papers, MS. 3233, Container 1, Folder 3 (Repository: Western Reserve Historical Society).

19. *Ibid.*

20. Arthur St. Clair, Address to the General Assembly of the Northwest Territory, November 5, 1800, printed in *Scioto Gazette*, November 13, 1800, available on microfilm (Repository: Western Reserve Historical Society).

21. *Ibid.*

22. *Laws of the Territory of the United States Northwest of the River Ohio*, Volume I, 1800–1801 (Chillicothe: Winship & Willis, 1801), pp. 61–63.

23. Letters Hannah Huntington to Samuel Huntington, September 6, 1800, and September 28, 1800, Letters of Hannah Huntington to her husband Samuel Huntington, Governor of Ohio, 1791–1811, MS. 884 (Repository: Western Reserve Historical Society).

24. Letter Hannah Huntington to Samuel Huntington, November 1, 1800, Letters of Hannah Huntington to her husband Samuel Huntington, Governor of Ohio, 1791–1811, MS. 884 (Repository: Western Reserve Historical Society).

Chapter Five

1. Quoted by Louisa Maria Edwards in *A Pioneer Homemaker, 1787–1866, A Sketch of the Life of Louisa Maria Montgomery* (n.p., 1903), p. 7.
2. William Law, Journal, MS. 596 (Repository: Western Reserve Historical Society), entry of June 14 [1799], no pagination.
3. Jonathan Law, Diary No. 5, October 12 to October 18, 1802, MS. 597 (Repository: Western Reserve Historical Society), entry of October 17, 1802, no pagination.
4. Letter Samuel Huntington to Reverend E. D. Griffin, January 10, 1801, MS. 2063, No. 2 (Repository: Western Reserve Historical Society).
5. Letter Samuel Huntington to Joseph Howland, June 10, 1800 (typescript copy, not catalogued), Howland Correspondence (Repository: Western Reserve Historical Society).
6. Letter Moses Cleaveland to Henry Champion, May 1, 1801, Moses Cleaveland Papers, MS. 3233, Container 1, Folder 4 (Repository: Western Reserve Historical Society).
7. Letter Hannah Huntington to Samuel Huntington, July 27, 1800, Letters of Hannah Huntington to her husband Samuel Huntington, Governor of Ohio, 1791–1811, MS. 884 (Repository: Western Reserve Historical Society).
8. Letter Christopher Leffingwell to Daniel L. Coit, May 7, 1801, Coit-Huntington Correspondence (Repository: Connecticut Historical Society).
9. *Ibid.*
10. Letter Daniel L. Coit to Simon Perkins, October 29, 1801, Simon Perkins Papers, Letterbox 8 (Repository: Western Reserve Historical Society).
11. Letter Samuel Huntington to Daniel L. Coit, December 25, 1801, Coit-Huntington Correspondence (Repository: Connecticut Historical Society).
12. Letter Daniel L. Coit to Simon Perkins, August 19, 1805, Simon Perkins Papers, Letterbox 8 (Repository: Western Reserve Historical Society).
13. Simon Perkins, Account with the Erie Company, 1800, MS., Simon Perkins Papers, Container 94, Folder 1 (Repository: Western Reserve Historical Society), no pagination.
14. *Ibid.* It is interesting to note that the Erie Company allowed these items on Simon's expense account but would not allow his charge for time spent in drawing maps and writing field notes.
15. Letter Joseph Howland to Simon Perkins, February 10, 1802, Simon Perkins Papers, Letterbox 17 (Repository: Western Reserve Historical Society).
16. The boundaries of the eastern state were, on the west, a line drawn due north from the mouth of the Great Miami River to the territorial

line; on the south, the Ohio River; on the east, the Pennsylvania western border. A copy of the Northwest Ordinance may be found in *Documents of American History*, edited by Henry Steele Commager (Sixth edition; New York: Appleton-Century-Crofts, Inc., 1958), pp. 128–132.

17. The Act may be found in *Debates and Proceedings in the Congress of the United States*, *Annals of Congress*, December 7, 1801, to March 3, 1803, Seventh Congress (Washington: Gales and Seaton, 1851), pp. 1349–1350.
18. Jonathan Law, Diary No. 5, October 12 to October 18, 1802, MS. 597 (Repository: Western Reserve Historical Society), entry of October 12, 1802, no pagination.
19. Letter Joseph Perkins to Simon Perkins, December 31, 1804, Simon Perkins Papers, Letterbox 27 (Repository: Western Reserve Historical Society).
20. Jonathan Law, Diary No. 6, October 19 to October 30, 1802, MS. 597 (Repository: Western Reserve Historical Society), entry of October 23, 1800, no pagination.
21. Letter Samuel Huntington to Turhand Kirtland, December 3, 1802, Turhand Kirtland Papers, MS. 3237, Container 11, Folder 1 (Repository: Western Reserve Historical Society).
22. Letter Joseph Howland to Simon Perkins, August 2, 1806, Simon Perkins Papers, Letterbox 17 (Repository: Western Reserve Historical Society).
23. Letter Daniel L. Coit to Simon Perkins, January 8, 1807, Simon Perkins Papers, Letterbox 8 (Repository: Western Reserve Historical Society).
24. Letter Simon Perkins to Daniel L. Coit, December 5, 1805, Simon Perkins Papers, Letterbook 1805–1808, Container 80, Folder 1 (Repository: Western Reserve Historical Society).
25. Letter Simon Perkins to Daniel L. Coit, January 12, 1806, Simon Perkins Papers, Letterbook 1805–1808, Container 80, Folder 1 (Repository: Western Reserve Historical Society).
26. Letter Simon Perkins to Daniel L. Coit, December 5, 1805, Simon Perkins Papers, Letterbook 1805–1808, Container 80, Folder 1 (Repository: Western Reserve Historical Society).
27. Letter Simon Perkins to Joseph Howland, January 13, 1806, Simon Perkins Papers, Letterbook 1805–1808, Container 80, Folder 1 (Repository: Western Reserve Historical Society).
28. Simon Perkins, Account Books, Simon Perkins Papers, Container 75, Folders 7 and 8; Container 76, Book 1806–1836 and Book 1818–1834 (Repository: Western Reserve Historical Society).
29. Letter Simon Perkins to Benjamin Gorham, September 3, 1805, Simon Perkins Papers, Letterbook 1805–1808, Container 80, Folder 1 (Repository: Western Reserve Historical Society).
30. Joseph F. McFarland, *History of the City of Washington and of Washington County, Pennsylvania and Representative Citizens* (Chi-

cago: Richmond-Arnold Publishing Company, 1910), p. 146. In addition, Harry Marlin Tinkcom notes in *The Republicans and Federalists in Pennsylvania, 1790–1801, A Study in National Stimulus and Local Response* (Harrisburg: Pennsylvania Historical and Museum Commission, 1950), p. 184, that "The dominance of Republicanism in western Pennsylvania was well illustrated in the Congressional elections of 1798. Of the five counties, only Allegheny favored the Federalists."

31. Caleb Ensign, "History of Rootstown" (n.d.), MS. 595 (Repository: Western Reserve Historical Society), no pagination.
32. *Ibid.*
33. Letter Simon Perkins to Elias Perkins, February 20, 1809, Elias Perkins Papers (Repository: New London County Historical Society).
34. *Ibid.*
35. Letter Simon Perkins to Nancy Bishop, April 20, 1803, Letters to Nancy Bishop, MS. 3232, Folder 8 (Repository: Western Reserve Historical Society).
36. Letter Simon Perkins to Nancy Bishop, June 22, 1803, Letters to Nancy Bishop, MS. 3232, Folder 8 (Repository: Western Reserve Historical Society).
37. Letter Simon Perkins to Joseph Perkins, August 4, 1804, John Arnold Rockwell Papers HM–RO 1020 (Repository: Henry Huntington Library).
38. Letter Simon Perkins to Joseph Perkins, March 11, 1805, John Arnold Rockwell Papers HM–RO 104 (Repository: Henry Huntington Library).
39. Letter Simon Perkins to Daniel L. Coit, February 23, 1807, Simon Perkins Papers, Letterbook 1805–1808, Container 80, Folder 1 (Repository: Western Reserve Historical Society).
40. Letter Simon Perkins to Elias Perkins, February 20, 1809, Elias Perkins Papers (Repository: New London County Historical Society).
41. Letter Simon Perkins to Jonathan Brace and Enoch Perkins, April 9, 1811, Simon Perkins Papers, Letterbox 28 (Repository: Western Reserve Historical Society).
42. Letter Christopher Starr to Simon Perkins, May 9, 1805, Simon Perkins Papers, Letterbox 33 (Repository: Western Reserve Historical Society).
43. Letter Christopher Starr to Simon Perkins, April 13, 1813, Simon Perkins Papers, Letterbox 33 (Repository: Western Reserve Historical Society).
44. Leonard Case, "Memoranda of Incidents in the Life of Leonard Case," January, 1853 (typescript copy), MS. 2871 (Repository: Western Reserve Historical Society), p. 57.
45. Louisa Maria Edwards, *A Pioneer Homemaker*, p. 23.

Chapter Six

1. Letter Daniel L. Coit to Simon Perkins, February 1, 1802, Simon Perkins Papers, Letterbox 8 (Repository: Western Reserve Historical Society).
2. Francis Manwaring Caulkins, *History of Norwich, Connecticut* (Hartford: Case, Lockwood and Company, 1866), p. 476, p. 545, p. 547, *et passim*.
3. Timothy Dwight, *Travels in New-England and New-York*, Volume II (New Haven: Timothy Dwight, 1821), p. 43.
4. Francis Manwaring Caulkins, *History of Norwich*, p. 499.
5. *Ibid.*, p. 479.
6. Letter Hannah Huntington to Samuel Huntington, September 10, 1800, Letters of Hannah Huntington to her husband Samuel Huntington, Governor of Ohio, 1791–1811, MS. 884 (Repository: Western Reserve Historical Society).
7. Letter Hannah Huntington to Samuel Huntington, November 1, 1800, Letters of Hannah Huntington to her husband Samuel Huntington, Governor of Ohio, 1791–1811, MS. 884 (Repository: Western Reserve Historical Society).
8. *Ibid.*
9. Letter Simon Perkins to Joseph Williams Junior, March 19, 1806, Simon Perkins Papers, Letterbook 1805–1808, Container 80, Folder 1 (Repository: Western Reserve Historical Society).
10. Letter Simon Perkins to the Trumbull County Representation in the Legislature of the State of Ohio, November 19, 1806, Simon Perkins Papers, Letterbook 1805–1808, Container 80, Folder 1 (Repository: Western Reserve Historical Society).
11. Letter Joseph Williams Junior to Simon Perkins, February 24, 1817, Simon Perkins Papers, Letterbox 37 (Repository: Western Reserve Historical Society).
12. Letter Joseph Howland to Simon Perkins, October 7, 1806, Simon Perkins Papers, Letterbox 17 (Repository: Western Reserve Historical Society).
13. Letters Joseph Howland to Simon Perkins, July 17, 1811, and August 29, 1811, Simon Perkins Papers, Letterbox 17 (Repository: Western Reserve Historical Society).
14. Harlan Hatcher, *The Western Reserve* (Revised edition; Cleveland and New York: World Publishing Company, 1966), p. 77.
15. Samuel Henry Wandell, *Oliver Phelps*, a paper read before the New York State Historical Association, September 18, 1941 (n.p., n.d.), pp. 15–16.
16. In addition to the Phelps Family Land Papers at Western Reserve Historical Society, the Walter Hubbell Papers, which contain Phelps documents, at Princeton University Library were also examined, but neither collection reveals Phelps's exact fate.

17. See Phelps Family Land Papers, MS. 3236, Container 1, Folder 7 (Repository: Western Reserve Historical Society).
18. Anna Cornelia Clauder, *American Commerce as Affected by the Wars of the French Revolution and Napoleon, 1793–1812* (Philadelphia: n.p., 1932), pp. 134–135.
19. Nelson W. Evans, *History of Taxation in Ohio* (Cincinnati: Robert Clarke Company, 1906), p. 126.
20. It will be remembered that Simon aimed at a ten per cent down payment on land contracts and that Connecticut had required only a fifteen per cent down payment from the original proprietors, when the land was purchased in 1795. Therefore the settlers could owe, on interest, for ninety per cent of their land and the proprietors for eighty-five per cent.
21. The quantity of land in the Reserve is listed in Joseph Perkins' Scrapbook, MS. 907 (Repository: Western Reserve Historical Society), p. 130 as follows: Salt Springs Tract 25,450 acres; east of Cuyahoga 2,002,970 acres; west of Cuyahoga, exclusive of surplus lands and the islands, 827,291 acres; surplus lands 5,286 acres; six islands 5,924 acres; Firelands 500,000 acres.
22. In addition to payments made on Cleaveland's agreement with Brant, in 1805 the Company agreed to pay Oliver Phelps $25,000 for negotiating the treaty with the Indians for the land west of the Cuyahoga River. See Phelps Family Land Papers, MS. 3236, Container 1, Folder 2 (Repository: Western Reserve Historical Society) for copy of this agreement.
23. According to the terms of the May 10, 1800, Land Act a minimum price of $2.00 per acre was established for the public lands. One-fourth of the purchase money was to be paid in forty days, but the remaining part was spread over a four-year period with interest, at six per cent, on the last three payments. A copy of the Land Act of 1800 may be found in *Documents of American History*, edited by Henry Steele Commager (Sixth edition; New York: Appleton-Century-Crofts, Inc., 1958), pp. 185–186.
24. Harlan Hatcher, *The Western Reserve*, p. 75.
25. *Cleaveland Herald*, August 1, 1820 (Repository: Western Reserve Historical Society), p. 1.
26. *Ibid.*, p. 4.
27. Caleb Ensign, "History of Rootstown" (n.d.), MS. 595 (Repository: Western Reserve Historical Society), p. 1b.

Chapter Seven

1. Letter Elijah Wadsworth to Williams Eustis, August 27, 1812, available in the Western Reserve Historical Society's microfilm publication, "War of 1812" (Repository: Western Reserve Historical Society).
2. Warren H. Goodman, "Origins of the War of 1812," *Mississippi Valley Historical Review*, Volume XXVIII, Number 2 (September, 1941), pp. 171–186.
3. *Ibid.*, p. 171.
4. For a discussion of Randolph's charges see Julius W. Pratt, "Western Aims in the War of 1812," *Mississippi Valley Historical Review*, Volume XII, Number 1 (June, 1925), pp. 36–50.
5. Henry Adams, *History of the United States*, Volume VI (New York: Charles Scribner's Sons, 1890), p. 409.
6. Warren H. Goodman, "Origins of the War of 1812," *Mississippi Valley Historical Review*, Volume XXVIII, Number 2 (September, 1941), pp. 171–186.
7. *Ibid.*, pp. 185–186. For the studies of the War of 1812 summarized by Goodman see Julius W. Pratt, "Western Aims in the War of 1812," *Mississippi Valley Historical Review*, Volume XII, Number 1 (June, 1925), p. 46; Thomas Andrew Bailey, *A Diplomatic History of the American People* (New York: F. S. Crofts & Company, 1940), p. 133; Theodore Dwight, *History of the Hartford Convention with a Review of the Policy of the United States Government Which Led to the War of 1812* (New York: N. & J. White, 1833), pp. 228–229; Louis Morton Hacker, "Western Land Hunger and the War of 1812," *Mississippi Valley Historical Review*, Volume X, Number 4 (March, 1924), pp. 386–387; Richard Hildreth, *The History of the United States of America*, Volume VI (New York: Harper & Brothers, 1863), pp. 315–316; and Julius W. Pratt, *Expansionists of 1812* (New York: Macmillan Company, 1925), p. 58.
8. *Mississippi Valley Historical Review*, Volume XII, Number 1 (June, 1925), pp. 36–50.
9. *Ibid.*, p. 50.
10. *Ibid.*, p. 44.
11. Letter Samuel Huntington to Moses Cleaveland, November 15, 1801, Moses Cleaveland Papers, MS. 3233, Container 1, Folder 3 (Repository: Western Reserve Historical Society).
12. William Ganson Rose, *Cleveland, The Making of a City* (Cleveland: World Publishing Company, 1950), p. 53.
13. Letter Simon Perkins to Jonathan Brace, July 5, 1805, Simon Perkins Papers, Letterbook 1805–1808, Container 80, Folder 1 (Repository: Western Reserve Historical Society).
14. Louis Morton Hacker, "Western Land Hunger and the War of 1812," *Mississippi Valley Historical Review*, Volume X, Number 4 (March, 1924), pp. 363–395.
15. *Ibid.*, footnote, p. 384.

16. Letter Issachar Bates to Richard [McNemar], December 13, 1811, copy in Alonzo G. Hollister, Book of Pioneer Correspondence from the West, 1871, Shaker Collection, MS. BX9786/L6B7 (Repository: Western Reserve Historical Society), p. 35.
17. For a detailed account of the Shakers' experiences with Harrison and the Indians during the War of 1812, see Mary Lou Conlin, "The Lost Land of Busro," *Shaker Quarterly*, Volume III, Number 2 (Summer, 1963), pp. 44–60.
18. Letter Calvin Pease to George Tod, January 10, 1812, available in the Western Reserve Historical Society's microfilm publication, "George Tod Papers Relating to the War of 1812" (Repository: Western Reserve Historical Society).
19. William Ganson Rose, *Cleveland, The Making of a City*, p. 68.
20. *Trump of Fame*, April 14, 1813 (Repository: Western Reserve Historical Society), p. 2.
21. See Elijah Wadsworth-William Eustis correspondence of July and August, 1812, and Elijah Wadsworth-Return Jonathan Meigs correspondence, July, August, and September, 1812, available in the Western Reserve Historical Society's microfilm publication, "War of 1812" (Repository: Western Reserve Historical Society).
22. Letter John Hindman to Elijah Wadsworth, August 1, 1812, available in the Western Reserve Historical Society's microfilm publication, "War of 1812" (Repository: Western Reserve Historical Society).
23. Letter Elijah Wadsworth to Simon Perkins, August 26, 1812, Simon Perkins Papers, Letterbox 39 (Repository: Western Reserve Historical Society).
24. Letters Return Jonathan Meigs to Elijah Wadsworth, July 10, 1812, and August 2, 1812, Simon Perkins Papers, Letterbox 39 (Repository: Western Reserve Historical Society).
25. Letter John Armstrong to Artemas Baker, printed in *Trump of Fame*, April 21, 1813 (Repository: Western Reserve Historical Society), p. 3.
26. Letter Gideon Granger to Simon Perkins, December 5, 1807, Simon Perkins Papers, Letterbox 41 (Repository: Western Reserve Historical Society).
27. Elisha Whittlesey, "Simon Perkins," August 8, 1860, MS., Simon Perkins Papers, Container 75, Folder 2 (Repository: Western Reserve Historical Society), p. 8.
28. Letter Charles Shaler to Elisha Whittlesey, February 2, 1858, available in the Western Reserve Historical Society's microfilm publication, "George Tod Papers Relating to the War of 1812" (Repository: Western Reserve Historical Society).
29. *Ibid.*
30. Lewis Bond, "Journal of the Battle and Massacre of River Raisin, January 22 and 23, 1813, and the War of 1812" (typescript copy), MS. 1885 (Repository: Western Reserve Historical Society), p. 2.

31. Elisha Whittlesey, "Simon Perkins," August 8, 1860, MS., Simon Perkins Papers, Container 75, Folder 2 (Repository: Western Reserve Historical Society), p. 8.

32. Letter Albert Gallatin to Return Jonathan Meigs, August 27, 1812, Simon Perkins Papers, Letterbox 39 (Repository: Western Reserve Historical Society).

33. Letter Gaius Pease, Samuel Jones, Hiram Hanchett, Alfred Kelley, Lorenzo Carter, and Nathan Perry to Simon Perkins, August 22, 1812, Simon Perkins Papers, Letterbox 39 (Repository: Western Reserve Historical Society).

34. Letter Elijah Wadsworth to Simon Perkins, August 22, 1812, Simon Perkins Papers, Letterbox 39 (Repository: Western Reserve Historical Society).

35. Letter Elijah Wadsworth to Simon Perkins, August 26, 1812, Simon Perkins Papers, Letterbox 39 (Repository: Western Reserve Historical Society).

36. Letter Elijah Wadsworth to Return Jonathan Meigs, September 8, 1812, Simon Perkins Papers, Letterbox 39 (Repository: Western Reserve Historical Society).

37. Letter Elijah Wadsworth to Simon Perkins, August 27, 1812, Simon Perkins Papers, Letterbox 39 (Repository: Western Reserve Historical Society).

38. Wadsworth also committed himself personally for equipping the Militia, and his correspondence with the United States Treasury officials, which is available in the Western Reserve Historical Society's microfilm publication, "War of 1812" (Repository: Western Reserve Historical Society), indicates that he was never fully repaid for what he spent and that he was pressed hard by the Western Reserve merchants for payment of his agreements.

39. Equipment List, September 11, 1812, available in the Western Reserve Historical Society's microfilm publication, "War of 1812" (Repository: Western Reserve Historical Society).

40. Letter Elijah Wadsworth to Simon Perkins, September 6, 1812, Simon Perkins Papers, Letterbox 39 (Repository: Western Reserve Historical Society).

41. *Ibid.*

42. Elisha Whittlesey, "Simon Perkins," August 8, 1860, MS., Simon Perkins Papers, Container 75, Folder 2 (Repository: Western Reserve Historical Society), p. 12.

43. Letter Elijah Wadsworth to Simon Perkins, September 8, 1812, Simon Perkins Papers, Letterbox 39 (Repository: Western Reserve Historical Society).

44. Letter Elijah Wadsworth to Return Jonathan Meigs, September 9, 1812, Simon Perkins Papers, Letterbox 39 (Repository: Western Reserve Historical Society).

45. Letter Elijah Wadsworth to Simon Perkins, September 9, 1812, Simon Perkins Papers, Letterbox 39 (Repository: Western Reserve Historical Society).

46. *Ibid.*
47. Letter Simon Perkins to Elijah Wadsworth (n.d.), Simon Perkins Papers, Letterbox 39 (Repository: Western Reserve Historical Society).
48. Letter Richard Hayes to Simon Perkins, September 21, 1812, Simon Perkins Papers, Letterbox 39 (Repository: Western Reserve Historical Society).
49. Letter Elijah Wadsworth to Simon Perkins, September 25, 1812, Simon Perkins Papers, Letterbox 39 (Repository: Western Reserve Historical Society).
50. Elijah Wadsworth, Address to the Troops, August 27, 1812, Simon Perkins Papers, Letterbox 39 (Repository: Western Reserve Historical Society).
51. Caleb Ensign, "History of Rootstown" (n.d.), MS. 595 (Repository: Western Reserve Historical Society), no pagination.
52. Anna Cornelia Clauder, *American Commerce as Affected by the Wars of the French Revolution and Napoleon, 1793–1812* (Philadelphia: n.p., 1932), p. 244.
53. For the letters of Reasin Beall to Elijah Wadsworth see the Western Reserve Historical Society's microfilm publication, "George Tod Papers Relating to the War of 1812" (Repository: Western Reserve Historical Society).
54. Elijah Wadsworth, Charges against Reasin Beall, November 7, 1812, available in the Western Reserve Historical Society's microfilm publication, "War of 1812" (Repository: Western Reserve Historical Society).
55. John Wightman, Alphear Hill, Thomas Hilton, Peter Yalman, Elias Sperry, Shubel Adams, and John Craig, Complaint to the Commandant of the Forces at Camp Avery, October 2, 1812, available in the Western Reserve Historical Society's microfilm publication, "War of 1812" (Repository: Western Reserve Historical Society).
56. Lewis Bond, "Journal . . . War of 1812" (typescript copy), MS. 1885 (Repository: Western Reserve Historical Society), p. 9.
57. *Ibid.*
58. Elisha Whittlesey, "Simon Perkins," August 8, 1860, MS., Simon Perkins Papers, Container 75, Folder 2 (Repository: Western Reserve Historical Society), p. 13.
59. *Ibid.*, p. 17.
60. Letter James Winchester to Simon Perkins, January 18, 1813, quoted to Elisha Whittlesey, "Simon Perkins," August 8, 1860, MS., Simon Perkins Papers, Container 75, Folder 2 (Repository: Western Reserve Historical Society), p. 17.
61. Elisha Whittlesey, "Simon Perkins," August 8, 1860, MS., Simon Perkins Papers, Container 75, Folder 2 (Repository: Western Reserve Historical Society), p. 18.
62. *Ibid.*, p. 19.
63. *Ibid.*

64. Lewis Bond, "Journal . . . War of 1812" (typescript copy), MS. 1885 (Repository: Western Reserve Historical Society), p. 14.
65. *Ibid.*, pp. 14–15.
66. Elisha Whittlesey, "Simon Perkins," August 8, 1860, MS., Simon Perkins Papers, Container 75, Folder 2 (Repository: Western Reserve Historical Society), p. 21.
67. Lewis Bond, "Journal . . . War of 1812" (typescript copy), MS. 1885 (Repository: Western Reserve Historical Society), p. 15.
68. *Ibid.*, pp. 16–17.
69. It will be remembered that Harrrison knew Brace from the days of Brace's congressional fight for the title to the Western Reserve, and that Harrison had cooperated in securing the title to Connecticut.
70. Letter William Henry Harrison to Simon Perkins, February 26, 1813, Simon Perkins Papers, Letterbox 39a (Repository: Western Reserve Historical Society).
71. Letter Simon Perkins to Daniel L. Coit, March 14, 1813, Simon Perkins Papers, Letterbook June, 1811–December, 1813, Container 80, Folder 4 (Repository: Western Reserve Historical Society).
72. Letter Simon Perkins to Elias Perkins, March 16, 1813, Elias Perkins Papers (Repository: New London County Historical Society).
73. Letter Daniel L. Coit to Simon Perkins, September 12, 1812, Simon Perkins Papers, Lettterbox 39 (Repository: Western Reserve Historical Society).
74. Letter Samuel Church to Ensign Church, October 27, 1812, available in the Western Reserve Historical Society's microfilm publication, "War of 1812" (Repository: Western Reserve Historical Society).
75. This election was being held to replace John Stark Edwards, who had been elected to the post only the year before but had died in February, 1813, of what Simon called "buffalo fever or the putrid pleurisy," while on his way home from checking the Merino sheep he had pastured on Cunningham's [Kelley's] Island.
76. *Trump of Fame*, April 14, 1813 (Repository: Western Reserve Historical Society), p. 3.
77. *Ibid.*
78. *Trump of Fame*, April 21, 1813 (Repository: Western Reserve Historical Society), p. 3.
79. Newspaper clipping, for the [Cleveland] *Leader* (n.d.), Joseph Perkins' Scrapbook, MS. 907 (Repository: Western Reserve Historical Society), p. 300.
80. *Ibid.*
81. *Trump of Fame*, April 21, 1813 (Repository: Western Reserve Historical Society), p. 3.
82. As Noble E. Cunningham Junior notes in *The Jeffersonian Republicans: The Formation of Party Organization, 1789–1801*, published for the Institute of Early American History and Culture at Williamsburg, Virginia (Chapel Hill: University of North Carolina Press,

1957), pp. 206–208, electioneering was not acceptable to Connecticut Federalists in the 1800 period.

83. Letter Simon Perkins to Elias Perkins, July 19, 1813, Elias Perkins Papers (Repository: New London County Historical Society).

84. Letter Simon Perkins to John Armstrong, May 28, 1813, quoted by Elisha Whittlesey in "Simon Perkins," August 8, 1860, MS., Simon Perkins Papers, Container 75, Folder 2 (Repository: Western Reserve Historical Society), p. 24.

85. Letter Lewis Coss to Simon Perkins, June 1, 1813, Simon Perkins Papers, Letterbox 39a (Repository: Western Reserve Historical Society).

86. Letter Simon Perkins to General Lewis Coss (n.d.), Simon Perkins Papers, Letterbox 39, and Letter Lewis Coss to Simon Perkins, June 26, 1813, Simon Perkins Papers, Letterbox 39a (Repository: Western Reserve Historical Society).

87. Letter Simon Perkins to Elias Perkins, March 16, 1813, Elias Perkins Papers (Repository: New London County Historical Society).

88. Elijah Wadsworth, Address to the Troops, August 27, 1812, Simon Perkins Papers, Letterbox 39 (Repository: Western Reserve Historical Society).

Chapter Eight

1. Letter Daniel L. Coit to Simon Perkins, October 10, 1813, Simon Perkins Papers, Letterbox 8 (Repository: Western Reserve Historical Society).

2. Letter Joseph Perkins to Simon Perkins, June 17, 1803, Simon Perkins Papers, Letterbox 27 (Repository: Western Reserve Historical Society).

3. Leonard Case, Memoirs, 1853, MS. 2871 (Repository: Western Reserve Historical Society), p. 128.

4. Letter Simon Perkins to William Hart, April 8, 1812, Simon Perkins Papers, Letterbook 1811–1813, Container 80, Folder 4 (Repository: Western Reserve Historical Society).

5. Letter Joseph Perkins to Simon Perkins, August 8, 1811, Simon Perkins Papers, Letterbox 27 (Repository: Western Reserve Historical Society).

6. The name Portage was given to this area because it was here that the Indians ported their canoes between the Cuyahoga and Muskingum rivers.

7. Letter Joseph Perkins to Simon Perkins, July 20, 1811, Simon Perkins Papers, Letterbox 27 (Repository: Western Reserve Historical Society).

8. Letter Joseph Perkins to Simon Perkins, August 8, 1811, Simon Perkins Papers, Letterbox 27 (Repository: Western Reserve Historical Society).

9. Letter Joseph Perkins to Simon Perkins, February 7, 1812, Simon Perkins Papers, Letterbox 27 (Repository: Western Reserve Historical Society).

10. Letter Simon Perkins to Gardner Greene, March 22, 1813, Simon Perkins Papers, Letterbook 1811–1813, Container 80, Folder 4 (Repository: Western Reserve Historical Society).

11. Letter Simon Perkins to Justin Ely, October 4, 1813, Simon Perkins Papers, Letterbook 1811–1813, Container 80, Folder 4 (Repository: Western Reserve Historical Society).

12. At four o'clock on September 10, 1813, Perry wrote to William Henry Harrison, "We have met the enemy, and they are ours. . . ." For Perry's famous letter to Harrison see *The Battle of Lake Erie*, edited by Charles Oscar Paullin (Cleveland: Rowfant Club, 1918), p. 43.

13. Letter Simon Perkins to Gardner Greene, March 22, 1813, Simon Perkins Papers, Letterbook 1811–1813, Container 80, Folder 4 (Repository: Western Reserve Historical Society).

14. Letter Daniel L. Coit to Simon Perkins, December 25, 1813, Simon Perkins Papers, Letterbox 8 (Repository: Western Reserve Historical Society).

15. Letter Joseph Perkins to Simon Perkins, December 2, 1815, Simon Perkins Papers, Letterbox 27 (Repository: Western Reserve Historical Society).

16. According to Letter Joseph Perkins to Simon Perkins, August 11, 1814, Simon Perkins Papers, Letterbox 27 (Repository: Western Reserve Historical Society), the United States had "refused to permit the wife & 7 children of Mr. James Stuart late British Consul at N London to leave the Country," and the British fired on Stonington in retaliation.

17. Letter Daniel L. Coit to Simon Perkins, September 12, 1814, Simon Perkins Papers, Letterbox 9 (Repository: Western Reserve Historical Society).

18. Letter Daniel L. Coit to Simon Perkins, September 26, 1814, Simon Perkins Papers, Letterbox 9 (Repository: Western Reserve Historical Society).

19. Letter Daniel L. Coit to Simon Perkins, September 12, 1812, Simon Perkins Papers, Letterbox 39 (Repository: Western Reserve Historical Society).

20. Historians have generally found it difficult to explain New England opposition to a war that was presumably fought for free trade and sailors' rights, but the fact is, that at the time of the declaration of war, according to Anna Cornelia Clauder's *Commerce as Affected by the Wars of the French Revolution and Napoleon, 1793–1812* (Philadelphia: n.p., 1932), Plate III, "Tonnage in American Foreign Trade, 1791–1812," p. 25, shipping was at 950,000 tons in 1811–1812, a rate second only to the year 1806–1807 when it was 1,000,000 tons. Naturally New England commercial interests

disliked a war that had the result, as The Major observed (see page 98 of this book), of ruining commerce. Moreover, many New Englanders, it should be remembered, owned western lands. Such proprietors no doubt desired the removal of the Indian threat from their lands, but they could not have desired the addition of Canadian lands to an already too competitive land market.

21. According to Frank Maloy Anderson, "A Forgotten Phase of the New England Opposition to the War of 1812," *Proceedings of the Mississippi Valley Historical Association for the Year 1912–1913*, Volume VI (Cedar Rapids, Iowa: The Torch Press, 1913), pp. 176–188, there were twenty-four delegates from Massachusetts, Connecticut, Rhode Island, Vermont, and New Hampshire at the Hartford Convention, which met for about three weeks from December, 1814, to January, 1815. In addition to the secession talked about by Pickering's followers, as Anderson points out [p. 180], the then radical idea of state sovereignty was advanced during the convention. This was expressed in opposition to the President's right to call out the Militia of the states. Neither nullification nor secession was touched upon in the resolutions reached by the convention, but both ideas were eventually expressed by Calhoun and Davis in connection with the Civil War.

22. Letter Elisha Whittlesey to Elisha Sterling, January 23, 1815, Elisha Whittlesey Papers, Container 41, Folder 1 (Repository: Western Reserve Historical Society).

23. In his *Jefferson and Hamilton, The Struggle for Democracy in America* (Boston and New York: Houghton Mifflin Company, 1925), p. vi, Claude G. Bowers says of the Federalists: "Men of wonderful charm they were, but they were singularly lacking in an understanding of the spirit of their times and country. They fell, as we shall find, because they neither had nor sought contact with the average man, and sternly set themselves against the overwhelming current of democracy."

24. Letter Daniel L. Coit to Simon Perkins, May 13, 1817, Simon Perkins Papers, Letterbox 9 (Repository: Western Reserve Historical Society).

25. As Harlan Hatcher notes in *The Western Reserve* (Revised edition; Cleveland and New York: World Publishing Company, 1966), p. 3, the Tallmadge Congregational Church was chosen by *Life* for its November 20, 1944, cover picture because it symbolized the spirit of the Puritans who celebrated the first Thanksgiving. Because of its historic architecture, the church has been marked by the Ohio Historical Society and the Architects Society of Ohio.

26. Letter Elisha Whittlesey to W. W. Griswold, May 7, 1825, Elisha Whittlesey Papers, Container 41, Folder 2 (Repository: Western Reserve Historical Society).

27. Letter Calvin Pease to Charles Nelson (n.d.), 1801, Rice Papers (Repository: Ohio State Historical Society).

28. Letter Simon Perkins to James Pumpelly, July 31, 1816, Simon Perkins Papers. Letterbook 1816, Container 80, Folder 6 (Repository: Western Reserve Historical Society).

29. For further information concerning the Canfield, Ohio, homes of Elisha Whittlesey and Elijah Wadsworth, see Harlan Hatcher, *The Western Reserve*, p. 72 and pp. 171–172.

30. Diploma from Massachusetts Society for Promoting Agriculture, March, 1816, and Letter [?] Sullivan to Simon Perkins, March 31, 1816, Simon Perkins Papers, Container 75, Folder 4 (Repository: Western Reserve Historical Society).

31. Letter Simon Perkins to Zephaniah Swift, September 12, 1818, Simon Perkins Papers, Letterbox 28 (Repository: Western Reserve Historical Society).

32. Letter Simon Perkins to William Leffingwell, March 25, 1817, Simon Perkins Papers, Letterbook 1816–1817, Container 80, Folder 7 (Repository: Western Reserve Historical Society).

33. Fellow commissioners of the Western Reserve Bank were Robert Parkman, Turhand Kirtland, George Tod, John Ford, Comfort S. Mygatt, Calvin Austin, William Rayne, and John Kinsman. See the *Trump of Fame*, June 16–July 8, 1812 (Repository: Western Reserve Historical Society), for the act chartering the Western Reserve Bank.

34. Cf., for example, the payment provisions of the Miami Export Company, as noted by Harlan Hatcher, *The Western Reserve*, p. 102.

35. For copy of the act chartering the Western Reserve Bank see *Trump of Fame*, June 16–July 8, 1812 (Repository: Western Reserve Historical Society).

36. Letter Simon Perkins to Enoch Perkins, July 20, 1813, Simon Perkins Papers, Letterbook 1811–1813, Container 80, Folder 4 (Repository: Western Reserve Historical Society).

37. See Elisha Whittlesey, "Simon Perkins," August 8, 1860, MS., Simon Perkins Papers, Container 75, Folder 2 (Repository: Western Reserve Historical Society), p. 29.

38. Letter Joseph Perkins to Simon Perkins, August 11, 1814, Simon Perkins Papers, Letterbox 27 (Repository: Western Reserve Historical Society).

39. Letter Joseph Perkins to Simon Perkins, September 8, 1814, Simon Perkins Papers, Letterbox 27 (Repository: Western Reserve Historical Society).

40. Letter Joseph Perkins to Simon Perkins, December 2, 1815, Simon Perkins, Letterbox 27 (Repository: Western Reserve Historical Society).

41. Letter Simon Perkins to Joseph Wakeman, February 26, 1817, Simon Perkins Papers, Letterbook 1816–1817, Container 80, Folder 7 (Repository: Western Reserve Historical Society).

42. Bray Hammond, "Jackson, Biddle, and the Bank of the United States," *The Journal of Economic History*, Volume VII, Number 1 (May, 1947), (New York: New York University Press, 1947), p. 1.

43. Leonard Case, Memoirs, 1853, MS. 2871 (Repository: Western Reserve Historical Society), p. 149.
44. *Ibid.*
45. *Ibid.*, p. 150.
46. *Ibid.*, p. 154.
47. Samuel Reznick, "The Depression of 1819–1822, A Social History," *The American Historical Review*, Volume XXXIX, Number 1 (October, 1933), (New York: The Macmillan Company, 1934), p. 28.
48. Harlan Hatcher, *The Western Reserve*, p. 102.
49. Letter Daniel L. Coit to Simon Perkins, June 12, 1817, Simon Perkins Papers, Letterbox 9 (Repository: Western Reserve Historical Society).
50. Newspaper clipping (n.p., n.d.), Joseph Perkins' Scrapbook, MS. 907 (Repository: Western Reserve Historical Society), p. 301.

Chapter Nine

1. Judge Ross, Charge to the Grand Jury, Montgomery County, Pennsylvania, printed in the *Cleaveland Herald*, August 1, 1820 (Repository: Western Reserve Historical Society).
2. Samuel Reznick, "The Depression of 1819–1822, A Social History," *The American Historical Review*, Volume XXXIX, Number 1 (October, 1933), (New York: The Macmillan Company, 1934), p. 28.
3. A friend to all occupations and professions, *Cleaveland Herald*, September 12, 1820.
4. Letter Simon Perkins to Elias Perkins (n.d.), Simon Perkins Papers, Letterbook 1820–1821, Container 80 (Repository: Western Reserve Historical Society).
5. Letter Simon Perkins to Jonathan Brace, April 15, 1820, Simon Perkins Papers, Letterbook 1820–1821, Container 80 (Repository: Western Reserve Historical Society).
6. Harlan Hatcher, *The Western Reserve* (Revised edition; Cleveland and New York: World Publishing Company, 1966), footnote, p. 102.
7. Letter Simon Perkins to Cyrus Bosworth, December 10, 1823, Simon Perkins Papers, Letterbox 29 (Repository: Western Reserve Historical Society).
8. Charles C. Huntington, *Banking and Currency in Ohio Before the Civil War* (Columbus: Ohio State Archaeological and Historical Society, 1915), p. 65.
9. Letter Simon Perkins to Jonathan Brace, April 15, 1820, Simon Perkins Papers, Letterbook 1820–1821, Container 80 (Repository: Western Reserve Historical Society).
10. Letter Simon Perkins to George Mather, May 27, 1820, Simon Perkins Papers, Letterbook 1820–1821, Container 80 (Repository: Western Reserve Historical Society).

11. The Land Act of 1820 had reduced the price of public land from the $2 per acre minimum established in the Land Act of 1800 to $1.25 per acre. See *Documents of American History*, edited by Henry Steele Commager (Sixth edition; New York: Appleton-Century-Crofts, Inc., 1958), p. 227 for an excerpt from the Land Act of 1820.

12. Letter Elisha Whittlesey to W. W. Griswold, May 7, 1825, Elisha Whittlesey Papers, Container 41, Folder 2 (Repository: Western Reserve Historical Society).

13. Information relating to the Holmes-Coit partition of Claridon township may be found in the letters of Daniel L. Coit to Simon Perkins for the period 1800–1823, Simon Perkins Papers, Letterboxes 8 and 9; the letters of Simon Perkins to Daniel L. Coit for the period of 1805–1823, Simon Perkins Papers, Letterbooks 1805–1820, Container 80, Folders 1, 2, 3, 4, 5, 6, and 7, Letterbook 1820–1821, Container 80, and Letterbooks 1820–1825, Container 81; and the letters of Uriel Holmes to Ephraim Root for the period 1798–1813, Ephraim Root Papers, MS. 3235, Container 1, Folders 5 and 6 (Repository: Western Reserve Historical Society).

14. Letter Daniel L. Coit to Simon Perkins, January 16, 1823, Simon Perkins Papers, Letterbox 9 (Repository: Western Reserve Historical Society).

15. Daniel Lathrop Coit, Letterbook (Repository: Connecticut Historical Society), p. 122.

16. Letter Daniel L. Coit to Simon Perkins, February 19, 1821, Simon Perkins Papers, Letterbox 9 (Repository: Western Reserve Historical Society).

17. Letter Daniel L. Coit to Simon Perkins, May 27, 1825, Simon Perkins Papers, Letterbox 9 (Repository: Western Reserve Historical Society).

18. Letter Simon Perkins to George Blake, January 20, 1821, Simon Perkins Papers, Letterbook 1820–1821, Container 80 (Repository: Western Reserve Historical Society).

19. Letter Gardner Greene to Simon Perkins, April 15, 1810, Simon Perkins Papers, Letterbox 14 (Repository: Western Reserve Historical Society).

20. Letter Simon Perkins to Jonathan Brace and Enoch Perkins, April 9, 1811, Simon Perkins Papers, Letterbox 28 (Repository: Western Reserve Historical Society).

21. Letters Simon Perkins to Jonathan Brace and Enoch Perkins, November 18, 1805, and April 9, 1811, Simon Perkins Papers, Letterbox 28 (Repository: Western Reserve Historical Society).

22. Under the terms of the Land Ordinance of 1785, which served as the basis for United States land policy until the Homestead Act of 1862, United States lands were to be surveyed into townships of six miles square and then into subdivisions or lots of one mile square, or 640 acres. Lot No. 16 was then reserved for the maintenance of public schools in the township. The Western Reserve had no such provision

for schools, since the land was all privately owned; but on the basis of the acreage in the Western Reserve the state was granted an amount of land equal to that granted in the public domain for the benefit of schools. See *Documents of American History*, edited by Henry Steele Commager, pp. 123–124 for relevant excerpts from the Land Ordinance of 1785.

23. William Ganson Rose, *Cleveland, The Making of a City* (Cleveland: World Publishing Company, 1950), p. 56.

24. Letter Simon Perkins to Joseph Howland, August 12, 1811, Simon Perkins Papers, Letterbook 1811–1813, Container 80, Folder 4 (Repository: Western Reserve Historical Society).

25. Letter Joseph Howland to Simon Perkins, July 17, 1811, Simon Perkins Papers, Letterbox 17 (Repository: Western Reserve Historical Society).

26. Letter Ethan A. Brown to Simon Perkins, February 29, 1820, Simon Perkins Papers, Letterbox 43 (Repository: Western Reserve Historical Society).

27. Governor Ethan A. Brown, Message to the Legislature, December 5, 1820, *Public Documents Concerning the Ohio Canals*, compiled by John Kilbourn (Columbus : John Kilbourn, 1828), p. 14.

28. James Geddes, Report, December (n.d.), 1822, *Public Documents Concerning the Ohio Canals*, p. 40.

29. An Act to build Canals, February 8, 1825, *Public Documents Concerning the Ohio Canals*, p. 170.

30. *Western Reserve Chronicle*, March 11, 1825, (Repository: Western Reserve Historical Society).

31. Memorials and Resolutions, February 8, 1825, *Public Documents Concerning the Ohio Canals*, p. 172ff.

32. *Ibid.*

33. Letter Alfred Kelley to Simon Perkins, March 13, 1825, Simon Perkins Papers, Letterbox 43 (Repository: Western Reserve Historical Society).

34. Letter Alfred Kelley to Simon Perkins, February 21, 1825, Simon Perkins Papers, Letterbox 43 (Repository: Western Reserve Historical Society).

35. Letter Alfred Kelley to Simon Perkins, April 18, 1825, Simon Perkins Papers, Letterbox 43 (Repository: Western Reserve Historical Society).

36. Letter Alfred Kelley to Simon Perkins, January 22, 1836, and note enclosed, Simon Perkins Papers, Letterbox 43 (Repository: Western Reserve Historical Society).

37. Report of the Canal Commissioners, June 7, 1825, *Public Documents Concerning the Ohio Canals*, p. 176ff.

38. Letter Alfred Kelley to Simon Perkins, January 22, 1836, Simon Perkins Papers, Letterbox 43 (Repository: Western Reserve Historical Society).

39. Letter Simon Perkins to Joseph Howland, August 12, 1811, Simon Perkins Papers, Letterbook 1811–1813, Container 80, Folder 4 (Repository: Western Reserve Historical Society).

40. Letter Alfred Kelley to Simon Perkins, January 22, 1836, Simon Perkins Papers, Letterbox 43 (Repository: Western Reserve Historical Society).

41. Simon Perkins, Land Contracts, Volume B, Simon Perkins Papers, Container 73 (Repository: Western Reserve Historical Society), p. 343.

42. *A Centennial History of Akron*, published under auspices of The General Committee of The City's First Centennial Celebration, July 19–23, 1925 (n.p.: Summit County Historical Society, 1925), p. 13.

43. Simon Perkins, Land Contracts, Volume B, Simon Perkins Papers, Container 73 (Repository: Western Reserve Historical Society), p. 354 and p. 365.

44. *Ibid.*, p. 365.

45. Quoted by William Donohue Ellis in *The Cuyahoga* (New York, Chicago, San Francisco: Holt, Rinehart and Winston, 1966), p. 110.

46. John S. Still, "Brown and Ohio's Canals," *Ohio Historical Quarterly*, Volume 66, Number 1 (January, 1957), p. 49.

47. *Public Documents Concerning the Ohio Canals*, pp. 227–228.

48. *Western Reserve Chronicle*, July 12, 1827 (Repository: Western Reserve Historical Society).

49. Alfred Kelley, Memorandums to Simon Perkins, May 18, 1830, and January 25, 1831, Simon Perkins Papers, Letterbox 43 (Repository: Western Reserve Historical Society).

50. Letter Samuel MacCracken to Simon Perkins, February 26, 1833, Simon Perkins Papers, Letterbox 43 (Repository: Western Reserve Historical Society).

51. Bayrd Still, "Patterns of Mid-Nineteenth Century Urbanization in the Middle West," *Mississippi Valley Historical Review*, Volume XXVIII, Number 2 (September, 1941), footnote 5, p. 189.

52. Letter William C. Gilman to Simon Perkins, June 25, 1836, Simon Perkins Papers, Letterbox 14 (Repository: Western Reserve Historical Society).

Chapter Ten

1. Letter Jacob Perkins to his parents, February 14, 1835, not catalogued (Repository: Western Reserve Historical Society).

2. E. N. Harmon, *Norwich University: Its Founder and His Ideals* (Princeton: Princeton University Press, 1951), p. 12, *et passim*.

3. Letter Joseph Perkins to Simon Perkins, December 25, 1826, Simon Perkins Papers, Letterbox 28 (Repository: Western Reserve Historical Society).

4. George A. Perkins, *The Family of John Perkins of Ipswich*, Book III (Salem: Salem Press Publishing and Printing Company, 1889), p. 18.

5. Letter Simon Perkins to Joseph Perkins, June (n.d.), 1826, John Arnold Rockwell Papers HM–RO 1091 (Repository: Henry Huntington Library).

6. Letter Joseph Perkins to Simon Perkins, December 25, 1826, Simon Perkins Papers, Letterbox 28 (Repository: Western Reserve Historical Society).

7. *Ibid.*

8. *Ibid.*

9. Letter Simon Perkins to Joseph Perkins, January 20, 1827, John Arnold Rockwell Papers HM–RO 1094 (Repository: Henry Huntington Library).

10. Letter Joseph Perkins to Simon Perkins, January 3, 1828, Simon Perkins Papers, Letterbox 28 (Repository: Western Reserve Historical Society).

11. Letter Joseph Perkins to Simon Perkins, May 10, 1828, Simon Perkins Papers, Letterbox 28 (Repository: Western Reserve Historical Society).

12. Letter Joseph Perkins to Simon Perkins, December 20, 1827, Simon Perkins Papers, Letterbox 28 (Repository: Western Reserve Historical Society).

13. Letter Joseph Perkins to Simon Perkins, May 10, 1828, Simon Perkins Papers, Letterbox 28 (Repository: Western Reserve Historical Society).

14. Jacob Bishop Perkins, Notebook, MS. 3226 (Repository: Western Reserve Historical Society), p. 9.

15. Letter Joseph Perkins to Simon Perkins, May 20, 1829, Simon Perkins Papers, Letterbox 28 (Repository: Western Reserve Historical Society).

16. Letter Nancy Bishop Perkins to Alfred Perkins, August 15, 1828, not catalogued (Repository: Western Reserve Historical Society).

17. Letter Jacob Perkins to his mother, September 25, 1832 (copy), Jacob Bishop Perkins, Notebook, MS. 3226 (Repository: Western Reserve Historical Society).

18. Letter Jeremiah Day to Simon Perkins, February 11, 1833, not catalogued (Repository: Western Reserve Historical Society).

19. *Ibid.*

20. Letter Alfred Perkins to his parents, February 15, 1833, not catalogued (Repository: Western Reserve Historical Society).

21. Letter Simon Perkins to Alfred Perkins, February 25, 1833, not catalogued (Repository: Western Reserve Historical Society).

22. Letter Jacob Perkins to his mother, February 29, 1834, not catalogued (Repository: Western Reserve Historical Society).

23. Letter Jacob Perkins to his parents, September 26, 1835, not catalogued (Repository: Western Reserve Historical Society).

24. Letter Simon Perkins to John Arnold Rockwell (n.d.), John Arnold Rockwell Papers (Repository: Henry Huntington Library).

25. Frederick Clayton Waite, *Western Reserve University: The Hudson Era* (Cleveland: Western Reserve University Press, 1943), p. 201.

26. Edward A. Miller, "History of the Educational Legislation in Ohio from 1803 to 1850," *Ohio Archaeological and Historical Publications*, Volume XXVII (Columbus: Fred J. Heer, 1919), p. 162.

27. *Public Welfare in Ohio Today*, Annual Report, September, 1952 (Columbus: Department of Public Welfare, 1952), p. 95.

28. Daniel L. Coit, Letterbook (Repository: Connecticut Historical Society), p. 147.

29. Indenture between Daniel L. Coit, Joseph Perkins, William C. Gilman, and Simon Perkins, December 17, 1831, Simon Perkins Papers, Container 72, Folder 2 (Repository: Western Reserve Historical Society).

30. No documents have been discovered that detail this project of supplying Akron with water, and a few shakily written letters from the eccentric Crosby that are in the Simon Perkins Papers, Letterbox 10 (Repository: Western Reserve Historical Society), do not clarify the development of either the Cascade Mill Race, the use of the Little Cuyahoga, or the activities of the Portage Canal and Manufacturing Company—a business venture undertaken by Crosby, Simon Junior, and others—that was based on the use of the water brought to Akron by Crosby and Simon. According to *A Centennial History of Akron*, published under auspices of The General Committee of The City's First Centennial Celebration, July 19–23, 1925 (n.p.: Summit County Historical Society, 1925), p. 65, the Cascade Mill Race became the bed of the Pennsylvania and Ohio Canal.

31. Samuel Eliot Morison, *The Oxford History of the American People* (New York: Oxford University Press, 1965), p. 425.

32. Letter Elisha Whittlesey to Simon Perkins, January 24, 1830, Simon Perkins Papers, Letterbox 37 (Repository: Western Reserve Historical Society).

33. The Anti-Masonic party was one of the strangest third parties ever organized in the United States. This party developed following an investigation into the abduction of William Morgan, who had written a book disclosing some of the secrets of Masonry. In the course of the investigation Masons refused to testify on the ground that they could not be made to incriminate themselves; and Anti-Masons, who thought the Masons obstructed justice in the affair, decided Masonry was not consistent with American concepts. The party was strongly anti-Jackson. For an account of the Anti-Masons see Alice Felt Tyler, *Freedom's Ferment* (Harper Torchbook; New York: Harper & Brothers, 1962), pp. 351–358.

34. Letter Simon Perkins to Jonathan Warner, September 20, 1830, Simon Perkins Papers, Letterbook 1829–1831, Container 81 (Repository: Western Reserve Historical Society), p. 227.
35. Letter Elisha Whittlesey to Simon Perkins, January 10, 1831, Simon Perkins Papers, Letterbox 37 (Repository: Western Reserve Historical Society).

Chapter Eleven

1. Letter John Law to Martin Van Buren, May 28, 1836, Martin Van Buren Papers, Reel 15, Series 2 (Repository: Library of Congress).
2. Letter Simon Perkins to Alfred Kelley, January 26, 1836, Simon Perkins Papers, Letterbox 43 (Repository: Western Reserve Historical Society).
3. *Acts of a General Nature Passed at the First Session of the Thirty-Fourth General Assembly of the State of Ohio, Volume XXXIV, begun December 7, 1835, at Columbus* (Columbus: James B. Gardiner, 1836), p. 655.
4. Letter Simon Perkins to Governor Joseph Vance, February 13, 1838, Simon Perkins Papers, Letterbook 1836–1839, Container 82 (Repository: Western Reserve Historical Society), p. 269.
5. Letter John Welsh to Simon Perkins, August 18, 1823, Simon Perkins Papers, Letterbox 37 (Repository: Western Reserve Historical Society).
6. Letter John Welsh to Simon Perkins, August 23, 1828, Simon Perkins Papers, Letterbox 37 (Repository: Western Reserve Historical Society).
7. Letter John Welsh to Simon Perkins, October 30, 1829, Simon Perkins Papers, Letterbox 37 (Repository: Western Reserve Historical Society).
8. Deposition of Simon Perkins in *Simon Perkins et al and John Welsh et al*, May 5, 1834, Simon Perkins Papers, Container 40 (Repository: Western Reserve Historical Society).
9. Leicester King, Deposition, *Report of the Committee on the Judiciary in Relation to the Official Conduct of Judge Hitchcock, presented by Mr. Collins, House, March 12, 1838* (n.p., n.d.), p. 7.
10. See *Report of the Committee on the Judiciary . . . March 12, 1838*, for a record of this investigation.
11. Letter Simon Perkins to Elisha Whittlesey, December 29, 1831, Elisha Whittlesey Papers, Container 23, Folder "Perkins" (Repository: Western Reserve Historical Society).
12. *Ibid.*
13. Hostility to the Second Bank of the United States was, in fact, extremely strong in Ohio, largely due to the strangle hold gained by

the Cincinnati branch on real estate. In 1819 the Ohio Legislature imposed a $50,000 tax on the Chillicothe and Cincinnati branches of the bank, collected the tax by force, and in 1824 carried the issue of the state's right to tax the bank to the Supreme Court in the case of *Osborn vs. Bank of the United States.* For accounts of this affair see Ralph C. H. Catterall, *The Second Bank of the United States* (Chicago: The University of Chicago Press, 1903), pp. 89–91; Bray Hammond, *Banks and Politics in America from the Revolution to the Civil War* (Princeton: Princeton University Press, 1957), pp. 266–268; and Walter Buckingham Smith, *Economic Aspects of the Second Bank of the United States* (Cambridge: Harvard University Press, 1953), p. 112.

14. Letter Simon Perkins to Elisha Whittlesey, December 29, 1831, Elisha Whittlesey Papers, Container 23, Folder "Perkins" (Repository: Western Reserve Historical Society).

15. In his *Banks and Politics in America,* pp. 323–324, Hammond states that the bank did, in fact, perform these functions.

On the part of the Bank [says Hammond], one is impressed in this period [1822–1828] by its performance of a rounded and complete central banking function. It acted . . . as the balance wheel of the banking system. It regulated the supply of money; restrained the expansion of bank credit; governed the exchanges; safeguarded the investment market; protected the money market from the disturbing force of Treasury operations and of payments on balance, interregional and international; and facilitated Treasury operation *vis-a-vis* the rest of the economy. It was in train to become the sole bank of issue and repository of the country's specie reserve. It even approximated . . . the constructive rather than merely regulatory role of modern central banks.

Hammond contends (p. vii) that the Second Bank bore an "obvious resemblance . . . to modern central banks," and played a part in the evolution of the present-day Federal Reserve System.

16. *Documents of American History,* edited by Henry Steele Commager (Sixth edition; New York: Appleton-Century-Crofts, 1958), p. 270.

17. Letter Elisha Whittlesey to Simon Perkins, February 18, 1836, Simon Perkins Papers, Letterbox 37 (Repository: Western Reserve Historical Society).

18. Letter Elisha Whittlesey to Simon Perkins, February 20, 1836, Simon Perkins Papers, Letterbox 37 (Repository: Western Reserve Historical Society).

19. Letter Elisha Whittlesey to Simon Perkins, September 12, 1838, Simon Perkins Papers, Letterbox 40 (Repository: Western Reserve Historical Society).

20. Martin Van Buren Papers, Reel 13, Series 2 (Repository: Library of Congress).

21. Letter John H. Groesbeck to Martin Van Buren, March 11, 1836, Martin Van Buren Papers, Reel 15, Series 2 (Repository: Library of Congress).

22. Letter Moses Dawson to Martin Van Buren, March 25, 1836, Martin Van Buren Papers, Reel 15, Series 2 (Repository: Library of Congress).

23. *Second Report of the Master Commissioner in the Matter of the Ohio Life Insurance and Trust Company, December Term, 1836* (Cincinnati: Looker, Ramsay & Company, 1837), pp. 16–17.

24. Letter Elisha Whittlesey to Simon Perkins, September 12, 1838, Simon Perkins Papers, Letterbox 40 (Repository: Western Reserve Historical Society).

25. Letter Simon Perkins to J. N. Perkins, October 3, 1840, Simon Perkins Papers, Letterbook 1839–1843, Container 83 (Repository: Western Reserve Historical Society), pp. 111–113.

26. In addition to depositing Treasury funds in his "pet" banks, Jackson had distributed surplus Treasury funds, and a boom in public land sales in the West resulted. In an effort to check excessive credit, Jackson directed the Secretary of the Treasury to draft the Specie Circular of July 11, 1836, which limited payment for public lands to specie. For terms of the Specie Circular, see *Documents of American History*, p. 283.

27. Newspaper clipping (n.p., n.d.), Joseph Perkins' Scrapbook, MS. 907 (Repository: Western Reserve Historical Society), p. 301.

28. Letter Simon Perkins to Elisha Whittlesey, February 24, 1834, Elisha Whittlesey Papers, Container 23, Folder "Perkins" (Repository: Western Reserve Historical Society).

29. *Ibid.*

30. Letter William Henry Harrison to Simon Perkins, February 12, 1835, Simon Perkins Papers, Letterbox 15 (Repository: Western Reserve Historical Society).

31. Letter Simon Perkins to William Henry Harrison, March 9, 1835, Simon Perkins Papers, Letterbook 1833–1836, Container 82 (Repository: Western Reserve Historical Society), p. 311.

32. Letter Simon Perkins to Elisha Whittlesey, October 20, 1836, Elisha Whittlesey Papers, Container 23, Folder "Perkins" (Repository: Western Reserve Historical Society).

33. The Locofocos, the radical Democrats of the day, got their name when they produced candles and "locofoco" matches, as the newly invented friction matches were called, at a meeting in 1835 in Tammany Hall and continued to meet after the conservatives had turned out the gas. For an account of the origin and concepts of the Locofocos, see Lee Benson, *The Concept of Jacksonian Democracy* (Princeton: Princeton University Press, 1961), pp. 94–97.

34. Letter Simon Perkins to Daniel Kilgore, appended to Letter Simon Perkins to Samuel MacCracken, May 22, 1840, Simon Perkins Papers, Letterbox 43 (Repository: Western Reserve Historical Society).

35. *Western Reserve Chronicle*, February 4, 1840 (Repository: Western Reserve Historical Society).

36. Letter Simon Perkins to "Gentlemen," July 25, 1840, Simon Perkins Papers, Letterbook 1839–1843, Container 83 (Repository: Western Reserve Historical Society), pp. 93–94.
37. Samuel Eliot Morison, *The Oxford History of the American People* (New York: Oxford University Press, 1965), p. 456.
38. William Ganson Rose, *Cleveland: The Making of a City* (Cleveland: World Publishing Company, 1950), p. 176.
39. Letter Simon Perkins to William Henry Harrison, July 22, 1840, Simon Perkins Papers, Letterbook 1839–1843, Container 83 (Repository: Western Reserve Historical Society), pp. 92–93.
40. *Western Reserve Chronicle*, September 8, 1840 (Repository: Western Reserve Historical Society).
41. Letter Simon Perkins to William Henry Harrison, July 22, 1840, Simon Perkins Papers, Letterbook 1839–1843, Container 83 (Repository: Western Reserve Historical Society), pp. 92–93.
42. Letter Francis P. Clair to Andrew Jackson, September 10, 1840, *Correspondence of Andrew Jackson*, edited by John Spencer Bassett, Volume 6 (Washington: Carnegie Institute of Washington, 1933), p. 76.
43. Letter Andrew Jackson to Martin Van Buren, November 12, 1840, *Correspondence of Andrew Jackson*, p. 82.
44. *Western Reserve Chronicle*, November 17, 1840 (Repository: Western Reserve Historical Society).
45. Letter Elisha Whittlesey to Simon Perkins (n.d.), Simon Perkins Papers, Letterbox 37 (Repository: Western Reserve Historical Society).
46. This anonymous letter, postmarked from Cleveland, was casually marked on the back by Simon, "One interested May 19—40." See Simon Perkins Papers, Container 75, Folder 2 (Repository: Western Reserve Historical Society), for the letter.
47. Letter Simon Perkins Junior to Simon Perkins, April 4, 1842, Simon Perkins Papers, Letterbox 28 (Repository: Western Reserve Historical Society).
48. Letter Simon Perkins Junior to Simon Perkins, December 15, 1839, Simon Perkins Papers, Letterbox 28 (Repository: Western Reserve Historical Society).
49. Letter Simon Perkins Junior to Simon Perkins, January 27, 1840, Simon Perkins Papers, Letterbox 28 (Repository: Western Reserve Historical Society).
50. Letter John Crowell to Simon Perkins, January 9, 1841, Simon Perkins Papers, Letterbox 10 (Repository: Western Reserve Historical Society).
51. Harlan Hatcher, *The Western Reserve* (Revised edition; Cleveland and New York: World Publishing Company, 1966), p. 105.
52. Letter Simon Perkins to Elisha Whittlesey, October 9, 1841, Elisha Whittlesey Papers, Container 23, Folder "Perkins" (Repository: Western Reserve Historical Society).

53. Letter Simon Perkins to Judge Lane, December 9, 1842, Simon Perkins Papers, Letterbook 1839–1843, Container 83 (Repository: Western Reserve Historical Society).

Chapter Twelve

1. Letter Simon Perkins to James Kingsley, September 19, 1839, Simon Perkins Papers, Letterbook 1836–1839, Container 82 (Repository: Western Reserve Historical Society), pp. 439–440.
2. Letter Simon Perkins to Jacob Perkins, November 7, 1839, Simon Perkins Papers, Letterbook 1836–1839, Container 82 (Repository: Western Reserve Historical Society), p. 453.
3. Letter Jacob Perkins to Simon Perkins, December (n.d.), 1839, not catalogued (Repository: Western Reserve Historical Society).
4. Letter Jacob Perkins to his parents, December 24, 1839, not catalogued (Repository: Western Reserve Historical Society).
5. Letter Simon Perkins to cousin Mrs. Marsh, August 14, 1841, Simon Perkins Papers, Letterbook 1839–1843, Container 83 (Repository: Western Reserve Historical Society), pp. 230–231.
6. Letter Simon Perkins to cousin Mrs. Marsh, April 11, 1841, Simon Perkins Papers, Letterbook 1839–1843, Container 83 (Repository: Western Reserve Historical Society), p. 207.
7. Letter Elisha Whittlesey to Simon Perkins, February 10, 1842, Simon Perkins Papers, Letterbox 37 (Repository: Western Reserve Historical Society).
8. Letter Jacob Perkins to George Parkman, November 28, 1844, Simon Perkins Papers, Letterbook 1843–1847, Container 83 (Repository: Western Reserve Historical Society), p. 128.

Afterword

1. Simon Perkins, Last Will and Testament (MS. copy), Simon Perkins Papers, Record Book of Estate of Simon Perkins, Container 76 (Repository: Western Reserve Historical Society), p. 302.
2. *Ibid.*
3. Jacob Bishop Perkins, Notebook, MS. 3226 (Repository: Western Reserve Historical Society), pp. 11–14.
4. Harlan Hatcher, *The Western Reserve* (Revised edition; Cleveland and New York: World Publishing Company, 1966), p. 106.
5. E. O. Randall and D. J. Ryan, *History of Ohio, The Rise and Progress of an American State*, Volume VI (New York: The Century History Company, 1915), pp. 51–55.
6. *Ibid.*, pp. 48–51.

7. Jacob Bishop Perkins, Notebook, MS. 3226 (Repository: Western Reserve Historical Society), pp. 7–8.
8. Edmund H. Chapman, *Cleveland: Village to Metropolis* (Cleveland: The Western Reserve Historical Society and The Press of Western Reserve University, 1964), p. 92.
9. E. O. Randall and D. J. Ryan, *History of Ohio*, Volume VI, pp. 41–48.
10. Frederick Clayton Waite, *Western Reserve University: The Hudson Era* (Cleveland: Western Reserve University Press, 1943), p. 305 and p. 341.
11. Jacob Bishop Perkins, Notebook, MS. 3226 (Repository: Western Reserve Historical Society), pp. 8–9.
12. *Ibid.*, p. 11.
13. E. O. Randall and D. J. Ryan, *History of Ohio*, Volume VI, pp. 38–41.
14. Simon Perkins, Last Will and Testament, Simon Perkins Papers, Record Book of Estate of Simon Perkins, Container 76 (Repository: Western Reserve Historical Society), p. 302.

Bibliography

Manuscript Sources

Atwater, Amzi. Description of the Surveying Party of 1797, "Bound MSS. of the Western Reserve," Volume 21, Book 8. Repository: Western Reserve Historical Society.

———. Letter, January 5, 1846, "Bound MSS. of the Western Reserve," Volume 22, Book 7. Repository: Western Reserve Historical Society.

Barr, John. Memoranda, 1843, "Bound MSS. of the Western Reserve," Volume 19, Book 3. Repository: Western Reserve Historical Society.

———. Memoranda on history of Cleveland, 1795–1811, 1843, "Bound MSS. of the Western Reserve," Volume 19, Books 8 and 9. Repository: Western Reserve Historical Society.

———. Recollections of first few years in Wooster, Ohio, 1820. MS. 759. Repository: Western Reserve Historical Society.

Bates, Issachar. Letter to Richard [McNemar], December 13, 1811. Copy in Alonzo G. Hollister, Book of Pioneer Correspondence from the West, 1871, Shaker Collection, MS. BX9786/L6B7, p. 35. Repository: Western Reserve Historical Society.

Bond, Lewis. "Journal of the Battle and Massacre of River Raisin, January 22 and 23, 1813, and the War of 1812." MS. 1885 (typescript copy). Repository: Western Reserve Historical Society.

Case, Leonard. Local History of the Western Reserve, 1863. MS. 1014. Repository: Western Reserve Historical Society.

———. Memoirs, 1853. MS. 2871. Repository: Western Reserve Historical Society.

————. "Memoranda of Incidents in the Life of Leonard Case," January, 1853. MS. 2871 (typescript copy). Repository: Western Reserve Historical Society.

Cleaveland, Moses. Papers, 1796–1805. MS. 3233. 1 container. Repository: Western Reserve Historical Society.

Coit, Daniel L. and Samuel Huntington. Correspondence [1800–1815]. Repository: Connecticut Historical Society.

Coit, Daniel L. Diary, 1793. Repository: Connecticut State Library.

————. Letterbook [1818–1832]. Repository: Connecticut Historical Society.

Connecticut Land Company. Records, 1795–1809, "Bound MSS. of the Western Reserve," Volume 9, Books 4, 5, and 6; Volume 16, Books 3 and 5; Volume 17, Books 1, 2, and 10; Volume 18, Books 1, 4, and 6. Repository: Western Reserve Historical Society.

————. Records of the Connecticut Land Company originally at the Connecticut State Library (Records, Votes and Proceedings, Minutes of Meetings, Accounts, Correspondence). Microfilm, 3 reels. Repository: Western Reserve Historical Society.

————. Road contracts, 1798, not catalogued, Connecticut Land Company Miscellaneous Papers. Repository: Western Reserve Historical Society.

Day, Jeremiah. Letter to Simon Perkins, February 11, 1833, not catalogued. Repository: Western Reserve Historical Society.

Ensign, Caleb. "History of Rootstown" (n.d.). MS. 595. Repository: Western Reserve Historical Society.

Estate Records, Norwich District, Book 6, 305–306. MS. 8632. Repository: Connecticut State Library.

Excess Company. Memoranda relating to, 1796, "Bound MSS. of the Western Reserve," Volume 17, Book 3. Repository: Western Reserve Historical Society.

————. Agreement, September 5, 1795. MS. 2525. Repository: Western Reserve Historical Society.

Gilman, William C. Letters, 1905. MS. 3191, Folder 19. Repository: Western Reserve Historical Society.

Harmon Family Papers, 1766–1855. 13 containers. Repository: Western Reserve Historical Society.

Harrison, William Henry. Papers, 1734–1939. Repository: Library of Congress.

Hitchcock Family Papers, 1788–1898. 38 containers. Repository: Western Reserve Historical Society.

Howland, Joseph. Correspondence, not catalogued (typescript copies). Repository: Western Reserve Historical Society.

Hubbell, Walter. Papers, 1788–1848. Repository: Princeton University Library.

Huntington, Hannah. Letters to her husband, Samuel Huntington, Governor of Ohio, 1791–1811. MS. 884. Repository: Western Reserve Historical Society.

Huntington, Samuel. Agreement with Connecticut Land Company, 1801. MS. 915. Repository: Western Reserve Historical Society.

———. Letters to Reverend Edward D. Griffin, 1801–1804. MS. 2063, Numbers 1 and 2. Repository: Western Reserve Historical Society.

———. Letter to Turhand Kirtland, February 15, 1802. MS. 915. Repository: Western Reserve Historical Society.

Kirtland, Turhand. Diary, 1798–1800. MS. 737 (manuscript copy). Repository: Western Reserve Historical Society.

———. Papers, 1794–1868. MS. 3237. 13 containers. Repository: Western Reserve Historical Society.

Knox, Henry. Copies of Letters on the Harman Expedition, 1790. MS. 2404. Repository: Western Reserve Historical Society.

Law, Jonathan. Diary No. 5, October 12 to October 18, 1802. MS. 597. Repository: Western Reserve Historical Society.

———. Diary No. 6, October 19 to October 30, 1802. MS. 597. Repository: Western Reserve Historical Society.

Law, William. Journal [1799]. MS. 596. Repository: Western Reserve Historical Society.

Norwich Land Records, Volume 21. Repository: Connecticut State Library.

Pease, Calvin. Letter to Charles Nelson (n.d.), 1801. Rice Papers. Repository: Ohio State Historical Society.

———. Legal Papers, 1816–1829. MS. 827. Repository: Western Reserve Historical Society.

Pease, Seth. Extracts from Field Notes, 1797, "Bound MSS. of the Western Reserve," Volume 23, Book 5. Repository: Western Reserve Historical Society.

———. Papers, 1792–1807. MS. 3234. 1 container. Repository: Western Reserve Historical Society.

Perkins, Alfred. Letters, 1833–1839, not catalogued. Repository: Western Reserve Historical Society.

Perkins, Andrew and Joseph. Account Books of Andrew and Joseph Perkins of Norwich, Connecticut, 1783–1825, "Account Books of grocers (general storekeepers) in New England, 1685–1904." Repository: Baker Library, Harvard Business School, Harvard University.

Perkins, Elias. Papers [1795–1815]. Repository: New London County Historical Society.

Perkins, Jacob. Letters, 1832–1845, not catalogued. Repository: Western Reserve Historical Society.

Perkins, Jacob Bishop. Notebook (n.d.). MS. 3226. Repository: Western Reserve Historical Society.

Perkins, Joseph. Scrapbook (n.d.). MS. 907. Repository: Western Reserve Historical Society.

Perkins, Nancy Bishop. Letters, 1828, not catalogued. Repository: Western Reserve Historical Society.

Perkins, Lieutenant Simon. Inventory of Estate, November 28, 1778,

Estate Records, Norwich District, Book 6, 305–306. MS. 8632. Repository: Connecticut State Library.

Perkins, Simon. The Simon Perkins Papers, 1795–1896. 103 containers, 5 packages, and 5 bound volumes. Repository: Western Reserve Historical Society.

———. Survey of Coitsville, Ohio, 1798. MS. 707. Repository: Western Reserve Historical Society.

Phelps Family Land Papers, 1792–1879. 5 containers. Repository: Western Reserve Historical Society.

Phelps, Oliver. Letter to William Walker, October 31, 1795. MS. 747. Repository: Western Reserve Historical Society.

Porter, Augustus. Letter to John Barr, January 10, 1843, "Bound MSS. of the Western Reserve," Volume 22, Book 3. Repository: Western Reserve Historical Society.

Rockwell, John Arnold. Papers, 1791–1871. Repository: Henry Huntington Library.

Root, Ephraim. Papers, 1769–1837. MS. 3235. 3 containers. Repository: Western Reserve Historical Society.

Report of the Committee of General Assembly on the Sale of Western Lands to the General Assembly, convened at New Haven, 2d Thursday October, 1795, "Bound MSS. of the Western Reserve," Volume 18, Book 1. Repository: Western Reserve Historical Society.

Tappan, Abraham. "Biographical Sketches of the Surveyors," "Bound MSS. of the Western Reserve," Volume 23, Book 7. Repository: Western Reserve Historical Society.

———. "Sketch of the Surveys West of the Cuyahoga River in 1806–1807," October, 1850, "Bound MSS. of the Western Reserve," Volume 23, Book 8. Repository: Western Reserve Historical Society.

Tod, George. Papers, 1783–1834. MS. 3203. Repository: Western Reserve Historical Society.

———. "Papers Relating to the War of 1812." Microfilm. Repository: Western Reserve Historical Society.

Trimble, Allen. Family Papers, 1793–1868. MS. 3205. 4 containers. Repository: Western Reserve Historical Society.

Van Buren, Martin. Papers, 1703–1862. Repository: Library of Congress.

"War of 1812." Microfilm collection of papers of Simon Perkins, Elijah Wadsworth, Elisha Whittlesey, Lewis Bond, Return Jonathan Meigs, William Henry Harrison, Ensign Church, Charles Shaler, George Tod, Reasin Beall, and Calvin Pease, related to the War of 1812. Repository: Western Reserve Historical Society.

Webb, Thomas H. "A Partial Sketch of the History of the Land Titles and Origins of the Connecticut Western Reserve," Joseph Perkins' Scrapbook, 1–131. MS. 907. Repository: Western Reserve Historical Society.

Whittlesey, Elisha. Papers, 1769–1889. 76 containers. Repository: Western Reserve Historical Society.

Printed Sources

Acts of a General Nature Passed at the First Session of the Thirty-Fourth General Assembly of the State of Ohio, begun December 1, 1835, at Columbus, Ohio. Columbus: James B. Gardiner, 1836.

Adams, Henry. *History of the United States of America.* 9 volumes. New York: Charles Scribner's Sons, 1891–1896.

American State Papers, Public Lands. Volume I. Selected and edited by Asbury Dickins and John W. Fortney. Washington: Gales and Seaton, 1834.

Anderson, Frank Maloy. "A Forgotten Phase of the New England Opposition to the War of 1812," *Proceedings of the Mississippi Valley Historical Association for the Year 1912–1913,* Volume VI, 176–188. Cedar Rapids, Iowa: The Torch Press, 1913.

Bailey, Thomas Andrew. *A Diplomatic History of the American People.* New York: F. S. Crofts and Company, 1940.

Baldwin, Ebenezer. *Annals of Yale College.* New Haven: H. Howe, 1831.

Baldwin, William Edward. *Ohio School Laws.* Cleveland: Banks-Baldwin Company, 1943.

Bank of the United States, 1791–1811. Bibliography compiled by Appleton Prentiss Clark Griffin. Washington: Government Printing Office, 1908.

Bates, Albert C. "The Connecticut Gore Land Company," *Annual Report of the American Historical Association for the Year 1898.* Washington: Government Printing Office, 1899.

Bates, Clement. *The New Bates' Compact Digest of Ohio.* Cleveland: Baldwin Law Publishing Company, 1926.

The Battle of Lake Erie. Edited by Charles Oscar Paullin. Cleveland: The Rowfant Club, 1918.

Beard, Charles A. and Mary R. *The Rise of American Civilization.* 2 volumes. New York: The Macmillan Company, 1927.

Benson, Lee. *The Concept of Jacksonian Democracy, New York as a Test Case.* Princeton: Princeton University Press, 1961.

Bowers, Claude G. *Jefferson and Hamilton, The Struggle for Democracy in America.* Boston and New York: Houghton Mifflin Company, 1925.

Brinton, Clarence Crane, *Ideas and Men.* New York: Prentice-Hall, 1950.

Butler, Margaret Manor. *Pictorial History of the Western Reserve.* Cleveland: Western Reserve Historical Society and the Early Settlers Association of the Western Reserve, 1963.

Calendar of the Papers of Martin Van Buren. Prepared from the original manuscripts in the Library of Congress by Elizabeth Howard West, Division of Manuscripts. Washington: Government Printing Office, 1910.

Catalogue of the Sophomore Class of Yale College, 1795. Broadside 0.49. Repository: Western Reserve Historical Society.

Catterall, Ralph C. H. *The Second Bank of the United States.* The

Decennial Publications, Second Series, Volume II. Chicago: The University of Chicago Press, 1903.

Caulkins, Francis Manwaring. *History of Norwich, Connecticut*. Hartford: Case, Lockwood and Company, 1866.

Celebration of the Two Hundred and Fiftieth Anniversary of the Settlement of Suffield, Connecticut. Suffield: n.p., 1921.

A Centennial History of Akron. Published under auspices of The General Committee of The City's First Centennial Celebration, July 19–23, 1925. N.p.: Summit County Historical Society, 1925.

Chandler, Alfred N. *Land Title Origins, A Tale of Force and Fraud*. New York: Robert Schalkenbach Foundation, 1945.

Chapman, Edmund H. *Cleveland: Village to Metropolis*. Cleveland: Western Reserve Historical Society and The Press of Western Reserve University, 1964.

Charter of the Colony of Connecticut, 1662. Hartford: Case, Lockwood and Brainard Company, 1900.

Charter of the Portage Canal and Manufacturing Company. New York: Piekcy and Reed, 1837.

Cheetham, Jean Dick. "State Sovereignty in Ohio," *Ohio Archaeological and Historical Quarterly*, Volume IX, 290–302. Columbus: Fred J. Heer, 1901.

Clauder, Anna Cornelia. *American Commerce as Affected by the Wars of the French Revolution and Napoleon, 1793–1812*. Philadelphia: n.p., 1932.

Cleaveland Herald, 1820. Repository: Western Reserve Historical Society.

Colleges and the Public, 1787–1862. Edited by Theodore Rawson Crane. (Classics in Education, Number 15.) New York: Bureau of Publications, Columbia University, 1963.

Connecticut Gazette, 1798. Repository: Connecticut Historical Society.

Coover, Arthur B. *Ohio Banks from 1803–1861*. Columbus: Ohio State Numismatic Society, 1906.

Cunningham, Noble E. J. *The Jeffersonian Republicans in Power, Party Operations, 1801–1809*. Published for the Institute of Early American History and Culture at Williamsburg, Virginia. Chapel Hill: University of North Carolina Press, 1963.

———. *The Jeffersonian Republicans, The Formation of Party Organization, 1789–1801*. Published for the Institute of Early American History and Culture at Williamsburg. Chapel Hill: University of North Carolina Press, 1957.

Curti, Merle, Willard Thorp, and Carlos Baker. *American Issues, The Social Record*. Fourth edition. Chicago, Philadelphia, New York: J. B. Lippincott Company, 1960.

Curti, Merle. *Growth of American Thought*. New York, Evanston, and London: Harper and Row, Publishers, 1951.

Davis, Harold E. *The Pennsylvania–Ohio Canal, 1823–1877*. Publication of Hiram Historical Society, Number 1 (December, 1929), n.p., n.d.

Debates and Proceedings of the Congress of the United States, Annals of Congress, December 5, 1796, to March 3, 1797, Fourth Congress, Second Session. Washington: Gales and Seaton, 1849.

Debates and Proceedings of the Congress of the United States, Annals of Congress, May 15, 1797, to March 3, 1799, Fifth Congress. Volume I. Washington: Gales and Seaton, 1849.

Debates and Proceedings of the Congress of the United States, Annals of Congress, December 2, 1799, to March 3, 1801, Sixth Congress. Washington: Gales and Seaton, 1851.

Debates and Proceedings of the Congress of the United States, Annals of Congress, December 7, 1801, to March 3, 1803, Seventh Congress. Washington: Gales and Seaton, 1851.

Debates and Proceedings of the Congress of the United States, Annals of Congress, November 4, 1811, to July 6, 1812, Twelfth Congress, First Session. Part I, 1811–1812. Washington: Gales and Seaton, 1853.

Debates and Proceedings of the Congress of the United States, Annals of Congress, November 4, 1811, to July 6, 1812, Twelfth Congress, First Session. Part II, 1811–1812. Washington: Gales and Seaton, 1853.

Debates and Proceedings of the Congress of the United States, Annals of Congress, November 2, 1812, to March 3, 1813, Twelfth Congress, Second Session. Washington: Gales and Seaton, 1853.

Dexter, Franklin B. *Biographical Notices of Graduates of Yale College, 1816–1884*. New York: H. Holt and Company, 1911.

Dial, George White. "The Construction of the Ohio Canals," *Ohio Archaeological and Historical Society Publications*, Volume XIII, 460–481. Edited by E. O. Randall. Columbus: Fred J. Heer, 1904.

Documents of American History. Edited by Henry Steele Commager. Sixth Edition. New York: Appleton-Century-Crofts, 1958.

Documents Relating to New-England Federalism, 1800–1815. Edited by Henry Adams. Boston: Little, Brown, and Company, 1877.

Dwight, Theodore. *History of the Hartford Convention: with a Review of the Policy of the United States Which Led to the War of 1812*. New York: N. and J. White; Boston: Russell, Odiorne, and Company, 1833.

Dwight, Timothy. *Travels in New-England and New-York*. 2 volumes. New Haven: Timothy Dwight, 1821–1822.

Edwards, Louisa Maria. *A Pioneer Home Maker, 1787–1866, A Sketch of the Life of Louisa Maria Montgomery*. N.p., 1903.

Ellis, William D. *The Cuyahoga*. Rivers of America series, edited by Carl Carmer. New York, Chicago, and San Francisco: Holt, Rinehart and Winston, 1966.

Evans, Nelson W. *History of Taxation in Ohio*. Cincinnati: Robert Clarke Company, 1906.

Federal Writers Project. *Warren and Trumbull County*. N.p., 1938.

Gilkey, Elliot Howard. *The Ohio Hundred Year Book*. Columbus: F. J. Heer, 1901.

Gilman, Daniel Coit. "Historical Discourse," *The Norwich Jubilee*, 49–113. Norwich: John W. Stedman, 1859.

Gilman, William C. Paper read to the New London County Historical Society, September 1, 1905, printed in *Norwich Bulletin* (September 4, 1905). Repository: Western Reserve Historical Society.

Goodman, Warren H. "The Origins of the War of 1812: A Survey of Changing Interpretations," *Mississippi Valley Historical Review*, Volume XXVIII, Number 2 (September, 1941), 171–186.

Governor's Message to the General Assembly of Ohio, December 7, 1824 and other Ohio State Papers, 1824–1825. Columbus: P. H. Olmsted, 1824–1825.

Hacker, Louis Morton. "Western Land Hunger and the War of 1812," *Mississippi Valley Historical Review*, Volume X, Number 4 (March, 1924), 365–395.

Hall, Charles S. *Life and Letters of Samuel Holden Parsons*. Binghamton: Otseningo Publishing Company, 1905.

Hammond, Bray. *Banks and Politics in America from the Revolution to the Civil War*. Princeton: Princeton University Press, 1957.

Harmon, E. N. *Norwich University: Its Founder and His Ideals*. Princeton: Princeton University Press, 1951.

Hatcher, Harlan. *The Western Reserve*. Revised edition. Cleveland and New York: World Publishing Company, 1966.

Hibbard, Benjamin Horace. *A History of Public Land Policies*. New York: P. Smith, 1939.

Hildreth, Richard. *History of Banks*. Boston: Hilliard, Gray and Company, 1837.

Hildreth, Richard. *The History of the United States of America*. 6 volumes. New York: Harper and Brothers, 1856–1863.

Hildreth, S. P. *Pioneer History: Being an Account of the First Examinations of the Ohio Valley and the Early Settlement of the Northwest Territory*. Cincinnati: H. W. Derby and Company, Publishers; New York: A. S. Barnes and Company, 1848.

History of Summit County with an Outline Sketch of Ohio. Edited by William Henry Perrin. Chicago: Baskin and Battey, 1881.

History of the Courts and Lawyers of Ohio. Volume I. Editor-in-chief, Carrington T. Marshall. New York: American Historical Society, Inc., 1934.

Hofstadter, Richard. *The American Political Tradition*. New York: Vintage Books, 1948.

Holdsworth, John Thom and Davis R. Dewey. *The First and Second Banks of the United States*. Washington: Government Printing Office, 1910.

Howard, Benjamin C. *Reports of Cases Argued and Adjudged in the Supreme Court of the United States*, December Term, 1853, Volume XVI, 415–451. Second edition. Edited with notes and references to later decisions by Stewart Rapalje. New York: The Banks Law Publishing Company, 1906.

Howland, George S. "Trade and Manufactures of Norwich about 1800," *The Norwich Jubilee*, 297–299. Norwich: John W. Stedman, 1859.

Huntington, Charles C. *Banking and Currency in Ohio Before the Civil War*. Columbus: Ohio State Archaeological and Historical Society, 1915.

Index to the James Madison Papers in the Library of Congress. Presidents' Papers Index Series. Washington: United States Government Printing Office, 1965.

Index to the William H. Harrison Papers in the Library of Congress. Presidents' Papers Index Series. Washington: United States Government Printing Office, 1960.

Interrogatories of the Legislature of Ohio to the Banks of the State, with the answer of the Ohio Life Insurance and Trust Company, January 15, 1838. n.p., n.d.

Jackson, Andrew. *Correspondence of Andrew Jackson*. Edited by John Spencer Bassett. 6 volumes and index. Washington: Carnegie Institute of Washington, 1926–1935.

Jefferson, Thomas. *The Writings of Thomas Jefferson:* Being His Autobiography, Correspondence, Reports, Messages, Addresses, and Other Writings, Official and Private. Published by order of the Joint Committee of Congress on the Library, from the original manuscripts deposited in the Department of State. Edited by H. A. Washington. 9 volumes. Washington: Taylor and Maury, 1853–1854.

Jefferson, Thomas and Alexander Hamilton. *Jeffersonian Principles and Hamiltonian Principles*. Extracts from the writings of Thomas Jefferson and Alexander Hamilton, selected and edited by James Truslow Adams. Boston: Little, Brown, and Company, 1932.

Journals of the Continental Congress, 1774–1789. Volume XXX, January 2–July 31, 1786. Edited from the original records in the Library of Congress by John C. Fitzpatrick. Washington: United States Government Printing Office, 1934.

Journal of the Senate of the State of Ohio, First Session of Fourth General Assembly, begun December 2, 1805, at Chillicothe, Ohio. Chillicothe: T. G. Bradford & Company, 1805.

Journal of the Senate of the State of Ohio, Tenth General Assembly, begun December 2, 1811, at Zanesville, Ohio. Chillicothe: J. S. Collins and Company, 1811.

Journal of the Senate of the State of Ohio, First Session of the Thirty-Sixth General Assembly, begun December 4, 1837, at Columbus, Ohio. Columbus: Samuel Medary, 1837–1838.

Laws of the Territory of the United States Northwest of the River Ohio. 2 volumes. Chillicothe: Winship & Willis, 1801–1802.

Livermore, Shaw. *Early American Land Companies, Their Influence on Corporate Development*. London: H. Milford, Oxford University Press, 1939.

———. *The Twilight of Federalism: The Disintegration of the Federalist Party, 1815–1830*. Princeton: Princeton University Press, 1962.

Madison, James. *The Writings of James Madison*. Edited by Gaillard

Hunt. 9 volumes. New York and London: G. P. Putnam's Sons, 1900–1910.

Mathews, Alfred. *Ohio and Her Western Reserve*. New York: D. Appleton and Company, 1902.

McAlphine, William. "The Origin of Public Education in Ohio," *Ohio Archaeological and Historical Quarterly*, Volume XXXVIII, Number 3 (July, 1929), 409–447. Columbus: F. J. Heer Printing Company, 1929.

McClelland, C. P. and C. C. Huntington. *History of the Ohio Canals, Their Construction, Cost, Use and Partial Abandonment*. Columbus: F. J. Heer, 1905.

McFarland, Joseph F. *History of the City of Washington and of Washington County, Pennsylvania and Representative Citizens*. Chicago: Richmond–Arnold Publishing Company, 1910.

Miller, Edward A. "History of the Educational Legislation in Ohio from 1803–1850," *Ohio Archaeological and Historical Publications*, Volume XXVII, 1–127. Columbus: Fred J. Heer, 1919.

Mirsky, Jeannette and Allan Nevins. *The World of Eli Whitney*. New York: Collier Books, 1962.

Morison, Samuel Eliot. *The Oxford History of the American People*. New York: Oxford University Press, 1965.

Morison, Samuel Eliot and Henry Steele Commager. *The Growth of the American Republic*. 2 volumes. Fourth edition, revised. New York: Oxford University Press, 1960.

Nye, Russel Blaine. *The Cultural Life of the New Nation, 1776–1830*. New York, Evanston, and London: Harper & Brothers, 1960.

Oskison, John M. *Tecumseh and His Times, The Story of a Great Indian*. New York: G. P. Putnam's Sons, 1938.

Parrington, Vernon Louis. *Main Currents in American Thought*. 2 volumes. New York: Harcourt, Brace & World, Inc., 1927.

Perkins, George A. *The Family of John Perkins of Ipswich*. Salem: Salem Press Publishing and Printing Company, 1889.

Perkins, Mary E. *Old Houses of the Antient Town of Norwich, 1660–1800*. Norwich: Press of the Bulletin Company, 1895.

Pratt, Julius W. *Expansionists of 1812*. New York: Macmillan Company, 1925.

———. "Western Aims in the War of 1812," *Mississippi Valley Historical Review*, Volume XII, Number 1 (June, 1925), 36–50.

Public Documents Concerning the Ohio Canals. Compiled by John Kilbourn. Columbus: John Kilbourn, 1828.

Public Welfare in Ohio Today. Annual Report, 1952. Columbus: Department of Public Welfare, 1952.

Purcell, Richard J. "Uriah Tracy," *Dictionary of American Biography*, Volume XVIII, 624. Edited by Dumas Malone. New York: Charles Scribner's Sons, 1936.

———. "Zephaniah Swift," *Dictionary of American Biography*, Volume

XVII, 250. Edited by Dumas Malone. New York: Charles Scribner's Sons, 1936.

Randall, E. O. and D. J. Ryan. *History of Ohio, The Rise and Progress of an American State.* 6 volumes. Special edition. New York: Century History Company, 1912–1915.

Report of the Committee on Banks and the Currency in Relation to Small Bills and Other Matters, presented by Mr. [Thomas] Richmond, February 17, 1838. n.p., n.d.

Report of the Committee on the Judiciary in Relation to the Official Conduct of Judge [Peter] Hitchcock, presented by Mr. Collins, House, March 12, 1838. n.p., n.d.

Report of the Committee of Both Houses of the General Assembly of Ohio, on the Communication of the Auditor of State, upon the Subject of the Proceedings of the Bank of the United States against the Officers of State in the U. S. Circuit Court. Concord: Hill and Moore, 1821.

Report, United States Circuit Court, Southern District of Ohio, Bell and Grant vs. Ohio Life Insurance and Trust Company and others. n.p., n.d.

Reznick, Samuel. "The Depression of 1819–1822, A Social History," *The American Historical Review*, Volume XXXIX, Number 1 (October, 1933), 28–47. New York: The Macmillan Company, 1934.

———. "The Social History of an American Depression, 1837–1843," *American Historical Review*, Volume XL, Number 4 (July, 1935), 662–687. New York: The Macmillan Company, 1935.

Rhodes, James A. *A Short History of Ohio Land Grants.* n.p., n.d.

Roll of State Officers and Members of General Assembly of Connecticut, from 1776–1881. Published by Order of General Assembly. Hartford: Case, Lockwood and Brainard Company, 1881.

Rose, William Ganson. *Cleveland: The Making of a City.* Cleveland and New York: World Publishing Company, 1950.

Sakolski, Aaron Morton. *The Great American Land Bubble.* New York and London: Harper & Brothers Publishers, 1932.

Scheiber, Harry Noel. "The Ohio Canal Movement, 1820–1825," *Ohio Historical Quarterly*, Volume 69, Number 3 (August, 1960), 231–256. Columbus: F. J. Heer, 1960.

Schlesinger, Arthur M., Jr. *The Age of Jackson.* Boston: Little, Brown and Company, 1945.

Scioto Gazette, 1800. Repository: Western Reserve Historical Society.

Sears, Louis Martin. *Jefferson and the Embargo.* Durham: Duke University Press, 1927.

Second Report of the Master Commissioner in the Matter of the Ohio Life Insurance and Trust Company, December Term, 1836. Cincinnati: Looker, Ramsay and Company, 1837.

Slocum, Charles Elihu. *The Ohio Country between the Years 1783 and 1815.* New York and London: G. P. Putnam's Sons, 1910.

Smith, Walter Buckingham. *Economic Aspects of the Second Bank of the United States.* Cambridge: Harvard University Press, 1953.

Stephenson, George M. *The Political History of the Public Lands from 1840–1862: From Preemption to Homestead*. Boston: Richard G. Badger; Toronto: The Copp Clark Company, Limited, n.d.

Stickney, Lucy W. *The Kinsman Family*. Boston: Alfred Mudge & Son, 1876.

Still, Bayrd. "Patterns of Mid-Nineteenth Century Urbanization in the Middle West," *Mississippi Valley Historical Review*, Volume XXVIII, Number 2 (September, 1941), 187–206.

Still, John S. "Brown and Ohio's Canals," *Ohio Historical Quarterly*, Volume 66, Number 1 (January, 1957), 22–56. Columbus: Ohio Historical Society, 1957.

Stone, William L. *Life of Joseph Brant, Thayendanegea*. 2 volumes. Albany: Mumsell, 1865.

Taylor, James W. *History of the State of Ohio*. Cincinnati: H. W. Derby & Company, Publishers; Sandusky: C. L. Derby & Company, 1954.

Tinkcom, Harry Marlin. *The Republicans and Federalists in Pennsylvania, 1790–1801, A Study in National Stimulus and Local Response*. Harrisburg: Pennsylvania Historical and Museum Commission, 1950.

Treaties between the United States and the Indian Tribes, 1778–1837. Compiled and printed by the direction and under the supervision of the Commissioner of Indian affairs. Washington: D. C. Langtree and O. Sullivan, 1837.

Trump of Fame, 1800–1825. Repository: Western Reserve Historical Society.

Turner, Frederick Jackson. *The Frontier in American History*. New York: H. Holt and Company, 1920.

Turner, Orsamus. *History of the Pioneer Settlement of Phelps and Gorham's Purchase*. Rochester: William Alling, 1851.

Tyler, Alice Felt. *Freedom's Ferment*. Harper Torchbook. New York: Harper & Brothers, 1962.

Upton, Harriet Taylor. *A Twentieth Century History of Trumbull County*. 2 volumes. Chicago: Lewis Publishing Company, 1901.

———. *The Western Reserve*. 3 volumes. Chicago and New York: The Lewis Publishing Company, 1910.

Van Buren, Martin. *Inquiry into the Origin and Cause of Political Parties in the United States*. Edited by his sons. New York: Hurd and Houghton, 1867.

Waite, Frederick Clayton. *Western Reserve University: The Hudson Era*. Cleveland: Western Reserve University Press, 1943.

Wandell, Samuel Henry. *Oliver Phelps*. A paper read before the New York State Historical Association, September 18, 1941. n.p., n.d.

Western Reserve Chronicle, 1825–1844. Repository: Western Reserve Historical Society.

Whittlesey, Charles. *Early History of Cleveland, Ohio*. Cleveland: Fairbanks, Benedict & Company, 1867.

Wish, Harvey. *Society and Thought in Early America*. 2 volumes. New York: David McKay Company, Inc., 1962.

Zeisberger, David. *Diary of David Zeisberger, A Moravian Missionary Among the Indians of Ohio, 1781–1789.* Translated from the original German manuscript and edited by Eugene F. Bliss. 2 volumes. Cincinnati: Robert Clarke & Company for the Historical and Philosophical Society of Ohio, 1885.

Index

Adams, Asahel (Asael), 11, 14, 96, 100
Adams, Henry: *quoted*, 75
Adams, Jabez, 11, 14, 96
Adams, John, 34–35
Adams, John Quincy, 112
Akron, 118, 120, 129, 131, 133, 134–36, 143, 186n30
Akron & Middlebury Baptist Church and Society, 130
Alexandria Gazette, 51
Allegheny College, 129
Allen, John W., 124
American House, 142
American Literary, Scientific, and Military Academy, 121
American System, 112
Andrews, Lorrin, 121
Anti-Masonic Party, 132, 186n33
Armstrong, John, 93
Ashtabula, 110

Bacon, Reverend David, 62, 100
Badger, Reverend Joseph, 62, 63, 100
Banking conditions, 104–6
Bank of Geauga, 152
Bardwell, Reuben, 43
Bates, Issachar: *quoted*, 76
Beall, Reasin, 81, 82, 83, 84–85, 92
Belden's Tavern, 119
Berea (Kentucky) College, 152
Big Beaver Bridge Company, 112
Big Beaver Creek, 23
Bishop, 17–18, 63, 122
Bishop, Nancy. *See* Perkins, Nancy Bishop
Bissell, John Partridge, 21
Black River, 115, 116
Bond, Lewis: *quoted*, 79, 85, 87–88
Bonus Law (1816–25), 108–9
Bosworth, Cyrus, 108, 109

Bowers, Claude G.: *quoted*, 31, 179n23

Brace, Jonathan, 8, 30, 31–32, 33, 62, 89, 108, 109

Brant, Joseph, 25, 161n22, 161n23, 171n22

Brown, Ethan, 118

Brown, Henry, 24

Brown, John, 152

Brown, Mrs. Henry, 24, 51

Burr, Aaron, 54–55

Burr, Timothy, 161n22

Burton, 23

Burton Academy, 63, 100, 127

Caldwell, John, 8

Camp Avery, 82

Canals. *See* Ohio Canal, Erie Canal, Pennsylvania and Ohio Canal

Canfield, 56, 61–62

Canfield, Judson, 35

Cannonsburgh, 100

Canton township. *See* Claridon

Carter, Lorenzo, 23, 51

Carter's Hotel, 51

Cascade Mill Race, 131, 186n30

Case, Leonard: 64, 137; quoted, 39–41, 42, 96, 104–5

Chambersburgh, Pennsylvania, 101

Chapin, Israel, 25, 161n23

Chardon, 100

Charles II of England, 4

Chelsea Landing (Norwich, Connecticut), 3, 53, 66, 67, 99

Cheney, Penuel, 14

Chillicothe, 53, 55, 95

Citizens Savings, 152

Claridon, 18, 22, 110–11, 131

Clark, Lemuel, 21, 23

Clauder, Anna Cordelia: *quoted*, 84

Clay, Henry, 112

Cleaveland, Camden, 35

Cleaveland, Moses: 7, 18, 19, 21, 32, 35, 49, 64, 76

    Connecticut Land Company activities: contract with Joseph

Cleaveland, Moses (*Continued*)

    Brant, 25, 161–62n23; Director, 4; General Agent, 3; surveying trip of 1796, 3, 10, 24

    Description, 1–2

    Education, 3

    Erie Company activities, 2, 15, 25, 26

    Occupation, 3

Cleaveland, Mrs. Moses, 45

Cleveland, 21, 51, 52, 57, 62, 119, 120

Cleveland-Mahoning Railroad, 151, 152

Cleveland State Hospital, 151

Cleveland, Zanesville & Cincinnati Railroad, 152–53

Coit, Daniel Lathrop: 18, 26, 36, 43, 55, 61–62, 83, 90, 91, 99, 100, 101, 106, 148

    Claridon dispute, 110–11

    Connecticut Land Company proprietorship, 2, 18

    Description, 2

    Erie Company activities: Treasurer-Trustee, 2; dispute with Cleaveland, 25, 26

    Health, 111, 130

    Occupation, 2

    Quoted, 54–55, 59, 95, 98–99, 100

    Western Reserve: ideas for developing, 61–62; opinion of, 2, 50–51, 110, 111; visits to, 49, 83

Coit, Henry, 101

Coit, Joseph, 14, 35

Commager, Henry Steele: *quoted*, 137

Commercial Bank of Lake Erie, 104–5

Congregational church, 62

Conneaut Creek, 19, 20, 21

Connecticut: 5, 57, 60, 64, 65, 67

    School Fund, 6, 72

    Western Reserve: government of,

Connecticut (*Continued*)
27; sale of, 6–8; title to, 5, 8, 9, 27, 30–35
Connecticut colony:
Boundaries of, 4
Boundary disputes, 4, 33–34, 155n13
Charter of, 4
Reserves western lands, 4–5
Connecticut Gore Land Company, 33–34
Connecticut Land Company: 2, 8, 10, 18, 21, 23, 36, 44, 47, 49, 52, 57, 72
Cleaveland, relations with, 24–25
Government, Western Reserve, 8, 27
Indian negotiations, 25, 71, 161n23, 171n22
Partition mode of lands, 10–11
Partitions: 1798, 11–12; 1802, 57; 1807, 71; 1809, 71–72
Proprietors, number of, 8
Surveying parties of, 10, 20, 21
Title to Western Reserve, 8–9, 31, 32–33
Connecticut Missionary Society, 62, 66
Constitution of Ohio (1802), 58
Constitutional Convention (1802), 53–54
Continental Congress, 5
"Corrupt bargain" of 1825, 112
Coss, Lewis, 93
Cotgreave, William, 86, 91, 93
Court of Common Pleas, 68
Court of Quarter Sessions, 44
Crawford, William, 112
Crosby, Eliakiam, 131, 135, 186n30
Crowell, John: *quoted*, 144
Cunningham's (Kelley's) Island, 110
Cuyahoga and Big Beaver Land Company, 43
Cuyahoga County, 92

Cuyahoga Falls, 143
Cuyahoga and Muskingum Navigational Lottery, 113–14
Cuyahoga River, 36, 38, 44, 49, 51, 109, 113, 115, 116, 117

Day, Jeremiah: *quoted*, 126
Delaware County, New York, 103
Devotion, Jonathan, 47
Distillery, 49
Doan, Nathaniel, 23
Dwight, Timothy: *quoted*, 67

Education. *See* Perkins, Simon: Education, *and* Schools
Edwards, John Stark, 35–36, 45, 48, 53, 55, 64, 99, 164n61, 176n75
Edwards, Jonathan, 27, 49, 164n61
Edwards, Pierpont: 27, 35, 164n61; *quoted*, 48
Election, Constitutional Convention (1802), 53
Ellis, William D.: *quoted*, 118
Elyria, 62
Embargo of 1807, 70
Ensign, Caleb: 83–84; *quoted*, 58
Erie Canal, 113, 114
Erie Company: 26, 35, 49, 52, 57, 66, 111
Formation of, 2, 11
Instructions to Simon, 15–16
Land contracts of, 24, 28, 51
Land holdings of, 2, 12, 154n3
Liquidation of, 130–31
Problems of, 22, 25, 26, 65–66
Proprietors, 2, 13–14, 158n11
Trustees, 2–3
Excess agreement, 7, 156n27

Fairport Harbor, 112
Federalists, 30–31, 53, 176–77n82, 179n23
Filles brothers, 39, 40
Firelands, 6, 57
Firelands Company, 71, 72

First Congregational Society (Akron), 130
Forgason, Reuben, 18
Fort Industry (Toledo), 76
Fort McIntosh, 23, 29, 54
Fort Meigs, 89
Fowler, Jonathan, 35
Frances Hotel, 31
Franklin House, 119

Gallatin, Albert, 28, 33, 34, 80
Geauga County, 56
Geauga County Court, 110
Geddes, James, 114–15, 117
General Assembly of Ohio, 119, 120
Genessee, New York, 24
George, Captain, 40–41
Gifford, Richard, 29
Gilman, William C.: 111; *quoted*, 120
Girdled Road, 21
Gorham, Benjamin, 62, 104
Grace Park, 153
Grand River, 56, 115, 116
Granger, Erastus, 43
Granger, Gideon Junior: 7, 31, 50, 51; *quoted*, 31, 33, 78
Granville Literary and Theological Institute (Denison), 129
Great Miami River, 115
Greene, Gardner, 69, 112
Griswold, Sylvanus, 43
Gros Isle, Michigan, 103
Grosvenor, Nathan, 57
Gun, Elijah, 23
Gun, Mrs. Elijah, 23

Halsey, Jeremiah, 33
Hamilton, Alexander, 30–31
Hammond, Bray: *quoted*, 104
Harper, Alexander, 23
Harrison, William Henry: 31, 32, 143, 178n12
  Campaign of 1835, 141
  Election of 1840, 141–42

Harrison, William F tinued)
  Quoted, 89–90, 14
  War of 1812, 76, 88, 89, 98
Hart, Seth, 10
Hart, William, 7
Hartford, 101
Hartford Convention, 99, 103, 179n21
Hartford Court House (Connecticut), 18, 33
Hayes, Richard, 83
Henshaw, 64, 83, 95, 96, 118
Hillhouse, James, 27, 72
Hillman, James, 23, 24, 28, 41, 42
Hitchcock, Peter, 135
Holmes, Uriel: 18, 26, 64, 110; *quoted*, 33, 36
House of Representatives (Ohio), 134
Howland, 44, 52, 57
Howland, Joseph: 35, 47, 49, 51–52, 55, 56, 61, 69, 117
  Connecticut Land Company proprietorship, 2
  Erie Company proprietorship, 13
  Howland proprietor, 44
  Occupation, 13–14
  Quoted, 52, 54, 114
Hubbard, 100
Hughes, Robert, 56
Hull, General William, 74, 78–79, 80, 156n27
Huntington, Ebenezer, 7
Huntington, Erastus, 14, 35
Huntington, Hannah: 49–50, 64; *quoted*, 47, 50, 67
Huntington, Samuel (governor of Connecticut), 14
Huntington, Samuel Junior: 14, 31, 35, 45, 50–51, 52, 57, 59, 93, 164n61, 165n2
  Impeachment proceedings, 59
  Move to Western Reserve, 49–50
  Occupation, 14

Huntington, Samuel Junior (*Continued*)
  Politics, 14, 31, 49
  Quoted, 36, 41–42, 43, 51, 53–54, 76
Huntington, Thomas, 14
Hyde, Elisha, 7

Impeachment of Huntington, Pease, and Tod, 59
Independent Banking Act of 1845, 151
Indian paths, 23, 51
Indians:
  Murder of, at Salt Springs, 39–41
  Relations with, 38–39, 43, 76–77, 165n2
  River Raisin massacre, 88–89
  Tribes on Western Reserve, 38

Jackson, Andrew, 112, 131, 133, 142
Jackson-Biddle Bank War, 136–38
Jay's Treaty, 6
Jefferson, Thomas, 30–31
Jeffersonians, 53
John Welsh *vs.* Simon Perkins *et al.*, 135

Kelley, Alfred, 116–17, 133
Kendall, Simon, 43
Killbuck River, 115
King, Ashbell, 43
King, Ebenezer, 23, 35
King, Leicester, 135
Kingsbury (infant), 20
Kingsbury, James, 20, 23
Kingsbury, Mrs. James, 20, 23
Kingsley, James, 146
Kinsman, Frederick, 64, 129
Kinsman, John, 8, 14, 17, 30, 35
Kinsman, John, Jr., 64
Kinsman, Joseph, 64, 122
Kinsman, Rebecca Perkins, 17, 60
Kirtland, 127
Kirtland Turhand: 21, 23, 45, 53; *quoted*, 23, 35, 41

Ladd, Isaac, 100
Lake Erie, 113, 114, 115, 116
Land Act of 1800, 171n23
Land Act of 1820, 182n11
Land Ordinance of 1785, 182–83n22
Land, public, 171n23, 182n11
Land, Western Reserve:
  Price, 29, 70–71, 109
  Taxes, 70–71
  Terms of sale, 16, 28, 47, 65–66, 109, 171n20
Lathrop, Daniel, 14, 33
Law, John, 133
Law, Jonathan: 49; *quoted*, 53
Law, William, 21, 48
Law, William, Jr., 48–49
Leavitt, John, 23, 43
Leffingwell, Christopher: 13, 22, 35; *quoted*, 50
Liberty township, 52, 57
Lisbon, Connecticut, 1, 59, 60
Lisbon, 101
Litchfield, 101
Little Cuyahoga River, 120, 131, 186n30
Livingston, John, 7, 156n27
Locofocos, 141, 143, 189n33
Louisiana Purchase, 54
Loveland, Amos, 21, 24

MacCracken, Samuel, 120
Madison, James, 99
Mahoning County, 56
Mahoning River, 44, 95, 115, 116, 125
Major, The (cousin to Simon): 13, 18, 26, 29, 35, 59, 60–61, 63, 65–66, 111, 116, 148
  Connecticut Land Company proprietorship, 8
  Description, 2–3
  Erie Company proprietorship, 2
  Occupation, 3
  Opinion of Western Reserve, 110, 130
  Portage proprietorship, 97, 117

Major, The (*Continued*)
  Quoted, 32, 96, 97, 98, 122–23,
    124–25
Manufacturing, 62, 112, 120
Marietta College, 147, 148, 152
Marshall, John, 31, 32
Massachusetts, 65
Massachusetts Institute for Agri-
    culture, 101
Mather, Samuel, Jr., 7
Maumee River, 115
McCurdy, Lynde, 13, 14, 35
McMahon, Joseph, 23, 38, 39–41,
    42, 45
McMahon, Mrs. Joseph, 39
McQuigg, Daniel, 18
Meigs, Return Jonathan, 77–78,
    80
Miami Export Company, 180n*34*
Middletown, Connecticut, 127
Militia, Ohio, 83–84
Mississippi River, 29
Morgan, Elias, 2
Morgan, John, 2, 8
Morison, Samuel Eliot: *quoted*,
    131, 141
Mormons, 127
Muskingum River, 113, 115, 117

Naturalization Act of 1798, 56
Newberry, Roger, 31, 35
New Connecticut, 7, 54, 101. *See
    also* Western Reserve
New England settlers, 58
New England states, 65, 99, 178–
    79n*20*
Newent Society, 3
New Haven, 101
New Haven colony, 4
New London, Connecticut, 99
New Orleans, Louisiana, 29
Newton, 62
Niagara Falls, New York, 18
Nicholl, Matthias, 7
North Union Shaker colony, 127
Northwest Army, 102

Northwest Ordinance, 2
    68n*16*
Northwest Territory, 2
Norwich, Connecticut, 5
Norwich Court House
    cut), 13, 14

Oberlin College, 129, 152
Ohio Agricultural and Mechanical
    College, 151
Ohio Board of Charities, 152
Ohio Canal, 113–20, 124, 129,
    131, 133, 149
Ohio, land claims in, 155n*14*
Ohio Legislature, 68, 128, 131
Ohio Life Insurance and Trust
    Company, 138–40
Ohio River, 29, 114, 115
Ohio, statehood, 52–53, 159n*31*
O'Mick (Omique), 77
Osborn *vs.* Bank of the United
    States, 187–88n*13*
Oswego, New York, 18
Oviatt, Samuel, 62
Owego, New York, 18, 24, 103

Painesville, 57
Parkman, 57, 100, 129, 130
Parsons, Samuel Holden, 8–9, 11,
    38
Partridge, Captain Alden, 121
Patch, Nathaniel, 18, 110
Pease, Calvin: 45, 59; *quoted*, 76–
    77, 101
Pease, Seth, 10, 20, 21
Pennsylvania and Ohio Canal, 120,
    148, 152
Pennsylvania colony, 4
Pennsylvania democracy, 58–59
Pennsylvania settlers, 58
Perkins, Alfred (son of The Ma-
    jor), 122, 128
Perkins, Alfred (son of Simon),
    83, 121–24, 125–27, 145,
    147
Perkins, Andrew, 3

erkins, Andrew and Joseph Company, 3

Perkins, Anna Maria (daughter of Simon, wife of John W. Allen), 61, 121, 124

Perkins' Camp, 21–22

Perkins, Charles (son of Simon), 96, 127, 145, 147

"Perkins Crotch," 3

Perkins, Daniel Bishop (brother to Simon). *See* Bishop

Perkins, Elias, 90, 93, 108

Perkins, Enoch, 62

Perkins, family, 3

Perkins, Henry Bishop (son of Simon), 96, 148, 151

Perkins, Jacob (son of Simon): 96, 127–28, 145–47, 149, 151; *quoted*, 127

Perkins, Jacob Bishop (grandson of Simon): 151; *quoted*, 152

Perkins, Joanna (sister to Simon, wife of Samuel Lovett), 17

Perkins, J. N., 139

Perkins, John, 3

Perkins, Joseph (cousin to Simon). *See* Major, The

Perkins, Joseph (grandfather of Simon), 17, 122

Perkins, Joseph (son of Simon), 96, 147, 152

Perkins, (Lieutenant) Simon (father of Simon), 16

Perkins, Martha (daughter of Simon), 96

Perkins, Mary (daughter of The Major), 128

Perkins, Nancy Bishop (wife of Simon): 60, 83, 95, 96, 121, 150; *quoted:* 125

Perkins, Olive (daughter of Simon, wife of Frederick Kinsman), 61, 121, 129, 145

Perkins, Olive (sister to Simon, wife of Christopher Starr), 17

Perkins, Olive Douglass (mother of Simon), 16, 61

Perkins, Rebecca (sister of Simon, wife of John Kinsman). *See* Kinsman, Rebecca Perkins

Perkins, Simon: 1, 18, 19, 24, 28, 29, 35, 44, 49, 52, 95–96, 101, 102, 148, 149, 150

Arbiter, 28

Banking, 102–4, 105–6, 108, 136–37, 140, 143–44

Canal Fund Commissioner, 118–19, 120, 134

Canals, 113–20

Connecticut Land Company, 57

Contributions, 129, 130

Education, 62–63, 64, 113, 122, 129, 182–83n22

Family, 3, 16–18, 59–60, 96, 122–23, 125–26, 127–28, 145–48

Indian negotiations, 79

Internal improvements, 112–13

Jurist, 45

Land agent activities, 1, 12, 15, 16, 21, 22, 24–26, 27–28, 29, 30, 37, 51, 64, 68, 71, 102–3, 109

Land holdings of, 57, 103, 130–31

Manufacturing interest, 62, 112, 120

Military, 74, 80–90, 93

Opinion of Western Reserve, 111–12

Opinions about, 3, 92, 110, 118, 143

Politics, 55–56, 91–92, 132, 141–42

Postal activities, 78, 113, 131

Quoted, 27, 30, 36, 37, 44, 45–46, 55–56, 57, 97, 101, 102, 104, 139–40

Perkins, Simon, Jr.: 61, 125, 129–30, 152–53; *quoted*, 143, 144

Perkins Park (Akron), 153

Perkins Professorship of Physics and Astronomy, 152

Perry, Oliver H., 97–98, 178n12

Phelps, Oliver, 6–8, 31, 69, 71, 72, 109, 161n23, 171n22
Pickering, Timothy, 99
"Pioneer," 119
Pittsburg, Pennsylvania, 23, 29, 45, 50, 96, 102
Plainfield Academy, 123
Portage Canal and Manufacturing Company, 186n30
Portage Path, 10, 114, 117, 129
Portage township, 22, 97, 110, 116
Port Independence. See Conneaut Creek
Pottery manufacture, 61–62
Presque Isle, Pennsylvania, 18, 24
Prophet, The, 76
Proprietors, Western Reserve. See Connecticut Land Company and Erie Company
Pumpelly, James, 18, 101
Put-in-Bay Island, 98

Queen Esther, 4
Quinby, Ephraim, 23, 36, 39, 40, 42, 43, 44, 55, 60, 148

Randolph, John, of Roanoke, 34, 75
Republicans (Democrats), 30–31, 168–69n30
Reznick, Samuel: quoted, 105, 107
Rhode Island colony, 4
Rockwell, John Arnold, 128
Root, Ephraim, 12, 18, 32, 36, 51, 57, 72–73, 109

St. Clair, Arthur: 5, 8, 35–36, 45, 55; quoted, 46
Salt, 62
Salt Springs, 5, 11, 21, 38, 39–41, 51
Salt Springs road, 43–44
Salt works, 38
Sample, Steel, 45
Sandusky, 115
Schools, 62–63. See also Perkins, Simon: Education

Scioto River, 115
Second Bank of the United States, 104, 105, 136–37, 187–88n13, 188n15
Settlers, Western Reserve, 55
Shakers, 76, 127
Shaler, Charles, 79
Sheehy, Daniel, 23, 28, 56
Sheldon, Oliver, 43
Sheldon, Thomas, 23
Shipping routes, 29, 113
Smith, Martain, 18, 110
Society for Savings, 152
Spafford, Amos, 21, 23
Specie circular, 140, 189n26
Spicer, Amos, 97
Spicer, Miner, 97, 110
"Spotted John." See Winslow, John
Starr, Christopher, 17, 53, 63
"State of Ohio," 119
Stiles, Job, 23
Stiles, Mrs. Job, 23
Still, John: quoted, 118
Stonington, Connecticut, 98, 178n16
Storer, Richard, 23, 39, 41, 42, 45
Stow, Joshua, 20
Stow's Castle, 20
Sufferers' Lands. See Firelands
"Surplus Lands," 57, 71–72
Susquehanna Land Company, 4, 27
Swift, Zephaniah: 14, 16, 25, 32, 101; quoted, 9–10

Tallmadge Congregational Church, 100, 179n25
Tallmadge, 62
Tappan, Benjamin, 45
Tecumseh, 76
Thomson, Matthew, 43
Tioga, New York, 103
Tod, George, 45, 59
Tod, Grace, 129
Town 1 Range 1 (Poland), 23
Town 1 Range 4 (Elsworth), 57
Town 1 Range 11 (Coventry), 115
Town 1 Range 17 (Homer), 57

Town 2 Range 1 (Coitsville), 29, 52
Town 2 Range 2. *See* Youngstown
Town 2 Range 5 (Milton), 57
Town 2 Range 11. *See* Portage township
Town 3 Range 2 (Liberty), 29
Town 3 Range 3 (Weathersfield). *See* Salt Springs
Town 4 Range 3. *See* Howland
Town 4 Range 4. *See* Warren
Town 4 Range 15 (Liverpool), 101
Town 4 Range 18 (Pittsfield), 116, 129
Town 6 Range 6. *See* Parkman
Town 7 Range 7 (Burton), 21
Town 7 Range 12. *See* Cleveland
Town 8 Range 7 (Canton-Claridon). *See* Claridon
Town 9 Range 8 (Chardon), 57
Town 10 Range 8 (Concord), 21, 29, 57
Town 11 Range 5 (Harpersfield), 23
Town 13 Range 1 (Litchfield), 21
Town 14 Range 1. *See* Conneaut Creek
Tracy, Uriah, 14, 27, 30, 31, 35
Travel routes, 29
Treaty of Brownstown, 79
Treaty of Detroit, 79
Treaty of Greenville, 6
Trenton Federal Court, 4
Trumbull-Ashtabula Turnpike Company, 112
Trumbull County, 36, 43–44, 47, 53, 55
Trumbull County Agricultural Society, 151
Trumbull, Jonathan, 35
Trump of Fame, 74
Tuscarawas River, 115
Tuttle, Lucius, 21

Umberville, Thomas, 23
Union Park, 153

Uniontown, Pennsylvania, 62
United States Congress, 25, 27, 53

Van Buren, Martin, 133, 138–39, 140
Virginia Military Lands, 155n14
Viva voce voting, 46, 53

Wadsworth, Elijah: 74, 77, 80–81, 82, 84–85, 93, 101, 174n38; *quoted*, 94
Walworth, John, 78–79
Ward, Andrew, 33
War of 1812, 74–90, 97, 98–99, 178n16. *See also* Perkins, Simon: Military
Warren, 23, 29, 43–44, 55–56, 57, 60, 100, 127, 129
Washington County, Pennsylvania, 23, 29, 58
Washington, George, 161n15
Wayne, Anthony, 6
Webb, Isaac, 127, 146
Webb, Thomas, 134–35
Welsh, John, 134–35. *See also* John Welsh *vs.* Simon Perkins *et al.*
Western Reserve: 29, 55–56, 57–59, 80, 100, 102, 171n21
    Boundaries of, 4–5
    Cession of Jurisdiction Act (April 28, 1800), 34–35
    Description, land, 22
    Government, 5, 26–27, 34–35
    History of, 4–6
    Partition, mode of, 10–11
    Proprietors of, 30, 33, 66. *See also* Connecticut Land Company and Erie Company
    Settlement of, 23, 29, 32–33, 51, 52, 97, 98–101, 120
    Surveying mode, 20
    Title to, 4–5, 8–9, 27, 30–35
Western Reserve Bank, 74, 102, 103, 105, 106, 108, 144, 149, 151, 152; 180n33. *See also*

Western Reserve Bank (*Continued*)
  Perkins, Simon: banking, *and* Banking conditions
Western Reserve College, 129. *See also* Western Reserve University
Western Reserve University, 151, 152. *See also* Western Reserve College
Whisky Rebellion, 58
Whittlesey, Elisha: 82, 86, 93, 101, 113, 116, 145; *quoted*, 18, 99, 101, 109–10, 131–32, 137–38, 139, 143, 148
Williams, Isaac, 67, 68
Williams, Joseph, 13–14, 35, 47, 66–68, 72

Williams, Joseph, Jr., 68
Williams, Paul, 97, 116, 117, 118
Williams, William Wheeler, 14, 15–16, 22
Winchester, General James, 85–86, 87–88
Winslow, John, 40–41
Wyoming Valley colony, 4, 27, 33

Yale, 122, 123, 125, 127, 128, 145, 146, 147
Young, John, 21, 23, 28, 35, 42–43, 49, 55
Young, Mrs. John, 51
Youngstown, 23, 29, 41, 42–43, 45, 49, 52, 55–56